ANXIETY, LEARNING, AND INSTRUCTION

JOAN E. SIEBER
CALIFORNIA STATE UNIVERSITY, HAYWARD

HAROLD F. O'NEIL, JR.
DEFENSE ADVANCED RESEARCH PROJECTS AGENCY

SIGMUND TOBIAS
CITY UNIVERSITY OF NEW YORK

 LAWRENCE ERLBAUM ASSOCIATES, PUBLISHERS
1977   Hillsdale, New Jersey

DISTRIBUTED BY THE HALSTED PRESS DIVISION OF

JOHN WILEY & SONS

New York   Toronto   London   Sydney

40227

Copyright © 1977 by Lawrence Erlbaum Associates, Inc.
All rights reserved. No part of this book may be reproduced in any form, by photostat, microform, retrieval system, or any other means, without the prior written permission of the publisher.

Lawrence Erlbaum Associates, Inc., Publishers
62 Maria Drive
Hillsdale, New Jersey 07642

Distributed solely by Halsted Press Division
John Wiley & Sons, Inc., New York

ISBN 0-470-99299-9

Library of Congress Catalog Card Number: 77-11127

Printed in the United States of America

Contents

40227   iii

Preface

Several years ago, each of the authors independently initiated research to find ways of reducing the undesirable effects of anxiety[1] on intellectual performance. These research programs were based on the assumption that anxiety is a complex process, parts of which can be modified through training or curriculum change so that the anxious individual can function more adaptively. The aim of this book is to summarize the research and ideas that have emerged from these programs. It is both a progress report on the approaches we have developed for reducing anxiety or its undesirable effects, and a means of sharing our insights concerning better ways of accomplishing these goals in the future.

The approaches that have been developed depart considerably from the mainstream of research on anxiety. The practical value of these approaches has been demonstrated and further development is now needed if they are to prove maximally useful. Consequently, this is an appropriate time for us to summarize our ideas and work, as a way of sharing them with advanced students and researchers in educational psychology, human development, personality, cognition, learning, instruction, and curriculum design.

Our work departs from the mainstream of research on anxiety in the following ways:

1. We do not seek to eliminate anxiety. We actively employ the premise that anxiety is a basic part of the human condition and has adaptive as well as maladaptive effects on cognition, performance, and personality.

2. We regard anxiety as a set of processes having to do with awareness of the possibility of failure (by whatever subjective standard), and with attempts to

---

[1]We use the term *anxiety*, and sometimes *evaluative anxiety* to denote anxiety about one's performance in educational settings. Sarason, Mandler, and others who have done research with versions of the test anxiety scale for children have used the term *test anxiety* to denote the same phenomenon.

resist that awareness, or to cope. We have sought to define this set of processes and to discover how some of the processes can be altered, through training or improved instructional technology, to enable the anxious student to function more adaptively. Some of the processes we have examined are memory, attention, probability estimation, and organization of concepts. We have not proceeded with any fixed idea about the nature of these processes; we began with a few simple ideas and went where our observations led us.

3. We have sought to reduce anxiety and its undesirable effects *without* focusing on the details of its origin or development.

4. Our research has been guided by a commitment to establish useful, generalizable principles for enabling anxious students to respond adaptively to evaluation.

5. We have used basic experimental techniques and aptitude-treatment interaction research designs to investigate treatments intended to modify the effects of anxiety on specific processes of cognition and performance.

6. We have used computer-based instruction in the research and development of these treatments. Computer-based instruction has limitations, some of which are pinpointed in this volume. But it also has advantages. It delivers the intended treatment to every student, and measures the results with objectivity and precision, without interfering in peculiar ways with the pedagogical procedures that the student considers normal. Curriculum that has been developed for research purposes can be packaged for large-scale instructional use. Finally, computer-based instruction offers systematic means of developing and evaluating curriculum that seems to have potential for helping anxious students.

For reader convenience, we have divided this book into four sections: introduction; anxiety-treatment interaction; computer-based instruction and anxiety; and recommendations for future research. Each section lays ground-work for succeeding ones, but sections may be read independently without very much loss of meaning.

Section 1 contains four chapters on the conceptual and methodological framework of our research. In Chapter 1, our mentor, Wilbert McKeachie, outlines the major contributions of this monograph and offers his critique. In Chapter 2, the historical development of the concept of anxiety is presented. Chapter 3 deals with problems of choosing operational definitions of anxiety. In Chapter 4, the research paradigm we employ is discussed, and examples are presented. Section 2 introduces the reader to the complexities of adapting actual instruction to the individual's level of anxiety (Chapter 5) and reports research on anxiety-treatment interactions (Chapter 6). Section 3 introduces the concept of computer-based instruction as an aid to research on anxiety and instruction. In Chapter 7, Charles Spielberger, who guided and encouraged the early computer-based research, provides an overview and critique of computer-based research on anxiety. This is followed by a description of computer-based learning environments (Chapter 8) and reports of computer-based research on instructional approaches designed to reduce anxiety or its undesirable effects (Chapter 9). Also within the computer-based instruction framework, a personalized clinical program to reduce anxiety is presented and tested (Chapter 10), and a series of basic and applied studies on the relation of anxiety to learning and performance are reviewed (Chapter 11). In Section 4, the shortcomings of the models and methods we have employed are discussed and recommendations are made for future research.

The research and ideas presented are largely our own, but this book could hardly have come into existence without the help and encouragement of many others. As the individual chapters reveal, we have benefitted greatly from our working relationship with Jeri D. Wine, Frank C. Richardson, John J. Hedl, Jr., Wilson A. Judd, and Richard D. Grant, Jr. Jeri Wine's work is extensively discussed in Chapter 3. Richardson, Hedl, Judd, and Grant have been closely associated with Harry O'Neil in programs of computer-based research on anxiety and instruction. They share authorship of some of the chapters in Section 3 with Harry O'Neil. We are exceedingly grateful for the encouragement received from Wayne Holzman, Bill McKeachie, and Charlie Spielberger. It was they who encouraged us in our early work on anxiety, who served as speakers at symposia on our work, and who ultimately suggested to us that we present a summary of our research in a volume. We acknowledge the help and inspiration we have received from many dedicated students, including Susan B. Crockenberg, Leon Paulson, Larry Kameya, Patricia Engle, and Barbara McCombs. We also acknowledge with gratitude the institutions that supported this work. The studies reported in this book were conducted at the Florida State University, University of Texas, at Austin, Stanford University, California State University, Hayward, and City University of New York Graduate Center, with the aid of grants from the U. S. Office of Education, the National Science Foundation, the Office of Naval Research, and the Research Foundation of California State University, Hayward. Finally, we acknowledge our appreciation of the help and moral support we have received from the staff of Lawrence Erlbaum Associates, and in particular Larry Erlbaum, himself.

We have already received many intellectual and emotional rewards in connection with our work. We have enjoyed trying out our new ideas, and we have some happy and less anxious students to show for our efforts. What we hope to gain through this book are colleagues who will share with us the pleasure and excitement of conceptualizing and developing some interesting, generalizable, and *useful* procedures for helping students to master learning and to enjoy demonstrating their mastery. We hope that we can succeed in interesting advanced students and researchers in psychology, education, and human development in this endeavor.

J.E.S.
H.F.O'N., Jr.
S.T.

Part I

INTRODUCTION

This book reports the theoretical and practical results of several related programs of applied research on evaluative anxiety. The aim of this research is to find ways to reduce evaluative anxiety or its undesirable effects on intellectual performance. It is based on the assumptions that individual components of the process of anxiety can be modified toward more adaptive functioning by means of training or curriculum changes, and such minor modifications may, in turn, have constructive effects on the entire process of anxiety and on performance.

Since this approach to the treatment of evaluative anxiety is new, the first section of this book is devoted to the conceptual framework within which this work was conducted. Chapter 1 contains an overview and critique of the concepts and methods employed in this book. Chapter 2 provides the reader who has limited knowledge in this area with an historical perspective on the concept of anxiety and how it has evolved into the set of contemporary theoretical constructs from which we have drawn.

In Chapter 3, these theoretical constructs are taxonomized according to the way in which test anxiety is operationally defined. Four kinds of definitions of anxiety are identified: those dealing with the phenomenology of anxiety; those dealing with its physiological correlates; those dealing with its effects on performance or behavior, and those dealing with the internal and external stimuli of anxiety (factors that increase or decrease anxiety). Chapter 3 also provides the reader with a brief overview of the way in which some of the research presented in subsequent chapters derives from one or more of these four kinds of definitions.

In Chapter 4, the major research approaches that have been employed here are described. The rationale of each approach is discussed, and illustrative examples are presented.

1
Overview and Critique

Wilbert J. McKeachie

University of Michigan

Anxiety has a bad name. No one wants to be anxious; parents try not to raise anxious children; teachers are warned against arousing anxiety; psychotherapists are well paid for their efforts to alleviate irrational fear; and millions of tranquilizers are consumed each day to reduce tension and anxiety. Yet, from an evolutionary viewpoint, anxiety must have some functional value for it to have evolved as an inherent response potential in the human species.

The chapters in this volume represent a major advance in the analysis of anxiety as a theoretical concept and, especially, in demonstrating the effects of anxiety on learning and intellectual performance. By a careful operational definition of anxiety, including specification of the stimuli of anxiety, the authors have made possible a tighter conceptualization than is typical of the field, and they have clearly identified a number of important research questions. Such an approach is vital, for only by approaching anxiety analytically can we determine when it is functional, when it is dysfunctional, and what can be done to optimize the effects of anxiety on performance.

Many of the studies in this volume approach anxiety in terms of attribute–treatment interactions. This approach makes sense theoretically. Its historical antecedents go back at least to the Yerkes–Dodson law. As applied to anxiety and performance, the Yerkes–Dodson law predicts that an increase in anxiety results in improved performance and effectiveness up to a point, and that further increases in anxiety result in decrements in performance. The precise relation between anxiety and performance seems to depend on the difficulty or complexity of the task. The research reported in this volume suggests, unfortunately, that the elegant conceptualization proposed in the Yerkes–Dodson law is either too simple or simply wrong. The authors raise theoretical and methodological issues which broaden our understanding of the relation between anxiety and performance.

My goal in this chapter is to highlight some of these theoretical and methodological issues that I believe to be important in research on the effects of anxiety on the performance of complex learning tasks. In raising these issues, I refer specifically to the contents and issues raised in the first five chapters of this volume, but the problems noted are ones of general importance.

METHODOLOGICAL PROBLEMS

It may be, of course, that the Yerkes–Dodson theory is right and that we have simply failed to test it adequately. Certainly one problem area in the test of any theory is that of measurement. The differentiation of trait and state anxiety is an important step forward, but each of these concepts would seem to need further differentiation. For example, trait anxiety is defined in terms of the disposition "to perceive a wide range of stimulus situations as dangerous or threatening and to respond to such threats with high state anxiety." May it be that the breadth of situations viewed as dangerous, and the intensity of anxiety experienced could usefully be differentiated?

Perhaps we need to have one instrument sampling a range of potentially anxiety producing situations; another instrument tapping the intensity of anxiety typically elicited; and perhaps still another dealing with styles of reacting to anxiety such as withdrawal, worry, or impulsive disorganization. Some anxious persons may respond to anxiety by attending to their physical symptoms; others may perseverate on thoughts about the future consequences of failure; still others may work harder. This is essentially the approach taken in S. Sarason's (1966) studies of defensiveness. The analysis in Chapter 4 of dimensions of self-report measures is particularly important as evidence emerges that the different concomitants of anxiety are not invariably associated; in fact Lacey's (1959) research suggests that different physiological symptoms are not even highly correlated with one another.

If Freudian theory is at all valid, we have yet another difficulty with self-report measures. According to theory, one should expect anxiety beyond a certain level to be repressed. Thus a low score on an anxiety scale may indicate the absence of anxiety or the denial or repression of intense anxiety. If anxiety scores drop under increased stress, we might suspect that some such mechanism is operating. Sarason's (1966) work dealt with the self-reported differences in defensiveness of individuals at the same level of self-reported anxiety. But the anxiety scores themselves may mean different things for defensive individuals. To identify defensiveness in a single anxiety questionnaire would be difficult but perhaps not impossible. For example, if items were scaled in terms of the degree to which they cue reports of anxiety, we might, in a trait-anxiety inventory, order the items systematically. Suppose that a student reports anxiety on low-cue items early in the questionnaire but denies anxiety in responses to later items scaled as higher in anxiety cues. We might infer defensiveness, and presumably predict different performance for these students than for students with patterns that were internally consistent.

If anxiety builds up as a result of successive cues and at some point triggers defensive reacting, we might well expect many measures of test reliability to yield low indices. A low-reliability coefficient indicates a problem but is not necessarily a sign of inadequacy of the measure. I would argue that any reliability coefficient is, in at least some sense, simply a special case of construct validity. Theories about psychological constructs have, as one of their most basic predictions, that a measure of the construct should correlate with itself or with another test of the same construct. We usually worry about this when the test doesn't correlate very well with anything else that we would expect it to. But in some cases we might expect it to correlate better with other behaviors than with a repetition of itself. This seems to be the case with tests of anxiety and need achievement. In these cases one's theory leads one to expect that items are not responded to independently of one another, but rather that the response to an item depends upon the items preceding it and upon the state of the individual when taking the test. Thus, the increased understanding gained through the experiments reported in the following chapters needs to be applied not only to the effects of anxiety on other behaviors, but also to the effects of anxiety on measures of anxiety.

Testing anxiety is itself an intervention which may have effects not only on test scores but also on later behavior. This may be a problem for those using measures of state anxiety, even though the use of such measures seems to me generally to be a major advance.

Finally, state anxiety scores may not directly parallel the effects of anxiety on behavior. As researchers uncover greater complexities in information processing, it becomes clear that the cognitive functions involved in answering a questionnaire may not be affected by changes in anxiety in the same way as the cognitive functions involved in the dependent variables studied.

RESEARCH DESIGN

Even if we had the measurement problem solved, we would not have surmounted all technical barriers. The hypothesized curvilinear relationship makes for difficulties in design and analysis. As Tobias points out in Chapter 6, our usual statistical techniques may be inadequate if we expect curvilinear relationships. Suppose, for example, that we compare the performance of two groups differing in anxiety level. Our results are likely to differ, depending on the cutting point used, since we may in one group be getting individuals on both sides of the point of inflection of the curve. If individuals who differ in level of anxiety are grouped together, potentially valuable information is lost. The computation of regression slopes within groups is also unsatisfactory if one of the two groups runs over the inflection point. Researchers typically use extreme groups to get around this problem, but this often loses significant portions of the potential sample. A test of linearity with use of a quadratic term may help. Tobias has a good discussion of the awesome complexities of analysis in Chapter 7.

A second problem in research design and particularly in interpretation of results is that it is usually much easier to administer a questionnaire to measure individual differences in anxiety than it is to manipulate anxiety. We compare the performance of high- and low-anxiety groups and attribute any differences found to anxiety. This leap from correlation to causation is natural, but to really pin down the effects of anxiety, we probably need to carry out comparable studies in which anxiety is manipulated. Unfortunately this doesn't always work (see studies of the Spence–Taylor theory of interaction between anxiety and task complexity, e.g. Spielberger & Smith, 1966; Spence, 1958). Neither measures of trait anxiety nor experimental manipulations are reliable predictors of differences in performance. This is one reason why measures of state anxiety are useful.

NATURE OF THE TASK

Researchers who study anxiety, more than most other researchers, encounter the problems of systematic versus representative design of experiments. With potential interactions between trait anxiety, state anxiety, treatment, and the nature of the task, the problem of representative sampling of all these variables becomes virtually impossible. As Tobias points out in Chapter 5, programmed and computer-assisted instruction provide convenient and well-controlled tasks for research on interactions between anxiety and instructional methods. However, a possible limitation on the generality of these studies is that the error rate is typically very low. Thus the usefulness of a particular technique of facilitating performance of highly anxious individuals may not be generalizable to tasks of greater difficulty. And, as reported in Chapter 5, interactions with anxiety may not occur consistently.

It is at this point that I am inclined to disagree mildly with Tobias' rejection of Cronbach and Snow's (1976) suggestion that the traditional criteria for levels of statistical significance not be followed too rigidly. Like Tobias, I have always taken replicability as the ultimate test of significance, but Cronbach and Snow have persuaded me that lack of replicability may point to the influence of variables that otherwise might be overlooked. I am less inclined than Tobias to weigh heavily the costs to Type 1 errors.

MEASURING LEARNING

A difficulty we run into when we try to determine the effects of anxiety on learning is that we expect anxiety to affect both learning and performance, in testing situations evaluating learning. Even if these effects are additive, one has no way of determining how much of the difference in test scores between high- and low-anxious individuals is due to differences in learning and how much to differences in test performance of individuals with equal learning. This is pointed up in the studies by Leherissey, O'Neil, Heinrich, and Hansen (1973) reported in Chapter 5. Different results were obtained from a paper-and-pencil posttest than from a posttest administered by computer. Constructed responding apparently was superior only on a test requiring the same response as required in the program, but was not superior when the learners were required to demonstrate transfer by drawing a tracing which they had previously learned to reproduce by punching keys on a computer terminal.

In most studies we make the reasonable assumption that manipulations of the learning situation affect the learning. Conceivably, however, manipulations of the learning situation may also affect the learner's approach to the testing. (Tobias notes this in Chapter 7.) Since we know that reassurance and encouragement to write comments facilitate the test performance of anxious students (McKeachie, Pollie, & Speisman, 1955), it may be that such techniques should be used to increase the likelihood that scores on the test more nearly approach a true measure of the learning of the anxious students.

IMPROVING PERFORMANCE

Assuming that we can measure anxiety with at least minimal adequacy, what situations facilitate performance of anxious persons and what situations are detrimental? One approach to this question is to analyze the components of anxiety and to devise conditions which will modify them. Chapter 4 gives a nice analysis of three such components, and the later chapters illustrate approaches directed at one or another of those components. The research has produced enough positive results to encourage continuation of this approach. In fact, as Chapter 4 indicates, positive results have been reported for a variety of techniques, including:

1. Reducing anxiety by:
   a. changing the situation to reduce stress by redefining the task or by modification of the social interactions;
   b. changing the anxious person's reaction by desensitization;
2. Providing mechanisms for coping with responses detrimental to performance by:

a. focusing attention;
b. giving memory support;
c. reducing task-irrelevant responses;
d. preventing premature closure;
e. teaching needed skills.

One wonders whether the subject's expectation that a treatment will work is responsible, in part, for the positive results. Perhaps we need a placebo control in more of our experiments.

Another approach is to conceive of situations in which one or more of the components of anxiety is functional. Perhaps we have been too ready to accept the view that anxiety responses are inevitably damaging to performance. Although we tend to emphasize the detrimental effects of anxiety, several studies have found superior performance by high-anxious individuals on learning programs of low difficulty.

My impression is that some of the situations in which anxious students excel were ones in which greater persistence or more work could result in better performance. One suspects that anxious college students have reached the college level by responding to anxiety with increased perseverance and effort. This was illustrated in Oosthoek and Acker's (1972) finding that high-anxiety students reviewed an audiotape more frequently than low-anxiety students. When a clear course of action is available to anxious students, I would expect them to use it. I attribute the poor performance of anxious students in student-centered classes (Domino, 1974; Dowaliby & Schumer, 1973) to a lack of clarity about the activities necessary to achievement.

Tobias presents a thoughtful discussion that constructed responding with feedback yields higher levels of state anxiety than other modes of responding in programmed instruction. He suggests that any condition in which the learner may find him/herself to be incorrect is likely to evoke higher levels of anxiety than nonevaluative conditions. This hypothesis seems likely and Tobias supplies some supporting evidence (1973b). However, alternative explanation might be derived from Atkinson's theory of achievement motivation. According to Atkinson's theory, the area of maximal motivation is where the probability of success is about .5. Thus, if an anxious individual enters the learning situation with a low subjective probability of success, experience with 80% incidence of correct responses gradually moves that individual from a nonthreatening low expectation of success into the region that is maximally anxiety arousing. If Atkinson is right, longer experiments would then move the learner past the 50–50 point into the less threatening region of expectancy of 80% success.

INTERACTIONS WITH OTHER INDIVIDUAL DIFFERENCES

Good progress is being made on analysis of some of the cognitive variables involved in the performance of anxious individuals. I hope this continues. At the same time, analysis of interactions of anxiety and other personality or individual difference variables may be useful in identifying ways of facilitating learning and performance.

Sex. I am pleased that the authors typically have reported the sex composition of their samples and often have examined differences in relationships found for men compared to those for women. I believe that some of the inconsistent results found earlier were due to ignoring sex as a source of variance. Now we know that it makes a difference, but we still don't know how and why. Some years ago (McKeachie, 1958), I suggested that males in our culture were likely to be trained to cope with anxiety by denying it and by autonomic preparation for physical activity, so that a muscle relaxant was actually a disturbing, rather than calming, influence. Females, on the other hand, were, I suggested, more likely to be trained to acknowledge anxiety and to express dependency. Thus answers to an anxiety questionnaire might mean quite different things for the two sexes, and their respective styles of coping with anxiety might also affect performance differently. Such sex differences may well be reduced as our child-rearing patterns change, but in the meantime, they may provide some handles for getting at the psychological variables affecting the relationship between anxiety and performance.

Need for approval. The research reported in Chapters 4 and 5 on the particular effectiveness of social reinforcement for anxious children suggests that study of the social psychological aspects of evaluative anxiety could yield positive results. If one examines the relationship of the anxious learner to teachers and peers in the learning and testing situation, what dimensions affect performance? Schmuck and Van Egmond (1965) found that the school achievement of boys depended upon the degree to which they felt *respected* by their peers while the school achievement of girls was positively related to the degree to which they felt *liked* by their peers. Thus the interpersonal aspects of educational and evaluative situations may have important consequences in determining anxiety and its effects.

Tobias, in Chapter 7, notes that results have more often conformed to theoretical predictions in full-semester classroom studies than in briefer studies using computer-assisted instruction or programmed instruction. One possibility is that the classroom is a social situation and that evaluative anxiety is almost inextricably tied to interpersonal consequences of failure. If this should be so, computer-assisted instruction and programmed learning are poor situations in which to study the effects of anxiety.

The potency of motivational differences in brief experiments with specially constructed learning programs is further reduced in task situations where success or failure has low perceived instrumentality for future success. Raynor (1974) has shown that future orientation has important effects on behavior of individuals differing in need achievement and anxiety. Similarly I am intrigued by Tobias' suggestion that the effects of anxiety may depend upon the degree to which the situation is structured to permit external versus internal attribution of failure. We have only begun to tap important personality characteristics relevant to the effects of anxiety.

SUMMARY

The more we learn; the less we know. Continued investigation of anxiety and learning has revealed more and more complexity. Such complexity could arouse anxiety and withdrawal on the part of prospective researchers. I trust that, rather, it arouses interest and further research.

2

Development of
the Concept of Anxiety

Man's effort to escape anxiety is a major theme in human thought and experience. So pervasive is this unpleasant emotion in the lives of human beings that it would add little to this exposition to provide a common-sense definition of anxiety. We know from our own lives and from literature that persons experience a wide variety of diffuse negative emotions, some in connection with specific events such as test taking; and others that appear as fear and malaise without an object. What is needed here, however, before we proceed to more technical matters, is a brief discussion of major philosophical and scientific ideas about the nature of anxiety, so that the reader may see how the research reported has modified the conceptions of anxiety which originally stimulated the investigation. Existential philosophers have enriched our ideas about the nature of anxiety by providing vivid descriptions of its experiential aspects, but have dealt in concepts that are not of a scientific nature. Psychologists have measured anxiety and have theorized about its processes in ways that make it amenable to study, but which seem to some to overlook the essential role of anxiety in the human condition. What concepts about anxiety do these two disciplines hold in common? In what ways do they differ? Which of these ideas have been built upon in the research presented here?

As an introduction, a description of some major philosophical and scientific conceptions of anxiety is offered, followed by discussion of how the conception of anxiety in educationally relevant situations developed out of the more general conception of anxiety. Finally, the main concepts that emerge from this literature are summarized, and the ways in which our concept of anxiety relates to other conceptions of anxiety is outlined.

PHILOSOPHICAL CONCEPTIONS OF ANXIETY

Existential philosophy may seem foreign to scientific psychology. It attempts to analyze the data of consciousness and, perhaps of necessity, lacks the kinds of clear and simple definitions and principles that characterize much of science. Two other major ways in which existential philosophy differs from psychology are in the terminology that is employed and in the explanations that are given about the causes of anxiety. Psychologists tend to use terms such as "anxiety" and "stress." Existentialists usually use the terms "dread" or "anguish." Most psychologists (with the notable exception of Mowrer, 1966) employ concepts of physiology and learning to explain why an individual manifests anxiety in the presence of certain kinds of stimuli. However, existentialists regard religious and moral dilemmas as the causes of anxiety. To quote Sarte (1970):

> First, what do we mean by anguish? The existentialist frankly states that man in in anguish. His meaning is as follows: When a man commits himself to anything, fully realizing that he is not only choosing what he will be, but is thereby at the same time a legislator deciding for the whole of mankind—in such a moment a man cannot escape from the sense of complete and profound responsibility. There are many, indeed, who show no such anxiety. But we affirm that they are merely disguising their anguish or are in flight from it. Certainly, many people think that in what they are doing they commit no one but themselves to anything: and if you ask them, "What would happen if everyone did so?" they shrug their shoulders and reply, "Everyone does not do so." But in truth, one ought always to ask oneself what would happen if everyone did as one is doing; nor can one escape from that disturbing thought except by a kind of self-deception. The man who lies in self-excuse, by saying "Everyone will not do it" must be ill at ease in his conscience, for the act of lying implies the universal value which it denies. By its very disguise his anguish reveals itself. This is the anguish that Kierkegaard called "the anguish of Abraham." You know the story: An angel commanded Abraham to sacrifice his son: and obedience was obligatory, if it really was an angel who had appeared and said, "Thou, Abraham, shalt sacrifice thy son." But anyone in such a case would wonder, first, whether it was indeed an angel and secondly, whether I am really Abraham. Where are the proofs [pp. 370–371]?

Nevertheless, while existential philosophers regard moral and religious dilemmas as the cause of anxiety, it is also true that many of the ideas about anxiety discussed by the existential philosophers, Kierkegaard, Jaspers, Heidegger, and Sartre have found wide acceptance in psychology as well. Each of these philosophers has mentioned that physical symptoms such as dizziness, nausea, and sweating are part of anxiety and are salient in the thoughts of the anxious person. Each has characterized anxiety as a disturbing feeling that arises as a result of the lack of a clear standard of one's own, or of the possibility of failing to meet some perceived external standard (often one that is vaguely sensed rather than clearly defined). Each has emphasized that anxiety is a basic human emotion which cannot be avoided entirely. Finally, each has characterized anxiety as having negative as well as positive consequences. The negative consequences of anxiety include discomfort and counterproductive striving, often in the form of fear and avoidance of the unpleasant. Its positive consequences include the acquisition of new competence or the attainment of some higher stage of psychological development, such as a more satisfying perspective of one's life.

The ideas of Kierkegaard (1944), Heidegger (1949), and Jaspers (Schilpp, 1957) somewhat resemble those of the psychologist Levinson (1974), who has shown that most adults face life crises about every seven years. Levinson *et al.* regards these crises as characteristic of passage through adult developmental stages. Some of the developmental tasks that are to be mastered in the course of adulthood are leaving one's parents and establishing one's own identity; experimenting with careers and life styles and then making a commitment to the most appropriate of these; acquiring competence in one's chosen field of endeavor; broadening and accepting mature responsibility for one's goals and values; and accepting the challenges and limitations of one's self-imposed choices in life. The crises of adult life occur when passing from one stage to the next. They are severe when the individual has not dealt satisfactorily with the prior developmental tasks or does not perceive or accept his current task. Levinson, like Jaspers (cited in Schilpp, 1957), emphasizes that it is not psychologically satisfactory to try to avoid feelings of anxiety or crisis by throwing oneself into one's work or by seeking external causes of the crises, such as faults in one's employer or spouse.

Sartre has defined anxiety in ways that best coincide with the definition of the kind of anxiety which is the focus of this book. It is fear of failure to meet a standard, or fear that one does not hold the appropriate standard. In his work *Being and Nothingness,* Sartre (1956) provides a wealth of examples of the complex and self-destructive character of these ubiquitous fears. We turn now to the specific views of each of these philosophers.

Kierkegaard, in *The Concept of Dread* (1944) conceived of man as constantly striving toward a higher stage of existence in which he may overcome his alienation from God. He considered dread (anxiety) to be a natural emotion that pervades man's feelings and thoughts, and indicates to him when he is in an untenable position with respect to God. It is the emotion that precedes and accompanies his desire to leap to a higher state of existence. Kierkegaard distinguished between fear and dread; dread is experienced in the absence of a tangible source of danger, while fear involves a tangible source of danger.

Jaspers' views on dread are presented in English in *The Philosophy of Jaspers* (Schilpp, 1957). He holds a more differentiated view of dread than Kierkegaard, distinguishing four kinds: (1) a kind of perplexity which occurs to people when they ask philosophic questions about the significance of their own being: (2) dread in the face of freedom, such as occurs when people are suddenly freed from old rules or social norms and recognize that they must make basic decisions for themselves; (3) fear of death; and (4) existential dread or the sense of aimlessness and profound emptiness that arises when one feels uncertain that he exists in any meaningful way.

Jaspers' main concern has been with existential dread, which he regards not as a symptom of mental illness, but as a result of rejecting religious faith. He proposes that man's only way out of existential dread is through a "leap into faith" which reconciles man with himself and with God, and provides an experience of the absolute which transcends mere sense experience. Jaspers emphasized the positive aspect of existential dread—its power to motivate man to seek understanding of his innermost problems. Jaspers warns that existential dread cannot be removed by physical and economic security, though many seek relief in vain by trying to attain security, power, or wealth.

Jaspers recognized that a single symptom, anxiety, may accompany any of a variety of situations in which the individual perceives that he cannot readily arrive at a satisfactory decision (be it a decision on a course of action, or a set of values, or goals) regarding some aspect of his life that he considers important at that time. He also pointed out that man may develop defenses against anxiety by doing things that provide evidence of power, but that these defenses are diversionary and do not remove the source of anxiety; they merely delay and interfere with the eventual confrontation of it.

Heidegger's major ideas are outlined in *Existence and Being* (1949). Heidegger holds that each person's very existence in the world causes him to experience anxiety—irrespective of his social, political, economic, or religious position. In response to this anxiety, each seeks assurance by merging his or her identity with that of others, by conforming, or by becoming socialized. Socialization, however, brings a new source of anxiety, for when the individual merges so completely with society that he or she loses the sense of identity and integrity, he or she again feels a sense of dread and nothingness. Heidegger identifies several defensive activities that people employ to hide their anxiety. These include superficial attempts at self-analysis and "knowing it all" about the outside world. He also believes that this anxiety can, in some cases, bring humans into touch with their own individuality—can cause them to become aware of those values and acts for which the individual will claim responsibility.

Sartre, in *Being and Nothingness* (1956) distinguishes between fear, which has an external object, and anxiety, which has an internal object, namely, distrust of one's own ability to react well under duress. That is, anxiety has to do with holding values, and fear that one will not measure up to them. For example, a soldier who is about to go into battle may fear that he will be afraid. Or, an individual who has just been given some important new rank and responsibility may fear that he or she will not measure up fully to that role. Anxiety also occurs when one examines one's values and finds that they are not acceptable or absolute.

Sartre's notion of anxiety as fear of failure to measure up to internal or perceived external standards and as fear that one's own standards are not appropriate or "good enough" comes closest to the notion of anxiety to which I refer in this book.

SCIENTIFIC CONCEPTIONS OF ANXIETY

Two early contributions to science, those of Darwin and of Freud, established anxiety as a subject of scientific study. Subsequently, Hull, Spence, Taylor, Sarason, Spielberger, and their respective associates transformed the concept of anxiety into a measurable and useful psychological construct.

Darwin placed the study of Homo sapiens squarely in the realm of natural science by emphasizing continuity with other species. He made anxiety and fear (which he did not distinguish from one another) the subjects of scientific inquiry by describing and documenting their manifestations in man and animals. He pointed out that these manifestations among higher mammals (rapid heart beat, perspiration, dilation of the pupils, dryness of mouth, change in voice quality, trembling, and so on) are so clearly established that one can readily recognize these emotions in species other than one's own. In his book *The Expression of the Emotions in Man and Animals* (1872), Darwin argues that the reason this pattern of expression is universally found in man and animals is that it is highly adaptive—only those having evolved this mechanism are able to cope with or flee from sources of danger as required for survival.

Freud (1936), like the existential philosophers, stressed the distinction between anxiety and fear. His distinction differs from theirs, however. Freud proposed that there is an objective anxiety and a neurotic anxiety. Objective anxiety is somewhat more complex than fear, incorporating, in addition, a sense of helplessness and general malaise. Objective anxiety results from some source of danger in the external environment. It is usually based on a substantial history of learning about that danger. Neurotic anxiety has no source in the external world. Like fear, neurotic anxiety is a complex internal reaction to some perceived danger. It prepares the individual to flee or cope with the impending threat. However, it differs from fear in that it is based not on external danger, but on the individual's own history of traumatic experiences such as birth, the loss of a loved one, or punishment of socially disapproved urges. Its source is some impulse to act, acquired sometime in the individual's past, that cannot now be perceived because it was punished and then repressed from memory. An example illustrates this point:

Mr. X is extremely anxious whenever he finds himself thinking about wishing he owned something that others have. A Freudian attempt to explain Mr. X's anxiety would involve a search for childhood events such as the following:

1. *Impulses* on the part of Mr. X when he was very young to take things that belonged to others.

2. *Punishment* (real danger) inflicted on him by his parents when they discovered that he had taken things or was taking things that belonged to others.

3. *Fear* (objective anxiety) of more punishment occurring if he took things again (this fear arising each time he thinks about taking something of others.

4. *Repression* of his thoughts of stealing, or even of coveting the possessions of others, enabling him to reduce his fear of being punished.

5. *Partial breakdown of the repression,* which may occur from time to time when Mr. X's impulses to covet the possessions of others become salient again (this might occur when he feels particularly deprived and has reason to want more than he has).

6. *Neurotic anxiety* which Mr. X would feel during the partial breakdown of his repression. (This neurotic anxiety would be experienced as an objectless fear, since the punished impulses and the associated fear of parental punishment would remain repressed.

According to Freudian theory, the way to reduce neurotic anxiety is to engage in therapy which will bring the repressed material back to consciousness. Only when the individual is able to verbalize the danger cues and the fear they evoke can he gain control over his anxiety. Thus, if Mr. X could recognize that he has strong impulses to want things that others have, and that he fears punishment for stealing or even for coveting, he could overcome his anxiety.

Hull (1943) and his associate, Spence (1958), proposed an explanation of anxiety that built on Hull's learning theory, and ultimately led to the development by Taylor (1953) of an anxiety scale. The Hull–Spence conception of anxiety represents a radical departure from its predecessors and deserves mention here. A brief description of Hull's learning theory is provided in order to explain his conception of anxiety.

Hull's explanation of learning consists of relationships between hypothetical variables which can be operationally defined in behavioral terms. It does not deal with mental events such as repression. The purpose of Hull's theory is to explain and predict the learning of new responses.

Hull set out to account for the factors that affect the probability that the learned response will occur on any given occasion when the stimulus is presented. Hull's formulation regarding the basic variables, among others, affecting the occurrence of a response is

$$E = f(H{\times}D).$$

That is, the excitatory potential (E), or probability of occurrence of a response, is a multiplicative function of the strength of the learned habit (H) and the strength of the person's drive state (D).

Within the formulation $E = f(H \times D)$, many subtleties of learning and performance may be dealt with. For example, H, in turn, is affected by the number of learning trials that have occurred; and D is affected by such factors as the intensity of the stimulus and the emotional responsiveness of the individual.

Emotional responsiveness is the important variable for our purposes, since it is Hull's term for what is otherwise known as anxiety. Emotional responsiveness is a personality variable in the sense that there are consistent individual differences in the magnitude of reflex responses to a stimulus of given intensity. Another way of saying this, which illustrates its relevance to Freudian and Darwinian notions, is that highly emotional persons respond more strongly to stressful or aversive stimuli, have faster and more vigorous escape responses, and express and demonstrate more extreme emotional responses to stressful situations.

Taylor operationally defined this personality variable by developing a self-report test which measures the extent to which persons admit possessing manifest (overt) symptoms of emotionality. The Taylor Manifest Anxiety Scale has received wide use in laboratory research on learning, and in the study of personality and abnormal psychology where it has been used to explore problems of behavior such as those raised by Freud.

As in most other areas of empirical study, the development of a valid measuring instrument was a major step forward. It enabled subsequent researchers to examine the relationships between anxiety and other aspects of personality, behavior, and socialization. It has also provided a means of studying ways in which anxiety and its effects on behavior may be reduced, which is the central concern of this book. Finally, it paved the way for investigation of other conceptions and measures of anxiety, some of which is summarized in Chapter 3 and discussed in more detail in subsequent chapters.

Development of the Taylor Manifest Anxiety Scale

The items on the Taylor Manifest Anxiety Scale (Taylor, 1953) were developed by asking clinical psychologists to indicate which items on the Minnesota Multiphasic Personality Inventory they considered to be indicative of anxiety. To make it clearer what was meant by anxiety, the psychologists were also given Cameron's (1947) description of the behavior of chronically anxious people, which can only be violated by paraphrasing, so it is given here in full:

> The chronic anxiety reaction is characterized by the presence of persistently heightened skeletal and visceral tensions, which disturb a person's habitual rhythms of living and predispose him generally to give exaggerated and inappropriate responses on relatively slight provocation. In well-developed cases the patient's complaints and the examiner's findings together give a consistent clinical picture that is not difficult to recognize. The patient usually complains of tightness, aching or pain in his head, neck, shoulders, back and limbs which indicates increased muscular strain, particularly, but by no means exclusively in the main postural groups. The general increased reactivity of skeletal muscles can be clinically demonstrated in the brisk phasic stretch reflexes, the tremors in fingers, tongue and sometimes lips and eyelids. The patient usually looks or acts strained in walk and posture in facial expression, verbal reaction, gestures and other movements, and especially in response to intense or unexpected stimulation.
>
> The common visceral complaints are those which we would expect from our knowledge of the visceral components of ordinary anxiety reactions. Thus, the patient tells us of loss of appetite or continual hunger, of difficulty in getting food down, nausea and regurgitation, abdominal discomfort, spastic constipation or chronic mild diarrhea, or urinary frequency and urgency, cardiac irregularities, breathing difficulties, secretory changes and cold, clammy extremities, of menstrual disorders or changes in sex pace, of dyspareunia or relative impotence.

The chronically anxious patient usually states that he cannot think clearly, concentrate or remember as he once could, and that he cannot seem to stick to any one task for long. Although these claims are seldom corroborated objectively by ordinary test procedures, one is not justified in concluding that therefore they are unfounded. Most test situations call for a relatively brief period of application to a task set by someone else, who also provides special social motivation. The patient's difficulty is in setting his own tasks and providing sufficient motivation himself to keep at them until they are completed. He is usually irritable, fatigued, worried and discouraged. In his thoughts he may repeatedly return to problems facing him or ruminate in a mildly compulsive manner over his possible errors of omission and commission. Many of his choices and decisions are made actually in response to his tensions rather than to factors in the objective situation.

It is obvious to an observer that the patient cannot let go and relax. His tensions contribute to his restlessness and interfere with adequate satisfaction in anything, and his restlessness and frustration contribute further to his tension. He falls asleep with great difficulty and only after a long period of tossing in bed; he awakens easily and once awake finds trouble in getting to sleep again. His sleep is often disturbed by anxiety dreams, sometimes of awesome or horrible predicaments, sometimes of his daytime fantasies and conflicts, which he carries over into the sleeping phases of his life in more or less recognizable forms. With this general background of unrelieved tension and strain, the patient is prone to develop anxiety attacks now and then, occasionally in response to stress which he can identify at the time, but more often not [pp. 249–250].

Taylor found that on 65 of the items at least 4 out of 5 of the clinicians agreed that manifest anxiety was indicated. Bechtoldt (1953) carried out an item-analysis on these 65 items and discarded the 15 items having the lowest correlations with the total score. Some representative items of the resulting 50-item scale, with their scoring key, are as follows:

I have been afraid of things or people that I know could not hurt me. (T)
I wish I could be as happy as others. (T)
I have periods of such great restlessness that I cannot sit long in a chair. (T)
I frequently notice my hand shakes when I try to do something. (T)
I am entirely self-confident. (F)

The Taylor Manifest Anxiety Scale proved to be highly reliable over time. For example, Taylor (1953) found a test–retest reliability of .81 over 9 to 17 months, suggesting that manifest anxiety is an enduring characteristic.

Basic Construct Validation Research

Relationships have been observed between manifest anxiety scale scores and theoretically interesting variables, such as personality characteristics, learning speed, intelligence, and defensiveness. Brief summaries of some of these findings are presented.

Anxiety and personality. According to Freud, (1936), we may expect a high level of manifest anxiety in persons who feared separation from their parents during their childhood. To test this prediction, Sarason (1961) examined the relation between the Taylor Manifest Anxiety Scale and scores on a test indicating concern about whether one's parents loved and actively cared for one. He obtained significant correlations of .30 for males and .65 for females.

Freud (1936) also held that anxiety occurs when repression is not totally successful. Accordingly, Joy (1963) predicted that repressers would be less anxious than sensitizers, and tested this prediction by determining the correlation between scores on the Taylor Manifest Anxiety Scale and the represser–sensitizer scale, observing a correlation of .91.

Freud's (1936) view that neurotic symptoms serve to reduce anxiety has not been upheld although tests of this hypothesis are difficult to interpret. For example, Matarazzo, Matarazzo, and Saslow (1961) found that psychiatric patients at the University of Oregon Medical School obtained significantly higher scores on the Taylor Manifest-Anxiety Scale than did medical patients there. Perhaps persons who seek psychotherapy are ones whose neuroses are not working successfully. In a similar vein, one might expect that successful psychotherapy would result in heightened awareness of one's anxiety, coupled with a greater ability to cope with it. Lorr, McNair, Michaux, and Raskin (1962) found that patients who were given the Taylor Manifest Anxiety Scale at 4-month intervals beginning at the onset of therapy showed a gradual decline in level of anxiety which was significant after 12 months of therapy. Again, the results are ambiguous; has the therapy facilitated repression, reduced the salience of the anxiety, or removed the sources of stress that caused the anxiety?

Anxiety and learning. It has been noted that anxiety (emotional responsiveness) affects learning.

Hull (1943) and Spence (1958) postulated that anxious persons are emotionally responsive, and hence a well-learned response is most likely to be made, given the appropriate stimulus conditions, if the individual is anxious. However, complex and subtle learning tasks can be readily envisioned in which learned responses are to be given to various similar stimuli such that for each stimulus there are several competing responses from among which the correct response must be chosen. High anxiety or emotional responsiveness would only add to the confusion and difficulty of such tasks. Research supports this supposition, showing that anxiety and task complexity interact in their effect on performance: anxiety facilitates learning and performance of simple responses, and hinders that of complex responses. Reviews of this research may be found in Spence and Spence (1966) and Goulet (1968).

Anxiety and intelligence. Sarason, Lighthall, Davidson, Waite, and Ruebush (1960), in their study of anxiety in elementary school children, noted a decrease in measured IQ following increases in anxiety and an increase in measured IQ following reduction in anxiety. On the other hand, Spielberger (1966b), using college students, found that among the very brightest students, those who were highly anxious obtained slightly higher grades than those who were low anxious. Among the students with less ability, however, those who were highly anxious tended to obtain lower grades than those who were low anxious. Spielberger has pointed out that one plausible explanation of these results is that the course work on which these results were based was easy for the bright students and difficult for the less able students, hence the differential effects of anxiety on performance.

Anxiety, defensiveness, and learning. Another finding that deserves mention here is that of a relationship between defensiveness and learning in anxious children. Observations by Sarason, Hill, and Zimbardo (1964) suggests that while anxiety, per se, may have highly undesirable effects on the performance of school children, defensiveness may have additional bad effects on their performance. S. Sarason (1966) reasons as follows: ". . . anxiety is such a compelling experience that it can give rise to a pattern of reactions which, however painful and self-defeating in their consequences, reduces the likelihood of experiencing the anxiety again [p. 69]."

Sarason goes on to speculate that it is defensiveness, (ways of avoiding anxiety—and incidentally, of avoiding the problem itself) that may account for much of the decrement in learning and performance of anxious children. Sarason notes that defensiveness is a result of socialization to hide one's manifestations of anxiety, and begins to develop at about the onset of middle childhood. Hill and Sarason (1966) examined the relationship between various ability measures on the one hand, and anxiety and defensiveness on the other. As predicted, a high level of defensiveness, at every level of (admitted) anxiety was accompanied by a decrement in performance relative to the performance of low-defensive children.

Test Anxiety (Evaluative Anxiety)

Mandler and Sarason (1952) pioneered in the development of an anxiety scale designed specifically to measure test anxiety in children.[1] Unlike the manifest-anxiety scale, it refers specifically to school-relevant evaluation situations such as those an elementary school child would encounter. The manifestations of anxiety to which it refers are much the same, however: nightmares about tomorrow's test, fear of being called on, trembling of hands when taking a test, lack of confidence in one's school performance, unhappiness about being evaluated, fear that one will fail and be scolded by the teacher or by one's parents,

---

[1] Sarason and Mandler (1952) and others who have continued to do research with versions of the text-anxiety scale for children have used *"text anxiety"* to refer to anxiety about one's performance in evaluative settings. Consequently, to many readers, "research on test anxiety" means either research that is based on some version of the test–anxiety scale for children, or research within the program initiated by Mandler and Sarason (1952). The research reported in this book does not fall into either of these categories, but is concerned with the same phenomenon: anxiety about one's performance in evaluative settings. Therefore, to avoid confusion, we usually use "evaluative anxiety" or simply "anxiety," rather than "test anxiety."

and so on. This scale, the test-anxiety scale for children, has been validated extensively (see Hill & Sarason, 1966, for example), and has undergone various revisions in the hands of others (see Wallach & Kogan, 1965, for example).

The research of Sarason and his associates (Sarason, Hill & Zimbardo, 1966; Sarason, Lighthall, Davidson, Waite & Ruebush, 1960) on text anxiety opened the way for educational researchers to examine the effects of evaluative anxiety on learning and performance. These subsequent developments are reviewed in Chapter 3 and 5.

SUMMARY OF MAIN CONCEPTS

Anxiety has been defined by both existential philosophers and scientists as an unavoidable unpleasant experience having physiological, phenomenological, and behavioral manifestations.

It is regarded as adaptive insofar as it enables the individual to mobilize himself to cope with a problem, but unfortunately some of the forms of coping that one learns are maladaptive. Heidegger (1949) and Sarason (1966) have both stressed that socialization is likely to involve learning to employ superficial coping skills such as bravado, escape from the fear, and focusing on the fear rather than the problem that is evoking it—on what is to be avoided and how—rather than on the development of skills that will enable one to actually solve the problem. Freud (1936) has proposed that punishment and repression underlie the development of neurotic anxiety and that anxiety attacks occur when the repression is partially broken through.

The causes of anxiety have been variously defined, and indeed it seems likely that there are various kinds of anxiety, such that no single statement about the cause or stimulus of anxiety is sufficiently general. However, with a few modifications, the definition of anxiety proposed by Sartre (1970) serves present purposes quite well. Satre has defined anxiety as fear of failure to meet a standard, or fear that one does not hold the appropriate standard. This definition may be modified so that it deals only with standards concerning performance in school and other settings in which one perceives that performance is likely to be evaluated. Evaluative standards are, of course, internalized, so that evaluation may refer to self evaluation as well as to evaluation by others.

FOCUS

The work reported in this book concerns anxiety about evaluation in educational settings. It is assumed that anxiety is an important part of the human condition. We do not seek to do away with it. What the research and theory reported in this book has sought to do is to use the methods of experimental psychology to discover how anxiety affects intellectual performance, and how some aspects of the process of anxiety may be altered. Having gained some understanding of the effects of anxiety on such processes as memory and attention, training procedures and modifications in the learning environment were devised that enabled the student to reduce anxiety or some of the undesirable effects of anxiety on intellectual performance.

Before turning directly to that research, it is useful to examine some of the major ways in which anxiety has been defined, and to assess the usefulness of these definitions for developing treatments that reduce its debilitating effects. Chapter 3 is devoted to this problem.

3
How Shall Anxiety Be Defined?

The purpose of this chapter is to examine the major ways in which anxiety in evaluative situations may be defined, and to assess the usefulness of these definitions in developing treatments that reduce anxiety or its undesirable effects on performance. From this discussion, a number of questions are developed about relationships among the various components of anxiety that have served as operational definitions. Some hypotheses concerning ways in which the undesirable effects of anxiety may be reduced are advanced. Some of these hypotheses have been tested and are reported in subsequent chapters of this volume. Others remain to be tested.

This review is concerned primarily with conceptual definitions rather than operational definitions and with anxiety in evaluative settings rather than general anxiety. Some mention is made of general anxiety and of certain operational definitions, but only for purposes of clarifying the concept of anxiety in evaluative settings.

EVALUATIVE ANXIETY AND GENERAL ANXIETY

In the remainder of this book, the terms *evaluative anxiety* or *anxiety* used without a qualifying adjective will be used to refer to the set of phenomenological, physiological and behavioral responses that accompany concern about possible failure in any testing or evaluative situation. Evaluative anxiety is, in most respects, synonymous with the construct of test anxiety which Mandler and Sarason introduced in 1952 and defined operationally with the test-anxiety scale, and later with the test–anxiety scale for children (Sarason, Davidson, Lighthall, Waite & Ruebush, 1960). Since many operational definitions in addition to the test-anxiety scale have been employed in the research reported in this book, it seemed advisable to use the term "evaluative anxiety" rather than "test anxiety."

General anxiety is a more comprehensive construct that refers to the phenomenological, physiological, and behavioral responses that may accompany any event in which the individual perceives that he or she may be unable to deal easily and satisfactorily. For example, general anxiety may refer to the unpleasant feeling that accompanies individuals' uncertainties about values and goals and their ability to meet them. It may also refer to phobias and other neurotic anxieties such as those that Freud has identified, and to objective anxieties (again in Freud's sense of the term) that are based on a history of learning to expect certain events to be aversive. The development of the concept of general anxiety is reviewed briefly in Chapter 1 and in detail by Spielberger (1966a, 1972a,b).

Although evaluative anxiety is a form of general anxiety, the overlap between test or evaluative anxiety and general anxiety is not great enough to make the two concepts synonymous. Significant positive correlations usually are found between measures of test and general anxiety, such as the test-anxiety scale and the general-anxiety scale (Sarason, 1972). However, although correlations between measures of test anxiety and test performance generally are significant, correlations between measures of general anxiety and test performance generally are not (e.g., Sarason, 1960).

The empirically demonstrable differences between evaluative anxiety and general anxiety do not mean that the initial stimulus conditions that predispose a person to experience high evaluative anxiety are necessarily different from those of general anxiety. It is true that the immediate stimulus of evaluative anxiety is the imminence of actual evaluation; but why is the imminence of evaluation so much more anxiety arousing for some people than for others? Scientific psychology has precious little to offer in the way of sound information about the initial stimulus conditions that predispose individuals to experience anxiety. However, clinical observation coupled with much speculation has resulted in some interesting and highly plausible explanations about the development and generalization of anxiety and other forms of negative affect (e.g. Tomkins, 1963; I. Sarason, 1972). These explanations generally hold that evaluative and general anxiety may have some common antecedents. For example, the conditions that initially predispose a child to feel anxious might be parental expectations during early childhood of greater maturity and competence than the child could possibly meet. Such early experience might indicate to the child that he or she will never perform well enough to attain the security that comes of parental approval. This concern about inadequacy might generalize to many facets of the person's life: social, sexual, intellectual, and so on. And, if one of the person's concerns is an inability to do well enough in school, then any test might constitute a grave threat. As this hypothetical example suggests, inquiry into the nature and initial causes of general anxiety may yield some useful ideas about ways of helping students who experience debilitating levels of evaluative anxiety, and so we draw on this source of ideas occasionally.

PROBLEMS CONCERNING THE DEFINITION OF ANXIETY

A considerable research effort has been devoted to developing the construct of test or evaluative anxiety. However, it remains difficult to define this construct in a clear and simple fashion since its manifestations differ depending on the individual, the nature of the activity performed, and the level of anxiety experienced. It may be manifested through admission of worrying or denial of warranted fear; through perspiring, trembling, and rapid breathing; or little physiological reactivity; through avoidance of tasks; impulsive blundering, or meticulous caution. It may result, for example, in a decrement in ideational fluency under standard testing conditions, or in an increase in ideational fluency if specific instructions are given to generate ideas (Wallach & Kogan, 1965).

In view of the complexity of anxiety as manifested in evaluative settings, it is not surprising that there exist in the literature many differing explanations or descriptions of the process of anxiety. Briefly, a few of the explanations that have been proposed about the nature of anxiety are as follows:

1. Mandler and Watson (1966) have proposed that anxiety occurs when an individual is interrupted in the course of executing a desired behavior sequence and has no alternative course of action available. The result of the interruption is an emotion of helplessness and disorganization which we call anxiety. Competence, then, is the ability to control or prevent interruption.

2. Alpert and Haber (1960) have proposed that anxiety may facilitate or impair performance in evaluative situations depending on its nature.

3. Wine (1971b) and Sarason (1972) propose that anxiety be viewed primarily as an attentional phenomenon. The highly anxious person is one who attends to evaluative cues, to self-generated concern about ability to do well enough, and to feelings of physiological arousal. The low-anxious person attends to the task at hand and to the operations required for dealing with it effectively.

4. Wolpe (1966) regards anxiety as a conditioned emotional response that may be unlearned through such counterconditioning procedures as deep muscle relaxation.

5. Spence and Spence (1966) equate anxiety with drive level, and thus arrive at the well-known prediction of an interaction effect between anxiety and task difficulty on task performance.

These explanations are, for the most part, not contradictory but, rather, deal with different sets of variables. Because there has been no comprehensive integration of these many definitions and explanations, applied researchers have found it difficult to develop useful theory about the nature of anxiety. Some of the important questions that remain to be answered (and the respective chapters of this book that deal with them) are the following:

1. What characteristics of anxiety can be identified? (2,3)
2. In what ways do people experience anxiety? (1, 2, 3, 4, 7, 12)
3. How are the various manifestations of anxiety learned and unlearned? (1, 2, 3, 4, 10, 12)
4. Which cognitive processes are affected by anxiety and in what ways are they affected? How can the undesirable effects be reduced? (3, 4, 6, 11, 12)
5. What is the relation between methods of instruction and the occurrence of anxiety? How can learning and performance be optimized for both high- and low-anxious students? What methods of research design and data analysis enable us to answer these questions empirically? (5, 6)
6. How might students be directly instructed in ways of reducing their anxiety? (4, 10)
7. How can well-controlled applied research be performed on the use of anxiety-reduction procedures in instructional settings? (4, 7, 8, 9, 11, 12)

This book represents a progress report on current efforts to answer these questions. In Chapter 12 a summary if offered of what has been learned in the course of the research presented in this book. This summary does not take the form of a complete theory since much remains to be learned about the effects of anxiety on cognition and performance. Rather, it takes the form of a research model that is intended to assist researchers in taking into account what is already known and in building on that knowledge in an efficient way.

APPROACHES TO DEFINING ANXIETY

This chapter focuses on the first question: What characteristics of anxiety have been identified? The different ways of identifying or defining test anxiety provide alternative approaches to answering the other questions that have been raised here.

Anxiety is an emotional process which has several components. Since each component contributes to the definition of anxiety, it is useful for our purposes to specify these components and then to show how each may be used to define anxiety. Borrowing from Spielberger's (1972c) concept of anxiety as an emotional process, we may specify its components as follows:

1	2	3	4	5
Evaluative situation	Perception → of situation	Anxiety → state reaction	Cognitive → reappraisal	Coping, defensive → or avoidance behavior

1. An evaluative situation arises. This is a potential stressor or cause for anxiety.

2. The evaluative situation is perceived by the individual. Depending on the nature of the evaluative situation and the individual's prior learning, he may perceive it as dangerous, that is, as a situation in which he is likely to perform inadequately and perhaps fail and suffer a loss of self esteem.

3. An anxiety-state reaction occurs if the individual regards the situation as dangerous. The complex of responses that is known as the anxiety-state reaction involves a set of physiological responses, and a conscious preoccupation with these physiological changes and with the stressor. It also includes feelings of distress, helplessness, and worry about inability to do well, and sometimes a feeling of self-deprecation and shame.

4. Cognitive reappraisal follows. The individual reappraises the stressful conditions to try to find a way to deal with them. He may find a constructive coping mechanism for alleviating the stress, or may find a defensive or avoidance behavior that enables him to escape the anxiety arousing condition.

5. Coping, avoidance, or defensive behavior is then engaged. For example, the individual may find a way to solve the problem effectively; deny his feelings of anxiety and blunder ineffectively through the task; or leave the situation entirely.

Anxiety has been defined operationally in terms that relate to each of these components of the process of anxiety. For our purposes, it is convenient to regroup these components into four definitional categories as follows:

1. The phenomenology of anxiety: the individual's conscious awareness of the anxiety-state reaction (Part 3 of the process discussed). Typically it is measured by asking the individual to report which of the relevant symptoms he has experienced, for example, "Are you worried that you will not do well on this test?" Subscales measuring denial of awareness of a stressor are used to indicate defensiveness (Part 5).

2. The physiological responses of anxiety: the physiological aspects of the anxiety-state reaction (Part 3). These responses include heart rate and systolic-blood-pressure changes and are assessed with standard physiological measures.

3. Task performance: any measure of task performance, including measures of cognitive mediating processes. Such measures may be indicative of the nature of the cognitive reappraisal (Part 4) and the effectiveness of the coping mechanism (Part 5) that the individual employs following reappraisal. Any stage of the problem-solving process may be assessed, as well as the speed, accuracy, and efficiency with which it occurred.

4. The conditions (internal and external) which affect the anxiety process: the internal and external stimuli which affect the anxiety-state reaction. These conditions may be modified through training, instructions, or curriculum design. They include: the objective characteristics of the evaluative situation (Part 1), the prior learning of the individual insofar as this affects his perception of the evaluative situation (Part 2), the character of his anxiety state reaction (Part 3),

40227

the nature of reappraisal responses (Part 4), and the kind of coping, defensive or avoidance responses made (Part 5).

As an example of modification of the objective characteristics of the evaluative situation, the task instructions could include mention that the student would be given coaching and a second chance if he did poorly. As an example of modification of the anxiety-state reaction, the individual could be taught to focus attention on the task at hand rather than on feelings of worry and emotionality.

The last of the four definitional categories mentioned above—the conditions (internal and external) that affect the anxiety process—is the approach to defining anxiety that is of greatest practical interest in education, since it encompasses the modification of anxiety and of its effects through training, therapy, instructions and curriculum design. It is also the approach to defining anxiety about which the least is known at present and to which this book is primarily devoted. In this chapter, an attempt is made to show how an understanding of the first three kinds of definitions, phenomenological, physiological, and task performance, may contribute to a better understanding of the fourth, the conditions (internal and external) which affect the anxiety process. We turn now to the details of these four approaches to defining anxiety.

Phenomenological Or Self-Report Definitions

Test anxiety typically is defined as a state of worry and emotionality about the evaluation of one's performance. When persons are highly anxious, they tend to exaggerate and personalize the threat of evaluation inherent in any situation. Indeed, high-anxious individuals are *set* to search out cues that they can interpret as meaning that they may be evaluated negatively (Wine, 1971a). Then, in response to the perceived threat, the high-anxious person engages in self-absorbing activities that interfere with performance on the task at hand. These self-absorbing activities take the following forms: (1) Thinking of oneself as stupid or foolish and likely to fail ("When taking an exam, I find myself thinking of how much smarter other students are than I"); (2) Considering oneself likely to panic and hence be unable to use whatever skill or knowledge one does have ("I freeze up on things like intelligence tests and final exams"); (3) Dreading the occurrence of certain evaluative situations ("I dread courses in which the professor has the habit of giving "pop" quizzes"); (4) Noticing one's own physiological responses to threat of failure ("I sometimes feel my heart beating very fast during important tests").

A frequently used operational definition of anxiety consists of persons' own reports on their experiential states concerning evaluation. Test anxiety scales have assessed the following five kinds of conscious experience: (1) worry within an evaluative situation ("During tests I find myself thinking of the consequences of failing"); (2) worry owing to anticipation of, or reflection on, an evaluative situation that occurs at some other time ("I dread courses in which the professor gives surprise quizzes"); (3) nightmares about evaluation ("I sometimes have nightmares the night before a big test"); (4) concern over the fact of worrying more than most other persons do about tests and school ("The university should recognize that some students are more nervous than others about tests"); (5) the experience of physiological symptoms ("While taking an important exam, I perspire a great deal"). Most of these examples of anxiety scale items are taken from the test-anxiety scale (I. Sarason, 1972).

Liebert and Morris (1967) have divided anxiety items into two subscales: a worry scale dealing with cognitive concern over performance relative to that of other students; and an emotionality scale dealing with reported autonomic arousal elicited by the immediate testing situation. Research indicates that self-report items about worrying are more predictive of performance than are ones about emotionality or the experiencing of physiological symptoms (Dixon & Judd, 1974). Accordingly, many recent versions of anxiety scales deal solely with worry-type items. Three major dimensions of phenomenological or self-report scales are: (1) the state–trait dimension; (2) the facilitating–debilitating dimension; and (3) the anxiety–defensiveness dimension.

State and trait anxiety. Spielberger (1972c) and his associates have made a distinction between state anxiety and trait anxiety. An anxiety state is transitory. It is evoked when the individual perceives a stimulus as potentially harmful to him; otherwise, the level of state anxiety is low. Trait anxiety refers to stable personality differences in anxiety proneness. It is not manifested directly in behavior, rather it is inferred from the frequency and intensity of the individual's anxiety states.

What is high trait anxiety and how is it developed? Individuals who are high in trait anxiety are disposed to perceive a wide range of stimulus situations as dangerous or threatening and to respond to such threats with high state anxiety. They are more concerned with the evaluation of their performance than with details that are intrinsic to the performance itself. It is generally thought that this orientation is developed through a combination of observing the unpleasant consequences of other people's failure, and harsh personal encounters with failure.

With regard to observation of others' experiences with failure, Sarason (1972) has pointed out that the child who ". . . notices that his mother gets upset when he mentions he will have an arithmetic test tomorrow" (p. 396) or who on several occasions hears ". . . how Dad couldn't get a job he wanted because he couldn't pass the qualifying exam" (p. 396) is being given opportunities to learn to be anxious. Cognitively, he is learning to associate the idea of evaluation with a lowering of self-esteem and an expectation of failure. Physiologically, he is learning to alter certain autonomic activity (for example, systolic blood pressure, heart rate) in response to perceived threat of evaluation.

Regarding direct experience of failure, the clinical literature (e.g., Erikson, 1950; Freud, 1936; Maslow, 1954) suggests that children develop a predisposition to be highly anxious through direct experience in which unreasonable demands, threats, punishments, and frustrations of needs are imposed when they are still young and highly dependent. Clinicians lay emphasis on the role of ignoring early dependency needs, failing to help the child to attain success in his early pursuits, frequent threat of privation and punishment for failure to meet parental standards in the development of trait anxiety. Situations in which there is ambiguity as to what is to be achieved, whether help will be given, and what kind of threat exists should the child fail are believed to be particularly conducive to the development of anxiety.

Since children, especially anxious ones, are likely to regard any adult as an evaluator of their performance, their responses toward their parents as evaluators are likely to generalize to their teachers. Among these feelings, Sarason (1972) has speculated, is hostility toward those whom they believe are passing judgment on them. This hostility is in conflict with their dependency needs; hence it is not expressed, but is turned against the self, taking the form of self derogation. Consequently, the behavior that teachers are likely to observe in the anxious child are dependence, direction seeking, conformity, and social unresponsiveness.

Speilberger, Gorsuch, and Lushene (1970) have developed the state–trait anxiety inventory to provide self-report measures of both state and trait anxiety. The trait-anxiety scale asks the respondent to describe how he/she feels generally. The respondent replies to each item (for example, "I lack self confidence") by indicating "almost never," "sometimes," "often," or "almost always." The state-anxiety scale consists of a similar set of statements, and respondents are to indicate the extent to which they are experiencing each kind of feeling at that time. They are to respond to each item (for example, "I feel tense") by indicating "not at all," "somewhat," "moderately so," or "very much so." The scale, per se, does not refer specifically to evaluative anxiety. However, when it is used to assess evaluative anxiety, the trait-anxiety instructions require respondents to indicate how they feel generally when taking a test; and the state-anxiety instructions require them to indicate how they feel while actually taking a test. Thus, the situation in which this instrument is administered and a few words of instruction transform this general anxiety scale into an evaluative anxiety scale.

Spielberger (1972c) has proposed that the relation of anxiety states to trait anxiety is as follows:

1. Anxiety states are evoked when the individual perceives that he is in a threatening situation.

2. The intensity of the anxiety state is proportional to the severity of the threat the individual perceives.

3. The anxiety state will persist as long as the individual perceives that the threat is continuing.

4. High trait-anxious individuals perceive threats of failure or to self-esteem as more severe than do persons having low trait anxiety, and perceive more situations as threatening than do low trait anxious persons.

5. Elevations in state anxiety have stimulus and drive properties that may be expressed directly in behavior or that may serve to initiate psychological defenses that reduce anxiety.

6. Stressful situations that are often encountered may cause the individual to develop coping responses or defenses that reduce or minimize state anxiety.

Persons who are high in trait anxiety tend to be characterized by fear of failure (Atkinson, 1964) and by a tendency to become upset by whatever kinds of situations pose a threat to their self esteem (Sarason, 1960). Persons who are low on trait anxiety but who are currently experiencing high state anxiety respond differently to intellectual tasks than do persons who are high on trait anxiety and are currently experiencing high state anxiety. High trait-anxious persons perform best in nonevaluative situations, that is, in which failure or punishment are inevitable, or not contingent on performance. Persons who are low in trait anxiety perform best in evaluative situations in which their outcomes are within their control, and do less well in nonevaluative and noncontingent situations (Silverman & Blitz, 1956). The relationships are further complicated by interactions with intelligence and problem difficulty, which are discussed in detail by Spence and Spence (1966) and Spielberger (1966b).

Facilitating and debilitating anxiety. Sarason, Mandler, and Craighill (1952) proposed that anxiety, per se, does not necessarily lead to poor performance:

> When a stimulus situation contains elements which specifically arouse test or achievement anxiety, this increase in anxiety drive will lead to poorer performance in individuals who have test-irrelevant anxiety responses in their response repertory. For individuals without such response tendencies, these stimulus elements will raise their general drive level and result in improved performance. (p. 561)

In 1960, Alpert and Haber constructed the achievement-anxiety scale which took these two forms of anxiety into account. The achievement-anxiety scale consists of two subscales, the facilitating-anxiety subscale and the debilitating-anxiety subscale. The facilitating-anxiety subscale consists of items such as "Before a test, I become excited and alert, and this helps me to organize what I know." The debilitating-anxiety subscale consists of items such as "When I am about to take a test I get upset and forget a lot of things I have studied." In instructional situations, the debilitating-anxiety subscale has been shown to be more predictive of student performance than the facilitating-anxiety subscale (Grant, 1973) although, as expected, the facilitating anxiety subscale has a significant positive correlation with test scores, and the debilitating-anxiety subscale a negative correlation with test scores (Alpert & Haber, 1960; Carrier & Jewell, 1966).

"Facilitating anxiety" may well be a misnomer. It refers to a state of arousal or enthusiasm in the face of a challenging task, rather than to dread, worry or other unpleasant feelings that are normally considered to be defining criteria of anxiety. It is a pleasant form of anxiety-state response, followed by effective coping. Irrespective of whether it has been misnamed, the state of drive and enthusiasm that may accompany anticipation of evaluation is an interesting phenomenon, and has been examined in several of the experiments reported in Chapter 6.

Anxiety and defensiveness. A third dimension of self-report measures concerns defensiveness—whether the respondent denies or admits to *warranted* fears and anxieties.

Anxiety is typically defined as the reportable experience of dread and foreboding based on some diffuse or specific expectation of harm, rather than on an obvious external threat. Defensiveness refers to a distortion of these thoughts by unconscious mental processes such that the felt intensity of the anxiety state is reduced. Denial of fears and anxieties that everyone normally experiences is taken as evidence that the individual has both learned to be anxious and learned to use a set of techniques that reduces awareness of anxiety. They are thus rendered unable to confront consciously the source of the emotional stirrings, hence less able than nondefensive individuals to extinguish the unwarranted fears.

Defensiveness, or "lie" subscales have been devised to measure the extent to which persons deny the occurrence of negative experiences that are common to most persons. Two such instruments are the lie scale for children and the defensiveness scale for children (Sarason, Davidson, Lighthall, Waite, & Ruebush, 1960). The various defensiveness instruments differ in range and depth of areas sampled, but they generally include such things as experiencing momentary unhappiness, being dishonest, and having momentary fear or mild anxiety (for example, "I am never afraid"). Such denial is taken to mean that the individual is experiencing anxiety at some level, but is repressing conscious feelings about it.

The intellectual performance of highly defensive respondents closely resembles that of persons who report experiencing extensive trait anxiety. Wallach and Kogan (1965), in their book *Modes of Thinking in Young Children,* examined the effects of anxiety and defensiveness on children's thinking. They conclude that neither anxious children nor defensive children can bear the pain of failure or nonconformity. Both types are addicted to school achievement in the case of bright children; or regress away from intellectual pursuits into passive or childish social activities in the case of slow children. Both are relatively unable to engage in creative or fanciful thought.

Although defensiveness and lie scales have demonstrated that denial of anxiety is a commonly used defense that is accompanied by specific effects on cognitive processes (Sarason, Hill, & Zimbardo, 1964) there remains the conceptual problem of determining what psychological processes these scales signify. There is also a methodological problem connected with the use of defensiveness scales. Since the defensiveness scale is necessarily used in conjunction with an anxiety scale, each subject's data point falls somewhere on the anxiety dimension and somewhere on the defensiveness dimension. One way of using both pieces of information is to examine the relation between anxiety level and the dependent variable with defensiveness level partialed out (Sarason, Hill, & Zimbardo, 1964). Another way of using these two sets of scores is to characterize subjects roughly according to where their score appears in coordinate space (Wallach & Kogan, 1965). This leaves the researcher to decide what criterion to use to characterize subjects as, say, truly low anxious. Should it be, for example, only those who fall below the thirtieth percentile on both anxiety and defensiveness? How is the subject's overall anxiety score to be characterized? Are highly defensive subjects simply to be discarded from the analysis of data? On account of these and other problems, defensiveness subscales have not been employed in most of the research reported here. (For further discussion of defensiveness scales, their uses and their shortcomings, the reader is referred to S. B. Sarason, 1966, pp. 69–73.)

Physiological Measures

Some investigators have conceived of anxiety as an emotionally based drive state and consequently have operationally defined it by such measures of physiological arousal as systolic blood pressure and heart rate. This conception of anxiety derives in part from the work of Pavlov and such American psychologists as Gantt (1942) and Masserman (1943) on experimental neuroses. Their work led to the view that neurotic anxiety is nothing but a conditioned emotional habit. According to this view, it is established by simple conditioning of physiological responses and may be counterconditioned.

However, researchers have been unable to adduce conclusive evidence of any specific patterns of physiological activity that regularly accompany the phenomenological components of anxiety. As Endler and Hunt (1966) have shown, whether anxiety is manifested in physiological changes varies between individuals and is idiosyncratic to the eliciting stimulus within each individual. Many studies that have used physiological measures along with other measures of anxiety have noted no significant physiological differences as a function of other measures of anxiety (e.g., O'Neil, Spielberger & Hansen, 1969, using systolic blood pressure; Hodges, 1968, using heart rate). There is, in fact, evidence that persons who are physiologically highly reactive to stress experience little or no anxiety. For example, Lykken (1957) and Jones (1950) have noted that persons whom others judge as being extremely "cool," and calm are the most physiologically reactive to stressors. Schachter (1971) has found that this pattern of extreme physiological reactivity to stress accompanied by lack of emotionality is characteristic of criminals who have been characterized as psychopathic. He has tentatively concluded that persons who are highly reactive physiologically are insensitive to changes in their own physiological level of arousal. This insensitivity may be due either to adaptation to extremely high levels of arousal or to a failure to learn to associate emotionality with physiological cues in the first place.

Since physiological response to stress does not necessarily result in the conscious experience of anxiety and since anxiety may be experienced without apparent physiological changes, we must conclude that the kinds of physiological responses that have been measured are neither necessary nor sufficient conditions for the occurrence of anxiety. This is not to say that there is no physiological basis of anxiety. It does, however, raise various questions:

1. What is the role of physiological response conditioning in the development of anxiety? What is the potential role of physiological response conditioning in reducing anxiety and its undesirable effects?

2. What is the role of physiological responses in determining the experience of anxiety?

3. Does anxiety that includes such physiological manifestations as trembling, increased heart rate, increased galvanic skin response (GSR) or increased blood pressure have any different effects on intellectual performance than anxiety that does not involve such physiological responses?

These questions may turn out to be crucial to an ultimate understanding of the nature of test anxiety. However, most of the research reported in this book has not involved the use of physiological measures for several reasons:

1. As the research previously summarized has indicated, physiological measures of anxiety tend to be uncorrelated with one another and with phenomenological and performance measures of anxiety.

2. There are extensive problems of recording and interpreting physiological data due to such phenomena as "floor" and "ceiling" effects, physiological adaptation to the stimuli of anxiety, and artifacts due to various forms of electrical interference in even the most carefully controlled laboratory situations.

3. It is not feasible to locate physiological recording equipment in school settings, to have electrodes attached to students while they attempt to do academic work, or to require of students that they engage in the long waiting periods required to obtain steady baseline measures. Telemetric devices, which do not require the use of electrodes, are extremely expensive.

4. The cost of using such equipment and of obtaining the necessary staff of engineers and technicians to operate it would be prohibitive, particularly in field settings where most of this research was performed.

Task-Performance Measures

Some highly predictable effects of anxiety on intellectual functioning have been used as operational definitions of anxiety. For example, the quality of human-figure drawing is affected by anxiety in various predictable ways and consequently a human-figure-drawing test of anxiety has been developed and used. (A review of the use of this test is presented by Roback, 1968.) Some specific components of task performance, such as short-term memory, deployment of attention, incidental learning, and divergent thinking, are also affected by anxiety. Consequently, these cognitive variables are useful in defining the construct of test anxiety. Furthermore, an understanding of the effect of test anxiety on these cognitive processes is essential to the development of certain kinds of treatments aimed at reducing the undesirable effects of anxiety on performance, as we shall discuss subsequently. However, many of these effects are not reliable enough to serve as operational definitions of anxiety.

Both the general effects of anxiety on task performance and its effects on mediating component processes that underlie the performance are discussed here. The major findings concerning the relation between anxiety and performance as it interacts with task complexity and stage of learning will be reviewed. The cognitive and motivational processes that are believed to account for these results will be discussed along with consideration of the specific effects of anxiety on attention and memory.

Performance. It is well documented that anxiety tends to reduce performance on complex tasks, but to facilitate performance of simple or overlearned responses (e.g., Ruebush, 1960). The term, "complex task," is used here to refer to a task in which the person must make one or more difficult discriminations in order to select the correct response from the response hierarchy. This result has been explained in drive theory terms as follows. According to drive theory (Spence & Spence, 1966), behavior is determined by several factors, the most important of which are habit (sHr) and drive (D). It is proposed that D multiplies H to produce excitatory potential (sEr); that is, the strength of the tendency to respond with habit H. Consequently, a particular response tendency, sEr, is at zero when either D or H are at zero. At any given level of H above zero, an increase in drive will increase the tendency to respond, sEr. In the early stages of learning, the habit to be learned has zero or relatively low strength in relation to the other response tendencies that are aroused by the (to-be-conditioned) stimulus. Since drive and habit have a multiplicative relation to the tendency to respond in a particular way, an increase in drive without an accompanying increase in the strength of the habit to be learned results in a relative increase in the probability of evocation of one of the stronger existing (incorrect) responses. That is, the response to be learned is less likely to be evoked.

Spence (1958) has equated high anxiety with a state of heightened drive and hence proposed that tasks requiring a single overlearned response are performed relatively more rapidly and correctly by anxious persons because their anxiety (high drive) decreases the likelihood of selection of weaker response tendencies in the habit-family hierarchy (Spence & Spence, 1966). Conversely, the effect of anxiety is to decrease the availability of a response tendency that is weak or poorly differentiated from other similar responses.

One implication of the effect of drive or anxiety on response selection is that the effects of anxiety on learning depend on the stage of the learning process. Most research has shown that anxiety hinders performance early in learning, but may even facilitate performance in later stages (e.g., Lekarczyk & Hill, 1969). In the early stages of learning, when the correct response is not yet dominant in the hierarchy, heightened drive only serves to make the correct response relatively less accessible. However, after the correct habit has become dominant in the habit-family hierarchy, the heightened drive increases the strength of that habit relative to the others.

A related implication of the effect of anxiety on response selection and evaluation is that it is difficult for the highly anxious individual to generate a wide range of response alternatives and to evaluate their appropriateness in relation to his own prior knowledge. As cited previously, Wallach and Kogan (1965) found that highly anxious and highly defensive children are less facile than their counterparts in producing divergent responses to problems.

Even when the response alternatives are presented (as in multiple-choice problems), highly anxious persons are relatively less able to assess their state of knowledge and arrive at an appropriate determination of the probability of correctness of each alternative. Rather, as suggested by the Hull–Spence (Spence, 1958) formulation, they overestimate the probality of correctness of their preferred alternative and underestimate the probability of correctness of their less preferred alternatives (Sieber, 1974). A detailed discussion of these results is found in Chapter 4.

Memory. A specific process that appears to be influenced by anxiety is memory. Highly test-anxious persons tend to do relatively less well on problems requiring memory (for example, recalling the outcome of previous trials, or a set of facts that are to be used in a subsequent aspect of the problem). However, they perform at least as well as low-anxious persons when memory support is provided (Sieber, Kameya, & Paulson, 1970). This research is described in detail in Chapter 4.

Attention. Another process that appears to be influenced by anxiety is attention. Wine (1971b) has reviewed the literature on anxiety and suggested that anxious persons are more selective attenders than are nonanxious persons. Specifically, anxious individuals tend to focus their attention on the individual who is evaluating them, on their own concerns about failure, and on the task they are supposed to be doing. Their attention is thus limited to certain classes of cues, and incidental learning is relatively less likely to occur (Easterbrook, 1959). A discussion of further research by Wine on attentional patterns in relation to anxiety may be found in Chapter 4.

Other processes. What other processes are affected by anxiety? Receptor orientation to stimuli, span of apprehension, ability to mask out irrelevant stimuli, information search, self-instruction and planning, comparison processes? It remains for educational psychologists interested in the effects of anxiety on cognition to devise ways of ferreting out such effects as may exist.

Modification of Anxiety and Its Undesirable Effects

Several components and effects of the anxiety process have already been discussed, and obviously modification of anxiety may be conceptualized as the modification of these response components. Specifically, the modification of anxiety would involve modification of: (1) its phenomenology—expectations, self evaluations, attentional phenomena, and so on; (2) its physiology—autonomic response patterns characteristic of anxiety; or (3) its effects on cognitive processes, and in turn on task performance. The ways of modifying these components of anxiety are examined in this book. Obviously, one desirable aim of education is to create settings that do not engender anxiety in the first place. Our discussion is relevant to this aim, but focuses primarily on ways in which anxiety, once engendered, may be reduced. These include: modification of social interaction patterns, redefinition of task situations, redirection of attention during task performance, and strengthening or supplanting of required cognitive processes.

Modification of social-interaction patterns. As summarized in the previous discussion of trait anxiety, high trait anxiety, dependency and low self-esteem tend to develop when unreasonable demands for performance are made on the child and no help or emotional support is given. Phillips, Martin, and Meyers (1972) have pointed out that one important facet of treatment aimed at reducing test anxiety is acceptance of the individual's dependent behavior. Research has shown that nurturant, personal, and rewarding interaction does indeed improve the performance of anxious persons. The feedback "Good!" produces higher performance in anxious persons than does "Try harder" (Sarason & Harmatz, 1965). The word "Right" produces better performance in anxious persons than does a buzzer used as a reinforcer (Horowitz & Armentrout, 1965). Punishment for undesirable performance is ineffective with anxious children; giving attention or token reinforcement for desired behavior and ignoring undesired behavior are generally highly effective (Wolf, Risley, Johnston, Harris, & Allen, 1967). This is not surprising in view of the fact that highly anxious persons tend to be considerably more responsive to positive verbal reinforcement than are low-anxious persons (Sarason & Glanzer, 1963).

Sarason and Glanzer (1962) have shown that one of the effects of a regimen of positive reinforcement on the phenomenology of anxiety is an increase in positive self reference.

Redefinition of task situations. It is characteristic of persons with high trait anxiety to regard a relatively large number of situations as evaluative ones. Various approaches have been identified that are effective in reorienting the attention and interpretations of the anxious individual.

I. Sarason (1958a) has shown that what persons are told about the tasks they are asked to perform has large differential effects, depending on their anxiety level. Low trait-anxious individuals respond with good, highly motivated performance to challenges (for example, being told to try to attain a high level of success) while highly anxious persons do relatively poorly under challenging instructions. Highly anxious persons respond well, when reassured that they need not worry if at first they progress slowly and make mistakes, but such instructions produce poor performance in low-anxious persons. Sarason (1972) was later able to devise instructions that both motivated the low anxious to perform and refocused the attention of the highly anxious by emphasizing the intrinsic aspects of the task performance and playing down the nature of the task. In his particular experiment, the following instructions were used:

> This is an experiment concerning the shape of learning curves. Some people learn at a more rapid rate than do other people. Some people learn more during a given period of time than do others. I am really not interested in either of these aspects of learning. My concern is exclusively with the shape of the learning curves for certain types of tasks. What would help me the most would be for you to think of the task on which you are to perform as an opportunity to get practice in memorizing different sorts of material. You won't get to try out all of the tasks, but you will find your task interesting and food for thought. I think you will find working on this task worthwhile [Sarason, 1972, p. 388].

Presumably, the crucial aspects for both challenging and reassuring may be worked into any set of instructions.

A more direct and basic approach to the problem of attention has been undertaken by Wine (1973), and is reported in Chapter 4. Briefly, she instructed students in productive attentional behavior, and found that this both reduced self-reports of anxiety and improved performance in various tasks.

Obviously, the physiological responses of anxiety are not triggered when the individual has been so instructed that the situation is not seen as an evaluative one. However, the chain of events: interpretation of a situation as evaluative → evocation of physiological response → awareness of and preoccupation with one's own physiological responses → deterioration of performance, is not the only possible sequence. Awareness of physiological arousal may be interpreted by the individual in various ways. In a context that could reasonably be considered as evaluative, it is often considered an indication that the evaluation is to be feared (Schachter, 1966). Hence, the use of deep relaxation therapy or the relabeling of these physiological cues as indicators of achievement motivation might prove useful, although little has been done in this direction.

Strengthening or supplementing required cognitive processes. A final way of helping anxious persons to overcome their concern about failure, and to improve their performance is to create conditions under which they are, indeed, less likely to fail. There are two major instructional approaches that may be employed to this end.

One approach is to provide a direct program of instruction in study, learning, and performance skills. Two such instructional programs are described in this book. Chapter 10 is devoted to description and evaluation of an automated anxiety reduction program, and Chapter 4 contains a description of Wine's (1971a) instructional program for teaching and reinforcing attentional, learning, and performance skills.

The second approach is to modify existing curriculum and instruction in subject-matter areas so that the cognitive skills that are needed for successful performance are shaped and reinforced or are supplanted, as the student works.

The shaping and reinforcing of needed skills may be accomplished by providing the individual with an opportunity to overlearn the skills that are required and by teaching the realistic planning and structuring of work. Supplanting of the cognitive processes that are impaired by anxiety might be accomplished by providing memory support so that the student is not hindered by inability to keep track of feedback from prior trials, by providing explicit step-by-step plans or instructions, or otherwise structuring learning so that the impaired abilities are not needed.

SUMMARY

As this discussion indicates, the first three definitions of anxiety may be used in the service of the fourth, and none of the four classes of definitions *alone* is very useful to the educational researcher.

Phenomenological measures indicate what an individual is willing to divulge about feelings of anxiety. These measures, taken in conjunction with performance measures, provide information that is needed to construct and evaluate programs designed to reduce anxiety or its undesirable effects.

Physiological measures do not appear to be systematically related to other anxiety phenomena and they are extremely difficult to obtain reliably. However, a knowledge of possible physiological concomitants of anxiety has been of value in the designing of therapeutic programs that enable persons to deal with their feelings of anxiety (see Chapter 4 and 10).

Task-performance measures obtained on carefully designed problems provide the context for studying the effects of anxiety on performance and for determining what modification in instructional procedure will reduce anxiety or its undesirable effects. As such, this approach to defining anxiety has formed the cornerstone of the current effort.

Programmed instruction is designed to shape and reinforce subskills, chaining them together into successful performance of a complex task. It would appear to be a natural vehicle for strengthening required subskills and enhancing the performance of anxious students. There is little chance of failure, provided that the learner is highly motivated, which anxious persons are. Programmed instruction may take the form of computer-based instruction with its provision of feedback loops that permit relearning of subskills, distributed practice, and the display of additional information as desired. A major portion of this book is devoted to exploration of the potential of programmed instruction and computer-based instruction for reduction of anxiety and its undesirable effects on performance. Chapters 5 and 6 deal with the work of Tobias and his associates, and Chapters 8 through 11 are devoted to the work of O'Neil and his associates on these problems.

Four major ways in which anxiety may be defined have been discussed: physiological definitions, phenomenological or self-report definitions, task-performance definitions, and definitions stating the conditions under which anxiety is increased and decreased. Information bearing on four questions has been discussed: What are the varieties of evaluative anxiety that may be observed? How are they learned and unlearned? How do they affect cognitive and affective processes and performance? How can the undesirable effects of anxiety be done away with?

Where does the present research fall within this definitional framework? The following chapter is intended to show how our conceptualization of anxiety has developed and how the various definitions of anxiety—conceptual, operational, and construct—have evolved in the course of this work.

4

A Paradigm for Research
on Treatments Designed to
Modify Anxiety or its Effects

In Chapter 3, anxiety was defined as a many-faceted process which is adaptive if it culminates in effective coping. This chapter builds on these defining concepts and focuses on a paradigm for research on treatments designed to modify anxiety or its undesirable effects.

What do we mean when we speak of modifying anxiety or its effects? The process of anxiety (stress → perception of danger → the anxiety-state reaction → cognitive reappraisal → coping, avoidance, or defensive behavior) is an integral part of the human response to environmental demands. It is hard to imagine what kind of human being would be left if the entire process were extinguished. How would such a person function in a changing and sometimes hostile world? Anxiety is not a form of pathology that should be removed. Rather, it is an essential process, but one that does not always function in an optimally adaptive way. If anxiety is viewed from this perspective, then educational or clinical efforts to help anxious students would consist of modifications in the process of anxiety that help the individual to feel more comfortable and to accomplish what is desired with greater competence. The following concrete examples illustrate some ways of modifying the process of anxiety so that these objectives are met:

1. The individual might be taught more effective problem-solving skills (for example, to generate a variety of solution alternatives and to evaluate them, to organize information so that it is more easily retrieved from memory, and so on). The availability of such coping skills may enable the individual to approach problems confident of success. Thus, functioning at *all* stages of the anxiety process may become more adaptive, comfortable and otherwise characteristic of a competent person.

2. The individual might be taught to modify the pattern of attention so that the anxiety-state response involves less worrying about failure and more constructive focusing on the problem at hand. As a consequence, the anxiety

process would include a more competent reappraisal of the stressor and more effective coping. (Such a training program has been used successfully by Wine, 1972, and is described in a subsequent part of this chapter.)

3. The individual might be given test items that contain humor. A laughter response on the part of the test taker would be incompatible both with perception of the test as threatening and with an intensely unpleasant anxiety-state reaction. This procedure was found to facilitate performance in highly anxious students (Smith, Ascough, Ettinger, & Nelson, 1971).

4. The individual could be presented with problems in such a way so as not to require the use of cognitive processes that are adversely affected by anxiety. One such approach is to provide the student with external memory support. This approach has been found to enable highly anxious students to perform as well as their low-anxious counterparts (Sieber, Kameya, & Paulson, 1970).

The first two of these treatments might be regarded as modifications of maladative responses within the anxiety process, and the second two as ways of circumventing undesirable effects of anxiety on performance. However, the distinction between changing the process versus circumventing the effects of anxiety is difficult to defend in practice. For example, students given the option of using an external memory support in the course of instruction indicated a lowered anxiety-state reaction on subsequent trials (Collier, Poynor, O'Neil, & Judd, 1973). It seems reasonable to expect that most procedures that affect ability to perform affect, in turn, anxiety-state reaction and possibly other parts of the anxiety process as well, temporarily or for an indefinite period of time. Consequently, in the following discussion, no firm distinction is made between treatments that modify anxiety and those that modify its effects on performance.

Approaches to modifying the anxiety process or its effects on performance such as those four previously mentioned were difficult to conceptualize until about 1966, when process models of anxiety (e.g., Sieber, 1969; Spielberger, 1966a) began to appear in the literature. Prior to that time, anxiety generally was regarded as a trait. The trait conception led to severe conceptual and methodological problems for the researcher who sought to discover treatments that would help the anxious student. Problems with the trait conception and ways in which these problems are circumvented with the process model are reviewed here to provide historical perspective on the development of the conceptual and methodological approaches that have been employed in current research.

PROBLEMS WITH THE TRAIT CONCEPTION OF ANXIETY

When the construct of test anxiety was introduced by Mandler and Sarason (1952), the major models of anxiety extant in the psychological literature were and Freudian (1936) model and Hull–Spence (1943) model. Both of these models treat anxiety as a trait and are of little heuristic value to researchers seeking to conceive of effective treatment programs. Astute researchers were able to glean some understanding of the needs of anxious students from those models and from clinical experience with anxious students, but their ideas were rather global and difficult to test empirically. For example, in their excellent pioneering book, *Anxiety in Elementary School Children,* Sarason, Lighthall, Davidson, Waite, and Ruebush (1960) advised teachers to do the following:

1. Identify , with a test-anxiety scale, those children at all levels of ability who experience a high degree of anxiety.
2. Be sure to encourage them to express any uncertainty or difficulty they experience in trying to master school work.
3. Encourage them to express their dependency on the teacher for repetition and additional instruction.
4. Make sure they are not allowed to feel that their self-esteem, or the teacher's esteem for them, is dependent on their test performance.

No subsequent research has cast doubt on the soundness of this advice. However, subsequent developments have shown that more concrete and detailed advice can be formulated. Some of the specific kinds of responses that are to be enhanced or reduced have been identified and ways of accomplishing these aims have been developed. But this can only be done within the context of a process model of anxiety. For, when anxiety is regarded as a unitary trait, it follows that anxiety per se must be reduced in order to reduce its undesirable effects. And this assumption leads to several conceptual and methodological difficulties:

1. Elimination of anxiety does not necessarily lead to improved intellectual performance unless: (a) anxiety is debilitating; (b) anxiety is the cause of poor performance and not vice versa; and (c) reduction of anxiety improves intellectual performance. The first two assumptions are not always true, as documented by Spence and Spence (1966) and by Spielberger (1966b). And, if anxiety has any adaptive functions, the final assumption also must be false at times.
2. There is no single measure that adequately represents the trait of anxiety, thus it is difficult to specify operationally what is to be reduced.
3. If the researcher settles for a phenomenological measure of anxiety as an indicator of the trait, as most investigators have done, there remains the problem that phenomenological measures of trait anxiety are not sufficiently sensitive to indicate significant effects of any but very powerful and enduring treatments.

When anxiety is regarded as a process, each component of the process is viewed as possibly affecting each other component. Maladaptive functioning of any component of the process may result in any of the phenomenological, physiological, and performance manifestations of debilitating anxiety. The research approach dictated by this model consists of two basic steps:

1. Identification of a maladaptive mode of functioning of some component of the anxiety process. This involves basic research on the relation between level of anxiety and the functioning of a selected component.

2. Development of a treatment designed to bring about adaptive functioning of the treated component and of other interdependent components of the anxiety process. This involves development of a treatment designed to have a direct and desirable effect on the selected component, and evaluation of the effect of the treatment on that component and on others such as proficiency of task performance, and the individual's sense of well-being as indicated by a self-report measure of state anxiety.

What is the researcher seeking with this approach? Presumably, the ideal treatments are those which alter the anxiety process in ways that most fully meet educational objectives—that produce highly motivated, self-confident, competent, innovative problem solvers as quickly and conveniently as possible. Thus, treatments might be evaluated in terms of the extent to which they meet such criteria as these. We turn now to the details of such an approach.

A PARADIGM FOR APPLIED RESEARCH ON EVALUATIVE ANXIETY

Overview

The researcher begins with an hypothesis concerning the functioning of some cognitive or affective variable within one or more of the components of the anxiety process, and in the context of a particular kind of evaluative task. To use an example that has already been mentioned and that is subsequently developed in greater detail, one such hypothesis is that inability to remember previously developed information in the course of problem solving may be characteristic of highly anxious persons. This is detrimental to performance in tasks which necessitate keeping track of previously observed information in order to develop a correct solution.

To test an hypothesis such as this, the researcher might select individuals who indicate high trait anxiety on a self-report scale and compare their performance with that of low trait-anxiety individuals with respect to variables such as ability to recall crucial task information that has just been generated, and ability to attain a correct solution efficiently.

If highly anxious persons are found to function less adaptively at the task, relative to their low-anxious counterparts, the next step in the research is to seek to develop a treatment that will enable them to overcome the problems that have been identified. To continue with this example, any of several treatments might be tried. A curriculum might be devised such that external memory support is automatically available to the problem solver. For example, using computer-assisted instruction, a running record of prior solution attempts might

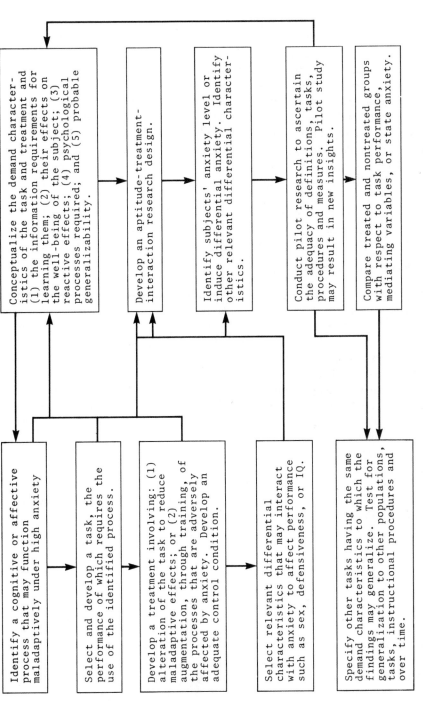

FIG. 4.1   A flow chart depicting some major problems involved in the conception, design and execution of anxiety-treatment interaction research.

45

be made available on the cathode-ray tube, at the student's request. Or, the student might be taught some heuristic techniques such as the use of mnemonic devices or note-taking skills. The effect of the treatment is then evaluated. If the treatment produces desired results, application may follow. Ways may be devised for incorporating the treatment into actual instructional programs.

This basic paradigm is obviously not original; it incorporates methods of experimental and applied psychology. It is new in that only recently have these methods been applied to research and development on anxiety, and adapted to deal with certain problems inherent in the study of anxiety. These elaborations are brought to the reader's attention in three ways in this chapter. In Figure 4.1, a flow chart is presented to show some of the problems that are involved in the conception, design, and application of research on anxiety. These and other problems are then discussed in some detail. Three examples are then given of research which employs all or part of this paradigm.

Selection of a Process and a Task

Any cognitive or affective process may turn out to be a reasonable candidate for investigation if it is frequently required in academic learning and performance settings. The research reported in this book no doubt deals with but a few of the processes that are altered when the individual is anxious. Furthermore, of the processes studied, it is not necessarily the case that the most fruitful level of analysis has been employed. (For example, as described in detail in Chapter 12, we have failed to make useful distinctions between input, processing, and output stages of learning behavior.) Where does one go from here in selecting cognitive and affective variables for further research? At what level of analysis should these variables be defined?

Six sources to which the researcher might turn for additional ideas about relevant cognitive variables are: (1) the literature on experimental research in cognition; (2) theory and research on cognitive development; (3) theory and research on problem solving and decision making (e.g., Newell, Shaw, and Simon, 1958; Maier, 1963); (4) the educational psychology literature dealing with the processes of learning and with educational objectives (e.g., Gagne, 1970; Bloom, 1956); (5) the school-curriculum literature dealing with specific areas of instruction and with the skills that are to be acquired with each (e.g., De Boer & Dallman, 1970; Grossnickle, Brueckner, & Reckzeh, 1968); (6) the literature on intellectual abilities and their nurture (e.g., Terman & Merrill, 1937; Meeker, 1969).

Likewise, to identify affective processes that might warrant study within this paradigm, there are various sources to which one might turn for ideas. These include the psychological literature on affect (e.g., Tomkins, 1962, 1963), the literature on anxiety (e.g., Spielberger, 1972a, b), and the literature on affective objectives in education (e.g., Krathwohl, Bloom, & Masia, 1964).

It might be argued, however, that there is a vast difference between the variables discussed in the curriculum literature and those discussed in the experimental-psychology literature. Which level of analysis is appropriate for research within the paradigm?

Whether one studies orienting responses, perception of one's own autonomic responses, ability to make accurate estimates, attention, memory, or discrimination ability—to name but a few variables that are candidates for research—each process may be differentiated into subprocesses and reduced to successively finer levels of analysis until the phenomenon bears little resemblance to processes we usually consider to be a part of learning or problem solving. Is such analysis or reduction of processes advantageous in anxiety-treatment research? For example, would the study of receiver-operator curve characteristics of individuals in relation to their anxiety levels provide useful practical information about the effects of anxiety on discrimination processes in many learning and problem-solving activities? This is an open question deserving consideration. However, the mere existence of a sophisticated model of signal detection or discrimination processes does not constitute grounds for using it in the present paradigm. While signal detection, in the context in which it is usually studied, bears little resemblance to most educational situations, it may be a basic process in school learning. Only a careful analysis of school learning tasks would provide information on this question. In any event, if the process does not occur regularly within a school-related task, it is obviously pointless to study the effects of anxiety on that process in the interest of helping anxious students. Ultimately, both the basic research and the development of useful treatments within the school curriculum depend on the selection of processes and tasks that are a regular part of the instructional program. Furthermore, the processes must be capable of being studied in the context of actual instructional settings. Some reasons for this have to do with research ethics, information background of subjects, reactive effects, sequential effects, and problems of generalizability.

Research ethics. According to the American Psychological Association publication entitled *Ethical Principles in the Conduct of Research with Human Participants* (1973):

> Ethical practice requires the investigator to inform the participant of all features of the research that reasonably might be expected to influence willingness to participate, and to explain all other aspects of the research about which the participant inquires. Failure to make full disclosure gives added emphasis to the investigator's responsibility to protect the welfare and dignity of the research participant.
>
> Openness and honesty are essential characteristics of the relationship between investigator and research participant. When the methodological requirements of a study necessitate concealment or deception, the investigator is required to ensure the participant's understanding of the reasons for this action and to restore the quality of the relationship with the investigator. [p. 29]

Before evaluative anxiety may be studied, it must be induced somehow: some individuals must be made to believe that they are being evaluated and that the outcome of the evaluation will have very important consequences for them. One problem faced by researchers in this area is that of finding ethical ways to induce anxiety. It is rare that anxiety can be induced by placing the individual in an evaluative situation that he knows has no serious consequences for his future. Perhaps an anxiety-prone young child may experience a state of high anxiety when told that a psychologist from a nearby university wants to see how well the child can perform. But anxiety-prone high-school or college students, in all probability, will not muster much anxiety for such an occasion. On the other hand, a fake Scholastic Aptitude Test or Graduate Record Examination session certainly would arouse state anxiety, but would be highly unethical. With sophisticated adolescents and adults, there are few ethical ways to create evaluative anxiety, short of conducting authentic evaluations in the course of school programs. Clearly, then, the process must be capable of being studied in the course of regular school instruction and evaluation procedures. It is true that some rather contrived tasks may be used for certain basic research purposes, if it is possible to arouse evaluative anxiety with those tasks within the ethical constraints of the American Psychological Association's guidelines. But before a full program of research can be completed, the process eventually must be studied within a school curriculum for other reasons to which we now turn.

Information background. To arouse anxiety, the difficulty level of the test material must be controlled to some extent so that it is neither too outlandishly difficult to be taken seriously, nor too easy to worry about. Furthermore, it should be a test of an ability that the student expects to be able to demonstrate; for example, a test of comprehension of physics principles would be more engaging for science students than for art students in most cases. The requirement that students have an appropriate kind and amount of background information to make the test one they will feel they should be able to deal with, but one for which the answers have not been overlearned can be met in two simple and convenient ways. A task, puzzle, or game, accompanied by a reasonably simple set of rules or instructions may be given to the student. Or, some educational materials may be presented that are to be learned immediately and used as the basis for answering questions or solving problems. If the materials are new to the student and somewhat challenging to persons of their ability level, then the requirement of roughly equal and appropriate information background will probably be met. There remains, however, the problem of motivation. Such a test may seem to the student to be of no serious consequence and, hence, may not engender anxiety unless presented under false pretexts— which raises some of the ethical problems discussed. The best way of assuring that students have roughly equal and adequate information and motivation to succeed is to use the curriculum materials and tests that are a part of their current academic work.

Reactive effects. Research tasks should be selected so that reactive effects are minimized. Reactive effects are responses created by the person's awareness of being tested and those which may invalidate the interpretation of results. Two reactive effects, the "guinea-pig" effect and "role selection," are particularly relevant to this paradigm. (For further discussion of reactive effects, the reader is referred to Webb, Campbell, Schwartz, & Sechrest, 1971.)

When the subject knows that he is a "guinea pig" in research, the subject is likely to behave in a special way: rebel; fake responses; try to make a good impression; develop an interest not previously demonstrated; or become extremely self-conscious. Guinea-pig responses, then, are new or atypical responses.

Role selection refers to selection of a role that is indeed typical of that person, but not necessarily typical in the kind of situation to which the researcher wishes to generalize. The subject selects the "proper" role for the situation. Thus, the subject who is told to solve some puzzles as part of a study of evaluative anxiety may decide to become the analytic self, or the carefree easy-going self, or the impulsive self. But perhaps none of these roles is one the subject typically takes when doing academic work or taking tests.

The obvious way to circumvent these reactive effects is to gather data in an actual instructional setting. Even the administration of a self-report anxiety scale is a rather natural event in that setting, since it is perfectly reasonable for an instructor to be concerned about the effects of coursework and evaluation on the feelings of the student. If data are required on such variables as reaction time, number of times the subject requests additional information, or number of trials to solution, a computer-assisted instruction environment may provide the necessary means of control and accurate recording without exposing to the student the obvious trappings of a research project.

Sequential effects. Anxiety level changes over time: adaptation occurs, defenses develop, constructive coping skills are learned, and additional sources of anxiety may begin to affect the individual and to have cumulative effects. Whether the subject is in the control group or the treatment group, the response to a series of evaluative situations is likely to change over time. Consequently, it is desirable to attempt to observe these sequential effects and to obtain asymptotic measures if an asymptote can be reached. To obtain such sequential data, a familiar evaluative setting and an extensive set of evaluative tasks are required. Again, the actual school learning situation appears to offer the best opportunity for creating such conditions.

Generalizability of results. For various reasons, results that have been carefully obtained in a given task setting may not be generalizable to other task settings. A brief summary of some of the factors that jeopardize external validity may assist the researcher in selecting research tasks and in estimating the generalizability of findings:

Selection effects. The students with whom the study is performed may differ from the populations to which results are generalized in ways that invalidate the conclusions. Research in natural settings, using highly heterogeneous samples of subjects will help to establish the variance or limits of generalizability due to population differences.

Nature, number, and salience of treatments. The experimental setting is likely to be simpler than the natural setting to which the researcher wishes to generalize with respect to the number of incidental or intended experiences the student has during or prior to an evaluative task. The additional events that occur in the natural setting may result in interactions or main effects which greatly deviate from the anticipated effects.

Nature, number and salience of processes. The experimental setting is likely to focus on fewer, and a somewhat different set, of cognitive or affective processes than are used in the natural setting. At worst, the setting to which findings are generalized may only *appear* to require the process that has been studied, or the task may be such that the particular process studied is very easy to perform and anxiety does not interfere with its functioning. Less disastrous to attempted applications of research findings and more typical is the case in which the process plays a less salient role in the setting to which the findings are generalized than it did in the experimental setting. The process of interest may indeed be required, and anxiety may interfere with the process. However, relative to the other processes required, its overall effect on performance may be rather insignificant.

These problems of generalizability constitute good reason for conducting research in the natural setting as early in the research program as is feasible. Unfortunately, however, research conducted in one natural setting may not generalize to another natural setting. One way to reduce this problem of generalizability is to know in detail the curriculum and instructional practices in the area to which the research will be applied, to understand the kinds of errors students typically make, and to analyze typical evaluative tasks in the curriculum to determine what processes are required.

Summary. The researcher seeks to find a cognitive or affective variable which is regularly affected by anxiety and which is frequently used in the course of studying and test taking. To avoid the difficulties that sometime accompany classroom research and to simplify the use of various means of control and manipulation in the exploratory stages of the research, it may be convenient to employ a contrived task. However, this may raise other kinds of problems. There are ethical considerations, problems of assuring equal and adequate information for all students, problems with reactive effects, and problems of measuring sequential effects—all of which may be unsolvable with contrived tasks. After preliminary investigation, the phenomenon is studied in a natural educational setting. The eventual treatment procedures will be of questionable usefulness unless they are employed and evaluated in the setting in which they will be used by the practitioner.

Measurement and Induction of Anxiety

Level of anxiety may be inferred by whatever means are considered valid. There are two basic means of inferring level of anxiety: measurement and induction.

Measurement typically is done via a self-report questionnaire or a projective test, administered sometime prior to the study. Apparently, the most appropriate time to measure anxiety is *just prior* to performance of the research task. Tennyson and Boutwell (1973) have shown that measurement of trait anxiety or of state anxiety prior to task performance provides a very poor estimate of task performance relative to measures of state anxiety during performance. This results from fluctuations in anxiety over time and to environmental changes.

Differential state-anxiety induction typically is accomplished by leading one group to expect an important test and leading the other group to expect a routine remedial exercise. If differential induction is used, it is desirable to check the effectiveness of the induction by administering a state-anxiety questionnaire to the subjects at some point following the induction and prior to, during, or just after the task. A very powerful anxiety-induction procedure can be expected to produce highly predictable differences in state anxiety and task performance between the high-anxiety induction group and the low-anxiety induction group. However, just as the theory of state and trait anxiety would predict, there is also tremendous variance in state anxiety within groups (Sieber, 1974).

Different assumptions underlie the procedures of anxiety measurement and induction. If trait anxiety is measured, it is assumed that in an evaluative setting, those high on trait anxiety will be in a state of high anxiety while those who are low on trait anxiety will be in a state of low anxiety. However, if anxiety is induced in one group by leading them to believe that they are facing a very important evaluation, it is generally assumed that all members of this group will experience a state of high anxiety. The contradiction in these two assumptions is obvious: the first assumption implies that only high trait-anxious people experience high anxiety in evaluative settings; the second implies that everyone is highly anxious when facing an important evaluation. The truth apparently lies close enough to the middle that both procedures seem to be valid for many research purposes.

Measurement of Other Relevant Differential Characteristics

Other variables such as IQ and defensiveness may be of interest because of their interaction with anxiety in its effect on performance. However, the usefulness of this additional information is limited by methodological difficulties. It is not highly desirable to match high- and low-anxious persons with respect to other variables, since matching procedures tend to result in nonrandom selection of subjects, especially when used with sets of variables that are not orthogonal.

Bellewicz (1965) has discussed in detail the disadvantages of matched designs involving quantitative responses, especially as the number of matching variables increases.

As discussed in Chapter 3, a procedure that is frequently used to combine anxiety and defensiveness scores is covariance, or partial correlation. However, such procedures are useful only when the covariate accounts for more than 9% of the variance on the dependent measure.

Selection of Dependent Variables

Two kinds of dependent variables may be assessed: mediating and performance variables. Since the paradigm is based on the assumption that anxiety affects mediating processes, which, in turn, affect performance, it would be desirable to examine the effects of anxiety on both the relevant mediating processes and on task performance. However, the ease with which the effects of anxiety on mediation can be directly examined depends on the particular process.

An example of a process that was easy to test can be found in the research of Wine (1972). She speculated that anxiety constricts attention so that highly anxious students attend primarily to the teacher or other authority figure and to a narrow aspect of their own work, whereas low-anxious students attend less to authority figures and more to a wide variety of cues around them that may give them ideas applicable to their work. To test this prediction, Wine simply observed and coded students' attending responses in relation to state anxiety and level of anxiety induction. After obtaining the predicted results, Wine then devised a treatment to train anxious students how to direct their attention more constructively. The treatment improved the performance of anxious students significantly.

An example of a process that is more difficult to observe directly is found in the work of Sieber, Kameya, and Paulson (1970), who tested the hypothesis that anxiety interferes with one or more short-term memory processes. They did not test directly the hypothesis that anxiety leads to forgetting of information that has just been developed in the course of attempted problem solving. Rather, they used two conditions in which memory support was varied. In one, external memory support was provided in the form of a running record of the prior solution attempts and their outcomes. In the other condition, no external memory support was provided. It was reasoned that if high-anxious subjects have greater difficulty solving the problems than their low-anxious counterparts on account of the interference of anxiety with memory, then the provision of memory support should enable the high-anxious students to perform as well as the low-anxious students—as indeed it did.

In comparison with the Wine (1972) study, the Sieber, Kameya, and Paulson (1970) study skipped a step. Rather than examining directly the effect of anxiety on memory, they first showed that anxious students without memory support performed less well than their low-anxious counterparts. They then showed that the treatment (memory support) enabled high-anxious students to perform as well as their low-anxious counterparts.

It may be useful to extend the memory-support research to study in a more direct way the effects of anxiety on memory, determining, for example, the effects of anxiety on information coding, storage, and retrieval, and to examine separately the effects of anxiety on short-term and long-term memory. Given the problems of control and data recording in instructional settings, a laboratory setting might be required for some of this research. The Sieber, Kameya, and Paulson (1970) research design was sufficient, however, to provide unequivocal evidence that memory support enhances the performance of anxious students. Whether more detailed analyses, such as those previously suggested, can provide an empirical basis for development of additional beneficial treatments remains to be seen.

A third, less critical, dependent variable that may be used in this paradigm is posttreatment state anxiety. As discussed in Chapter 9, the researcher may seek to demonstrate, in addition to performance improvement, a change in anxiety level as a result of the treatment. This paradigm is particularly well suited for the measurement of change in anxiety level since it involves a treatment and nontreatment group of high- and low-anxious students, respectively. It is recommended that "change" in anxiety level be measured by assessing state anxiety in all subjects during or immediately after performance, and then comparing treated students with nontreated students, within anxiety levels (for example, high-anxiety treated students with high-anxiety nontreated students). This method of measuring "change" in anxiety level due to treatment is superior to the use of "raw-change" scores obtained by subtracting pretest scores from posttest scores, for, as Cronbach and Furby (1970) have shown, the use of raw-change scores leads to invalid conclusions.

Development of an Attribute—Treatment-Interaction Design

The purpose of an attribute—treatment-interaction design is to demonstrate whether a given treatment and attribute (in this case, anxiety) interact such that the effect of the treatment depends on the attribute (anxiety) level of the individual. Detailed discussions of attribute-treatment-interaction research designs may be found in Chapters 5 and 6 and in Cronbach and Snow's (1976) work. Here, a few basic considerations relevant to the study of anxiety and intellectual performance are summarized.

The attribute—treatment-interaction design employed in this paradigm requires a control group of students differentiated with respect to anxiety, and a treatment group that is likewise differentiated. There are two basic versions of this design:

1. The attribute (anxiety) is treated as a continuous variable. Students are randomly assigned to two groups. One group receives the treatment and the task; the other group receives no treatment and the task.

2. The attribute is treated as a discrete variable. High- and low-anxious students are selected. The high-anxious students are randomly assigned to treatment and no treatment (control) groups as are the low-anxious students. The result is a 2 X 2 research design.

These basic versions may be elaborated by using more than two levels of the attribute or treatment; or additional attributes or treatments. The following examples indicate some aims of these elaborations and some procedural approaches that may be employed.

Additional levels of attributes or treatments typically are employed when curvilinear effects are anticipated. Thus, for example, it may be advisable in Version 2 to employ three levels of anxiety rather than two, since curvilinear relationships between anxiety and cognitive variables have been observed (e.g., Bloxom, 1964; Klein, Frederiksen, & Evans, 1969; Stennett, 1957). The same reasoning would lead to the use of an analysis for curvilinear effects in Version 1. More than one level of a given treatment might be employed (for example, short versus long treatment) to determine how to optimize the effects of treatment in relation to the level (and cost) of treatment and the level (and value) of performance improvement yielded.

Additional attributes typically are employed when it is believed that they interact with the main attribute and would result in confounding if they were not identified as distinct sources of variance. Some attributes that have been found to interact with anxiety in their effect on intellectual performance are intelligence (Spielberger, 1966b), defensiveness (Sarason et al., 1964), sex, and verbal ability (Klein et al., 1969).

Klein et al. (1969) provide an example of two procedural approaches to the use of additional atrributes. In one set of analyses, a three-factor factorial analysis of variance was used, involving three levels of anxiety (obtained by dividing the total anxiety-scale distribution into thirds), two levels of defensiveness (obtained by splitting the scale at the median), and two experimental treatments. In the second treatment, an analysis of covariance was used, employing three levels of anxiety, two treatments, and four covariates (Scholastic Achievement Test verbal scores, defensiveness, ideational fluency, and vocabulary knowledge). Additional treatments may be examined in combination or singly. If interactions among treatments are expected, factorial designs may be used to examine the effects of combinations of treatments.

Treatment and Control Groups

As discussed, the treatments used in this paradigm fall roughly into two categories: modifications of curriculum such that students are not required to perform operations that are interfered with by anxiety and modifications of maladaptive anxiety processes within the individual. Having selected a process with which anxiety is thought to interfere and a task within which to study the relation between anxiety and the functioning of that process, a treatment is then designed that seems likely to reduce the undesirable effects of anxiety on performance. In the section on selection of a process and a task, nine sources of information on processes vulnerable to anxiety were suggested. These same sources provide some insights into the kinds of treatments that may modify the processes. Little more can be suggested concerning the selection and development of treatments, except to provide some detailed examples in the final part of this chapter. However, the selection and use of control groups involves some specific problems that merit discussion.

The main problems in establishing a control group are to ascertain that both groups represent samples of a single population, and that the specified treatment is the only stimulus that is varied between the control and treatment groups. Several procedures for establishing control groups in anxiety–treatment-interaction research have been found to be satisfactory.

The simplest procedure is to pretest many students with respect to test anxiety and any other differential characteristics of interest (defensiveness, IQ, and so on), to select those students who would be appropriate subjects and to randomly assign these to treatment and control groups. This method is particularly appropriate when there are no problems of refusal to participate and when it is not obvious to either group that they are receiving special treatment. However, if students are free to refuse to participate and if some do refuse, there may be a differential willingness of treatment- and control-group members to participate, which would violate the assumption that both groups represent samples of the same population. In addition, if students perceive that a treatment has intervened between selection and performance for members of one group, reactive effects may occur.

Another procedure, called the "wait-list control," circumvents these problems of differential volunteering and of perceived special treatment. A group of students are pretested and those who would be appropriate for participation are selected, as in the prior procedure. Then, the selected students are contacted and asked if they will participate in the treatment group (using whatever terminology is needed to describe to them what is required of participants in the treatment group). When enough volunteers have been obtained to fill both groups, they then are randomly assigned to the control and treatment groups. The control-group students are treated in all respects like the treatment-group students except that they do not receive the treatment prior to performing the criterion tasks. They are told that they are on the list to receive the treatment—later. All of the other kinds of special treatment, interviewing, testing, performing the criterion tasks, and so on, are the same for both groups. To fulfill the researcher's agreement, the students who are on the wait list should be given the treatment after the experiment is completed. A wait-list control procedure is described in detail in Chapter 10, p. 195.

A third solution to the two major problems of establishing a control group is to give control students a placebo: a treatment purported to help them reduce their anxiety, but which is actually unrelated to the treatment of anxiety. Thus, members of the control group are led to believe that they have received the treatment, but have not received *the* treatment. In all other respects the two groups are treated in the same way until after the experiment is completed. Then, members of the control group are debriefed and given the real treatment if they want it.

Evaluating the Effectiveness of Treatment

Within this paradigm, the initial goals of anxiety-treatment-interaction research are to ascertain whether anxiety has a significant effect on the selected process and on overall intellectual performance; and whether the selected treatment results in significantly more adaptive behavior. If these aims are attained, it remains to be seen whether the treatment can be generalized effectively to important educational settings, and whether desirable effects of the treatment continue to occur over time. The research that is summarized in the remainder of this book exemplifies some important factors affecting the ultimate value of a treatment. Among these are the following: (a) the difficulty level of the tasks to which the treatment is generalized; (b) the particular way in which the treatment is offered (for example, the degree of personalization, and the extent to which the student has control over the availability of the treatment); (c) the anxiety level of students who are chosen for treatment; (d) the relevance of the treatment to enhancement of those particular task processes that are crucial to performance of the task.

THREE EXAMPLES OF USE OF THE PARADIGM

Three sets of studies are summarized to illustrate variations of the paradigm:

1. Two laboratory studies and two field studies examine the effects of anxiety and a memory support treatment on problem solving. Both laboratory studies consist of a simple anxiety-treatment-interaction design and show that the treatment improves the performance of anxious students. The treatment is then developed and evaluated in field experiments in which memory support is provided in computer-assisted instruction for college students.

2. The effects of anxiety on patterns of attention are studied. A standard anxiety-treatment-interaction design is not used because of the complexity of the initial investigation of the effects of anxiety on attention and because of the complexity of the treatment. Rather, field studies of attention as a function of trait and induced anxiety are conducted first to see if the predicted effects occur. They do occur, therefore the researcher develops and tests a complex therapeutic and instructional program designed to teach anxious students more adaptive patterns of attention.

3. The relation between anxiety and ability to estimate probabilities is studied in an incomplete version of the paradigm. The deleterious effect of anxiety on probability estimation revealed by this study is interesting since it provides an explanation for frequent findings of inability to make good decisions under stress. This is a deleterious effect that is still in search of a treatment. Suggestions are advanced regarding treatment approaches which might warrant investigation.

In each of the three examples that follow, the major considerations in the use of the paradigm are highlighted to give the reader a sense of how those research decisions were made.

Anxiety and Memory Support

Selection of a process and a task.   Until recently, research on the relationship between anxiety and problem solving yielded seemingly conflicting results. Waite (1959) found that highly anxious persons made fewer mistakes than low-anxious persons in solving the Porteus maze test when under no pressure to respond. In this task, all relevant information is displayed so as to allow the subject to compare all choice alternatives and their respective outcomes at any time the subject wishes. Waite attributed his results to anxious persons' tendency to be cautious and to acquire and consider more information before acting relative to the behavior of low-anxious persons. However, in studies that utilize tasks in which the necessary information is not available and organized in some external form, high-anxious persons do not behave in a cautious or accurate manner. Rather, they seek relatively less information, respond rapidly, and make more errors than do low-anxious persons (Castaneda, Palermo, & McCandless, 1956; Lanzetta, 1963; Stevenson & Odom, 1965).

Noting that each of the tasks used in these studies requires the problem solver to generate and select correctly from among various related sets of information, Sieber, Kameya, and Paulson (1970) hypothesized that the absence or presence of memory support is the crucial variable that accounts for the apparently conflicting results. They predicted that:

1. When information must be remembered in order to formulate a correct strategy, high-anxious persons make more wrong choices, commit more memory errors, and less frequently catch potential errors before they are fully committed than do low-anxious persons.

2. Provision of external memory support reduces the difference between high-anxious and low-anxious persons in these respects.

To test these hypotheses, two tasks were constructed which could be performed with or without external memory support. In the first task, the marble puzzle, the problem solver is presented with a board containing a row of nine small, evenly spaced holes. Four black marbles are placed over the four holes right of center and four white marbles are placed over the holds left of center.

The puzzle is solved when the marbles of the two respective colors have been moved to the end of the board opposite their starting position. Only two kinds of moves are permitted: marbles may be moved forward (toward the opposite end of the board) to an adjacent hole, or forward over one adjacent marble of the opposite color to an empty hole. A trial ends when the problem solver has successfully finished the task or when an impasse is reached. Incorrect moves may be retracted only if the problem solver's fingers are not removed from the incorrectly moved marble before retracting it. There is only one correct sequence of 24 moves; the task, then, is one of learning to avoid incorrect moves. Each move changes the configuration; prior configurations cannot be referred to unless they can be recalled from memory. If a given sequence of moves leads to an impasse, the ability to avoid repeating that mistake depends on remembering the marble configuration which existed one move prior to the point at which the impasse became obvious. Although simple in design, the task is difficult to execute.

An altered version of this task was developed in which external memory support is provided. There are three sets of marble boards and marbles. If a mistake is made, another attempt is made on a second board. The previously used board is kept intact for future reference so that the problem solver can avoid making similar mistakes. The problem solver continues to rotate boards until the correct solution is found.

The second task is a concept attainment task. The individual was shown cards from a deck of 4 X 6-inch cards that contain all possible combinations of three binary dimensions: size (large, small), shape (triangular, arrow) and color (red, black). The task is to state the rule used to group the cards; such a rule would be, "The figures are all the same size and that size is small." In the nonmemory support condition, the cards were exposed one at a time, for about 10–20 sec each. The first card was a positive exemplar, after which positive and negative exemplars were presented alternatively. With each positive exemplar, the experimenter said, "This card fits the rule. What do you think the rule is?" With each negative exemplar, the subject was told, "This card does not fit the rule." When a correct answer was given, a new deck with a new rule was started. A criterion of four successive correct responses was used, at which point testing was ended.

In the memory-support condition the presentation was cumulative. That is, the cards were left out of the deck so that the subject did not have to remember what was on them.

Selection of dependent variables. The two tasks were selected since they offered opportunities to study not only trials to criterion, but also failure to recognize errors in one's own thinking, failure to recall what information had been present in prior trials and failure to recall what information had been absent in prior trials. In the marble puzzle, failure to recognize errors in one's own thinking was defined as making an incorrect move of a marble and removing one's hand from the marble without recognizing the error. In the concept attainment task, failure to recall what information was present in a prior trial was defined as stating hypotheses involving stimulus dimensions that had been absent in the immediately preceeding positive exemplar. Failure to recall what information had been absent in prior trials was defined as stating hypotheses involving stimulus dimensions that had been present in the immediately preceeding negative exemplar.

Information background. Both tasks were created for the purpose of the experiment, hence were novel to the participants. Each participant was given the complete set of instructions and required to complete a trial correctly prior to the trials on which data were collected. This practice on each task was given to control for individual differences in prior experience with such tasks and to reduce the influence of variables other than short-term memory functioning. Thus, background factors were equalized and the major determiner of success in these two tasks was ability to recall the stimulus configuration on which a correct response could be based.

Research ethics. Given the strictness of the American Psychological Association ethical guidelines, it might seem out of the question to conduct research in which children are made highly anxious and required to try to solve difficult problems. Under what conditions can informed consent be obtained and ethical procedures for inducing anxiety be developed? In medical research, it is relatively easy to obtain permission to perform nonharmful research on persons who are already seriously diseased and who cannot be helped otherwise. But, to induce disease would be unacceptable. An analogous situation exists in anxiety–treatment-interaction research. In communities in which evaluative anxiety in school children is recognized as a serious problem and value is placed on attempts to discover ways to reduce evaluative anxiety, school administrators and parents may readily grant permission to study this problem, as was the case with the this research on anxiety and memory support.

The medical analogy extends to the problem of anxiety induction as well. When the anxiety already exists as the student's accustomed state in school activities, the researcher need do nothing more than ask the student to try to do well in order to make the anxiety manifest. In the case of the research described here, students were told ahead of time that they would be asked to participate in a research project that was being carried out to try to find ways to help students become better problem solvers. Then, students were called from their class, one at a time, to participate, and were told: "You are going to participate in a Stanford University research project. We are going to give you some problems to solve. It is very important that you do well on these tasks" (Sieber, Kameya, & Paulson, 1970, p. 161).

After participation, each child was thanked, told that the participation had been helpful, and that useful information would be provided on ways to improve problem solving after the entire study was completed. At the conclusion of the study, a letter of thanks and a pamphlet, *The Teacher and the Anxious Child* (Sieber & Crockenberg, 1970), which summarized the findings and other advice on helping the anxious child, was sent to the parents and faculty.

Reactive effects, sequential effects, and generalizability.   These issues all concern the external validity of the research: could the obtained effects be found in "real life" settings and would they persist over time? Since treatment- and control-group students were not aware of their differential status, there is no reason to suppose that students in the treatment group manifested reactive effects that were not also manifested by the control students. Perhaps, however, both groups manifested atypical behavior. Sequential effects of the treatment were not observed, but this is hardly surprising since the treatment trials lasted less than 15 min in most cases. The only adequate test of whether the obtained results were artifacts of reactive behavior or of behavior that would not persist over time would be to generalize the procedure to a problem-solving curriculum in which memory support could be provided to treatment-group students but not to control-group students. As reported subsequently in the discussion on evaluating the effectiveness of treatment, and in Chapter 9, the procedure was generalized to an actual curriculum.

Measurement of anxiety.   The participants in these two studies were selected from among a larger group of students who had completed a version of the text-anxiety scale for children a few weeks earlier. High- and low-anxious students were chosen from the upper and lower quartiles of this sample.

Development of treatment and control groups and of an anxiety—treatment interaction design.   The treatment employed in these two studies permitted the use of a simple anxiety X sex X treatment design. Memory support was provided by modifying the tasks so that the students were not required to remember the information they had generated in prior trials. Since the treatment was to receive a modified task rather than to have a mediating process modified, neither training nor any direct measurement of mediating processes was required. Students were randomly assigned to experimental and control groups and treated identically except for the provision of memory support. The experimenter was not aware of the anxiety level of individuals. Thus, there was no reason to doubt that both groups represented samples of a single population and that differences between groups were due solely to the provision of external memory support.

The anxiety—treatment-interaction design employed two attributes, anxiety and sex, and controlled for IQ. Because anxiety and its effects are not always orthogonal to IQ or sex, the upper quartile (highly anxious) students were then paired with the lower quartile students by matching them with respect to sex and IQ, until an equal number of matched pairs of boys and girls were obtained. For half of the pairs of boys, the low-anxious ones were assigned to the memory-support condition and the high-anxious ones were assigned to the no-memory-support condition. Of the other half of the pairs of boys, the high-anxious ones were assigned to the memory support condition and the low anxious ones were assigned to the nonmemory-support condition. Girls were assigned in the same way.

Evaluating the effectiveness of treatment. The effectiveness of the memory-support treatment was evaluated both in terms of the results of the two initial studies and by generalizing the treatment to two field settings. Using the defining concepts developed in Chapter 3, three classes of operational definitions of anxiety were used to evaluate treatment effectiveness: definitions dealing with task performance; definitions in terms of (external) conditions believed to affect anxiety; and definitions dealing with the phenomenology of anxiety. Task performance measures are reported first:

The major results of the two initial studies are shown in Tables 4.1 and 4.2. On all five performance measures, the students who received no treatment and who were deemed high anxious according to the self-report measure performed less well than did students who were low anxious or who received memory support. An analysis of variance of the number of errors committed on the marble puzzle showed that anxiety interacted with memory support as predicted: high-anxious students with no memory support made more errors than did members of the other three groups, ($F = 5.23$; $df = 1,16$; $p<.05$), and low-anxious students recognized more potential errors (began to make wrong moves, but retracted them) than did high-anxious students ($F = 22.00$; $df = 1,16$; $p<.01$). Likewise, in performing the concept attainment task, the highly anxious, no memory support group required significantly more trials to criterion than did the remaining 3 groups ($t = 3.76$; $df = 92$; $p<.001$). As shown in Table 2, high-anxious students

TABLE 4.1

Means and Standard Deviations of Raw Scores of High- and Low-Anxious Students as a Function of Memory Support

	Memory support		No memory support	
Kinds of memory errors	Mean	*SD*	Mean	*SD*
Marble puzzle				
Errors committed				
Low-anxious students	3.30	2.54	3.10	2.88
High-anxious students	3.00	2.58	7.00	2.26
Potential errors recognized				
Low-anxious students	.70	.48	.70	.48
High-anxious students	.30	.48	00	00
Concept Attainment Task				
Errors committed				
Low-anxious students	3.00	1.64	5.38	5.48
High-anxious students	3.46	3.59	10.08	10.43

TABLE 4.2
Mean Number of Positive- and Negative-Exemplar Memory Errors
for the Four Experimental Conditions

	Memory support		No memory support	
Kind of memory error	Low anxious	High anxious	Low anxious	High anxious
Negative exemplar	4	5	8	15
Positive exemplar	3	2	8	15

negative exemplars than did any other group. Low-anxious, no-memory-support students made more positive exemplar errors than did students in the two memory-support conditions, but such a difference was not observed for negative exemplar memory errors. No effects were observed for sex.

Lehrissey, O'Neil, and Hansen (1971) generalized this treatment to a field setting in which college students were required to solve mathematics problems in a computer-assisted instruction setting. The treatment group had a list of their previous errors displayed on a corner of the cathode-ray-tube screen and the control group did not. The predicted anxiety by memory—support interaction occurred; high state-anxious students in the memory—support condition performed about as well as low state-anxious students, whereas high state-anxious students who did not have memory support performed considerably less well. (This experiment is reported in full detail in Chapter 11, pages 206—208.)

Turning to operational definitions of anxiety, in terms of the conditions which are thought to modify the anxiety process, we see from the interactions of anxiety and treatment that the provision of memory support affects the performance of high-anxious students so that their task performance is about as good as that of low-anxious students.

Finally, we consider the definition of anxiety in terms of its phenomenology. When the high-anxious students (according to a self-report or phenomenological measure) were treated in a way designed to modify their anxiety process, and, as a result, performed tasks as well as their low-anxious counterparts, was their subjective state altered? In terms of Spielberger's (1972c) model of the anxiety process, the treated students were given a new coping tool, which presumably modified their perception of the task so that it became less threatening and hence reduced their anxiety-state response. Would measurement of their anxiety state during and after performance indicate that they experienced less anxiety as a result of the treatment? Collier, Poynor, O'Neil, and Judd (1973) performed a field experiment which indicated that the answer to this question is yes, under certain circumstances.

These investigators presented students with concept-learning tasks in a computer-assisted instruction setting. There were three learning groups: a control group that had no access to information from prior trials; a memory-support group that had a continual display of this information; and a learner-control group that could obtain this information at will. Both the learner-control and the memory-support groups outperformed the control group, but only in the learner-control group did students indicate that they felt less anxious. Apparently, being able to call for information that puts one in a position of greater competence is more anxiety reducing than having that information available at all times. (This study is reported in detail in Chapter 9, pages 157–163.)

These data suggest that highly anxious students may benefit from learning to use a variety of external memory supports, such as diagrams, notational systems, methods of outlining general ideas prior to the development of details, use of symbolic logic to provide a way of sorting and organizing complex information, and so on. In addition, internal memory-support devices which aid ability to remember and organize a material, (like mnemonic devices) may be useful to highly anxious persons. Such additional kinds of memory-support treatments remain to be developed and tested. The effects of memory-support treatments on the anxiety process over long periods of time also remain to be examined.

Anxiety and Attention

Selection of a Process and a Task

A review of the text-anxiety literature (Wine, 1971b) suggests that one explanation for the relatively poor performance of highly anxious students in evaluative settings lies in the different attentional focuses of high- and low-anxious persons during task performance. High-anxious individuals divide their attention between self-related and task-related concerns. They worry about their performance, about how others are doing and about how upset they are; they berate themselves for stupidity, long for the test to be over, and worry about what the important people in their life will think of their poor performance. The low anxious student focuses attention more fully on task-relevant material and is able to perform at a higher level. Wine (1971b) inferred from this literature review that anxious students might benefit from training designed to increase awareness of maladaptive attentional habits and to teach adaptive attentional habits.

However, before proceeding to develop such a treatment, it seemed desirable to test directly the hypothesis that high anxiety results in maladaptive attentional patterns. To test this hypothesis, Wine (1972) developed an ingenious field experiment. She reasoned that if anxiety affects the individual's attentional patterns, then there must be major differences between high- and low-anxious students in the kinds of classroom activities in which they choose to engage, and in the kinds of information they acquire. There existed no prior evidence regarding variations in overall classroom behavior as a function of anxiety level, but this lack of research was probably attributable to the fact that the pull of situational variables is so strong that it is quite difficult to make comparisons of children's behavior across classroom situations. For example, it is not meaningful to compare a child's behavior while taking a test with behavior in a reading class because the appropriate behavior in the two settings is different. However, Wine (1972) resolved this problem by manipulating evaluative stress within a single kind of class, an art class. Evaluative stress was introduced in one group by the anticipation of a classroom examination in the following class. The art class was chosen since it permitted the student to focus attention on a wide range of things: children, the teacher, objects in the room, the work of other children, and one's own work.

Selection of dependent variables.   Observer coding categories were developed within each of these activities. These coding categories included initiation of communication with the teacher, receipt of communication from the teacher, initiation of communication with another child, receipt of communication from another child, attention to teacher's communication to others, and attention to other children's conversations; also, individual activities such as working quietly, sitting idly, taking materials, standing, leaving desk, looking at camera; interaction with the teacher such as: hand raising, displaying work to the teacher, and receiving help or material from the teacher; interaction with other children such as: displaying work to another child, looking at another child's work, giving or receiving help, ideas, or materials, joking or laughing, and task-disruptive or aggressive behavior.

Information background.   Both the experimental and control classes were regular art classes, randomly assigned to groups. Students shared the same information background: those of regular art students in that program.

Anxiety induction and research ethics.   Anxiety was induced by informing students that they would receive a major examination in the next class (the class immediately following the art class). This was not a contrived induction; the announced test was a regular part of the school program. Hence, there was no deception and no special treatment on account of the experiment.

Selection of differential independent variables.   The effects of trait anxiety and sex were examined in addition to the effects of the anxiety induction. Trait anxiety was assessed prior to the experiment.

Results of the experiment.   Test anticipation had pervasive effects of attention despite trait-anxiety level. Overall, children who anticipated evaluation shifted towards more intense task orientation, greater concern for the teachers' evaluation, and more behavioral constriction. Both the boys and the girls in the anxiety-induced group sought more of the teacher's attention, displaying their work to the teacher more often than did children in the noninduced group. There were sex differences in a couple of teacher-child interactions in the anxiety-induced group: the teacher initiated more communication and gave more help to boys than to girls. Children listened to the teacher's communication to the class more in the anxiety-induced condition. This effect was most marked for the high state-anxiety children. However, low and medium state-anxiety children listened to the teacher's communication with other children more in the anxiety-induced group, while the high state-anxious student listened to this kind of communication slightly less in the anxiety-induced condition; the high state-anxious child listened only to communication specifically directed at that child; while the medium and low state-anxious child became more alert to a range of cues. Low- and medium-state-anxious students spent more time working quietly in the anxiety-induction group than in the noninduction group, while the high state-anxious students spent slightly less time working in the anxiety-induction group than in the noninduction group. The high state-anxious students looked at the work of others less than did the medium and low state-anxious students.

Although the obtained results were weak and have not yet been replicated, they are highly consistent with the hypothesis and warrant investigation of the effects of attentional training.

Development of treatment and control groups and of a research design. Having established that anxiety has a significant effect on attention in school settings, the next practical step seemed to be to develop a program of attentional training designed to reduce maladaptive patterns of attention. Wine (1972) developed attentional training programs for children and for college students. Preliminary research with college students has been completed and is described briefly here (more detailed information may be found in Wine, 1972).

This second set of studies was not concerned with demonstrating the wide variety of effects of anxiety on attention in school settings, but with establishing that training could alter at least some of the attentional habits of anxious students and reduce their feelings of anxiety as well as improve their test-taking performance.

The participants were obtained by advertising in the student newspaper, through the counseling service, and on bulletin boards that treatment for anxiety was available to students on an experimental basis. Only 19 students volunteered. They were administered the achievement-anxiety test (Alpert & Haber, 1960), and those 16 students who scored in the upper quartile on the debilitating-anxiety subscale, or in the lower quartile on the facilitating-anxiety subscale were accepted into the study. These 16 students were randomly assigned to each of 3 treatment groups, with the extra student going into Group 1. Each group received six hour-long sessions. Group 1 received attentional training. Group 2 received a combination of attentional and relaxation training. Group 3 was a placebo training group in which students received instruction to focus their attention of their feelings and self-related thoughts. This placebo condition was considered more appropriate than other control group options because it seemed less likely to result in differential attrition, and it differed from Groups 1 and 2 only with respect to the critical aspects of treatment. Presumably, the placebo treatment merely required anxious students to do what they ordinarily do when taking tests, hence provided no new treatment.

Attentional training (Group 1) was aimed at teaching students to focus their full attention on tasks while working on them. This was accomplished through three forms of instruction:

1. Students were given the following explanation. Anxious students do more poorly than nonanxious students on tests because they waste a lot of time worrying. This can be overcome by learning to focus full attention on the test. Physiological arousal may still be felt, but this need not interfere with performance; in fact, it may help.

2. Students were shown two videotapes. The first showed anxious and non-anxious students learning verbal material; the anxious students were making irrelevant, apologetic and self-deprecating remarks to themselves, and doing poorly. The nonanxious students were performing in a businesslike, effective way, and making task-relevant comments only. The second tape showed anxious students taking tests and demonstrating that they could turn off their worrying by instructing themselves to stop wasting time and pay attention to what they were doing.

3. The students were given intensive practice in working on a variety of tasks with instructions to attend fully to the tasks and to inhibit self-related thinking.

Attentional training plus relaxation (Group 2) emphasized both the role of attention and of physiological factors in anxiety. Students were given the same training as was provided for Group 1, with the following exceptions. They were *not* told that physiological arousal is irrelevant or helpful to performance, and they were given training in learning to relax while taking tests. A progressive relaxation technique (Paul, 1966) was administered via a tape recording. Students heard the tape in the first three sessions and were required to give themselves the instructions in the second three sessions. After each of the six sessions, they were asked to practice the exercises at least once daily, using them first in nonevaluative settings and then in evaluative settings.

The self-attention training (Group 3) was aimed at providing a placebo treatment that would appear to students as a credible treatment for anxiety. Students were told that it would foster self-awareness and insight into the origins of their anxiety. They performed the same tasks as did subjects in the other groups, but were instructed throughout to focus on their feelings.

Selection of tasks and dependent measures. Two sets of tasks were employed; one set provided a context for training and the other provided the dependent measures. The tasks used as a context for learning to focus attention as directed consisted of a variety of individually administered tests including a nonsense-syllable-learning test, various IQ scales (Wechsler Adult Intelligence Scale,

Stanford–Binet subtests, Otis Self-Administering Test of Mental Ability, Benton Test of Visual Retention, Verbal Reasoning, and Mechanical Reasoning scales of the Differential Aptitude Tests, Porteus Mazes). These tests are representative of some of the kinds of tasks to which it was hoped the training would generalize. They are self-contained in the sense that the instructions are easy for college students to read and follow, and they require an information background that is generally shared by college students.

The tasks used as dependent measures consisted of Forms 1 and 2 of the Wonderlic personnel test (Wonderlic, 1961) and alternate forms of a digit-symbol test which provided measures of ability to take mental tests, and the following six self-report measures of anxiety: the facilitating- and debilitating-anxiety subscales of the Achievement Anxiety Test (Alpert & Haber, 1960), the test-anxiety questionnaire (Mandler & Sarason, 1952), the worry and emotion-ality subscales of the Liebert–Morris scale (Liebert & Morris, 1967), and the trait anxiety inventory (Spielberger, Gorsuch, & Lushene, 1970). These measures were administered before and after the treatment to assess the effect of treatment on the phenomenology of anxiety and on task performance

Evaluation of the effectiveness of treatment. As shown in Table 4.3, Group 1 showed the greatest improvement in task performance, reduction of undesirable forms of anxiety and increase in facilitating anxiety. Group 2 also showed significant improvement in task performance but not on other measures. In contrast, Group 3 showed little change on any of the measures.

It is difficult to draw clear-cut conclusions from these findings, given the limitations in the design of the experiment. The treatments consisted of several

TABLE 4.3
Pre- to Posttest Difference Scores for the Three Treatment Groups

Treatment	Task							
	Wonder[a]	D/S[b]	Facil[c]	Debil[d]	TAQ[e]	Trait[f]	Worry[g]	Emotion[h]
Group 1	4.4**	10.8	10.6*	−7.4**	−8.6**	−6.0	−4.0	−2.6
Group 2	4.2*	16.4*	3.0	−4.2	−7.2	−2.4	−2.0	−6.2
Group 3	1.8*	3.3	2.3	−2.0	−2.8	−1.2	−1.2	−0.5

$*p < .05$, $**p < .01$ (one-tailed tests).
[a]Wonderlic Personnel Test.
[b]Digit symbol test.
[c]Facilitating anxiety subscale of the achievement anxiety test.
[d]Debilitating anxiety subscale of the achievement anxiety test.
[e]Test anxiety questionnaire.
[f]Trait anxiety inventory.
[g]Worry subscale of the Liebert Morris scale.
[h]Emotion subscale of the Liebert Morris scale.

manipulations each, making it impossible to determine which aspects of the treatments produced the effects. All of the treatments were administered by the experimenter, who knew the hypotheses of the study, and could possibly have produced experimenter expectancy effects (Rosenthal, 1966). The sample was extremely small. And, change scores rather than intergroup comparisons of posttreatment scores were used as dependent measures.

Anxiety and Subjective Uncertainty

Selection of a process and a task. Continued working at a problem until a correct solution is attained depends in part on whether the student has generated warranted subjective uncertainty.[1] If the student feels certain about the correctness of a solution, but does not actually have a correct answer, work on the problem will be terminated and the incorrect answer will be accepted. When this occurs, the student has incorrectly estimated the probability of correctness of the solution alternatives under consideration and consequently has incorrectly assessed his or her state of knowledge.

Failure to be uncertain when one is entertaining a wrong answer may be due to ignoring available information, failing to generate plausible alternatives, or failing to use previously acquired information. All of these behaviors that reduce the complexity and uncertainty of decisions are also behaviors that characterize anxious individuals (Wallach & Kogan, 1965; Wine, 1971). Sieber (1974) reasoned that if a way was found to learn more about how anxiety affects probability estimation and whether these effects of anxiety on subjective uncertainty and state-of-knowledge assessment are systematic and predictable, then it would be possible to design and test plausible treatment procedures for reducing these effects. An obvious context in which to require students to work on tasks under stress and to assign subjective-probability estimates to alternatives is a multiple-choice examination in which students are required to respond by indicating the probability of correctness that they would assign to each alternative. Done in the context of an actual course examination, this procedure would eliminate the major problems of anxiety induction, research ethics, information background, reactive effects, and generalizability cited previously.

Accordingly, a study was performed in a college course in the context of an optional midterm examination. Forty college students had chosen to take the

---

[1] An individual is in a state of subjective uncertainty when he considers two or more mutually exclusive choice alternatives; that is, when none of the choice alternatives are given a subjective probability of 1.00 of leading to a desired outcome. The level of uncertainty is warranted if the degree of confidence in choice alternatives corresponds to the frequency with which those alternatives turn out to be correct. If probability values are assigned so that 10% of the choice alternatives that are assigned a subjective probability of 0.10, 20% of the choice alternatives that are assigned a subjective probability of .20, . . . , etc; turn out to be true or adequate solutions, then the degree of subjective uncertainty would be warranted and the "state-of-knowledge" assessment would be perfectly accurate.

examination to try to improve their grades. They were instructed to use the Shuford, Albert, and Massengill (1966) multiple-choice confidence-estimation procedure, which eliminates blind guessing and gives credit for partial knowledge. The students had used this technique previously, but it was again explained to them via a programmed instruction booklet. The booklet provided instruction on how to assign subjective-probability values to choice alternatives and demonstrated that test scores would be maximized if the respondents gave their honest assessment of the likelihood of correctness of each alternative.

Anxiety measurement and induction. Students were randomly assigned to either a group in which anxiety was induced by expectation of an examination or a group in which no anxiety was induced. The anxiety-induction group was given the state-anxiety scale (Spielberger, Gorsuch, & Lushene, 1970) and the midterm examination. The no-anxiety-induction group was first told that they were not actually taking the midterms and that if they did not do well enough to get an A on the test they were about to take, their confidence-estimation data would be used to help in coaching them for a second test. They were given the anxiety scale and the examination. (Since the midterm examination accounted for only 10% of the grade, the use of two different procedures had very little effect on grades.)

Dependent measures. The following data were obtained: (1) confidence estimation scores based on a formula contained in the Shuford, Albert, and Massengill (1966) study which takes into account the student's accuracy in estimating confidence and accuracy in selecting correct answers; (2) traditional test scores computed by the usual method (the highest probability response was counted as the chosen alternative and that answer was then scored according to whether it was right or wrong); (3) improvement over score in traditional method through the use of the confidence-estimation procedure; (4) number of items on which uncertainty was indicated (on which probability = 1 was not assigned to any alternative); (5) state-anxiety scale scores. The two groups were compared on all five measures.

Results. As shown in Table 4.4, the anxiety induction had the predicted effects on confidence-estimation ability. Students' overall test performance, as revealed by their traditional test scores, did not differ significantly in relation to anxiety induction. However, no-anxiety-induced students distributed their probabilities (generated subjective uncertainty) significantly more frequently, had higher confidence estimation scores, and earned higher difference scores (made more accurate state-of-knowledge estimates) than did the students whose anxiety had been induced by knowledge that they were taking a real examination. Scores on the state-anxiety scale indicated that the effects of the induction were substantial, but that induction turned out to be a better predictor of performance than the state-anxiety-scale scores.

As shown in Figure 4.2, the anxiety-induced group tended to err most by overestimating high probabilities and underestimating low probabilities.

TABLE 4.4
Means, Standard Deviations and t-Test Comparisons of Differences
between Anxiety and No-Anxiety Groups on Five Dependent Measures

Measure	No anxiety		Anxiety			
	$\overline{X}$	SD	$\overline{X}$	SD	t	p
Confidence estimation	92.1	6.3	85.1	10.6	2.54	<.01
Traditional scoring	84.6	10.3	83.5	10.7	ns	−
Improvement	6.8	4.2	2.7	3.3	3.31	<.01
Number of distributed probability scores	4.1	2.0	2.1	2.3	2.71	<.01
State anxiety	42.6	33.2	66.6	32.1	ns	−

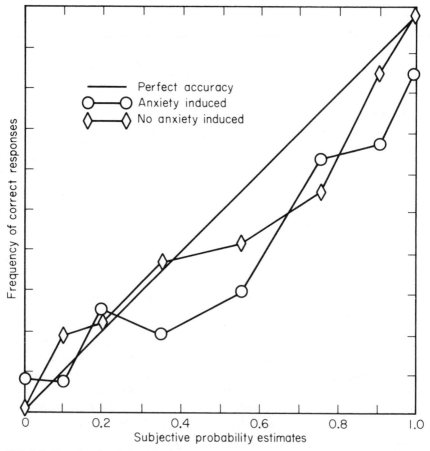

FIG. 4.2 Functional relationship between relative frequency of correct responses and subjective-probability estimates for two groups of students.

Obviously, students in the anxiety-induced group had difficulty making the best use of partial knowledge. The following illustrates this quite well. Students in five upper-division psychology sections were carefully instructed in the use of the confidence estimation procedure. They expressed enthusiasm at the prospect of using it in weekly quizzes. However, despite their previous enthusiasm, most of the students seemed unable to use the procedure rationally in the quizzes. Typically, they would assign a probability of 1.00 to some incorrect multiple-choice answers, then complain bitterly about being thrown off by the new scoring system. Further discussion with the instructor about the items missed usually showed that the student could generate plausible arguments in support of choice alternatives to which they had assigned a probability of .00. However, the student would typically claim having been unable to think "that way" while taking the quiz. This anecdote strongly suggests that when problem solvers are in a state of anxiety, confidence-estimation procedures do not help them to apply all of the information they have. If this is so, it is a troubling commentary on human ability to deal with important or threatening problems. Clearly, it would be desirable to find a way of treating this problem to reduce decision-maker irrationality.

Possible approaches to treatment. Other research has suggested ways of training students to deal with uncertainty under anxiety:

1. Informal observations by Shuford (1972) indicate that extensive practice with confidence-estimation procedures in which the student receives frequent feedback on the accuracy of state-of-knowledge assessments helps to build confidence estimation skills that are unaffected by high anxiety.

2. Sieber, Clark, Smith, and Depue (1976) experimented with a curriculum designed to teach elementary-school children how to handle problematic or uncertain situations. Results indicated major changes in children's intellectual and affective approaches to problematic issues following training. However, no formal study has been made to determine whether children's utilization of information under conditions of anxiety was increased as a result of the training.

3. The literature on group decision making (e.g., Delbecq & VandeVen, 1971) stresses the importance of leadership designed to evoke problem finding (for example, to discover a wide range of relevant information and to generate many solution alternatives prior to decision making). However, there has been no research on ability to generate warranted uncertainty under anxiety provoking conditions in relation to leadership style.

Thus, probability estimation remains a process in search of a treatment for the debilitating effects of anxiety. Only further research can determine whether maladaptive functioning of this and other psychological processes due to anxiety can be remedied by treatment.

Part II

ANXIETY-TREATMENT
INTERACTIONS

The purpose of this section is to discuss the use of anxiety as a variable in aptitude–treatment-interaction studies, and to review the existing literature in this area.

In Chapter 5, we discuss the role of anxiety in education. The notion of aptitude–treatment interaction is introduced, and types of aptitude–treatment interactions are defined.

In Chapter 6, a rationale for seeking interactions between anxiety and instructional methods is specified in detail. Individualized and conventional instructional practices are compared with respect to the anxiety–treatment interactions that might be expected to occur. The aptitude–treatment interaction literature in which anxiety is used as an independent variable and achievement is used as a dependent variable is reviewed in detail with major attention being given to interactions between anxiety and instructional methods.

5
Anxiety and Instructional
Methods: An Introduction

High anxiety is unpleasant and painful. It is, therefore, not surprising to note that high anxiety interferes significantly with the ability of students at all education levels to profit from instruction. If instruction can be modified so as to reduce interference by anxiety, an important step will have been taken in the prevention of a variety of academic and emotional difficulties. The purpose of this chapter is to review the possibilities of adapting instruction in order to minimize the disruptive effects of anxiety. Individualized instruction is introduced as a way of adapting instruction to anxiety status, followed by consideration of the type of evidence required in order to implement a truly individualized instruction which would be especially beneficial for high anxiety students. Finally, the specific type of statistical evidence required for such individualization will be reviewed.

INSTRUCTION AND ANXIETY

In the area of instruction, experimental psychologists and psychologists with experience in training programs of various kinds have begun to apply their knowledge and skills to educational problems, often for the first time. A drive to establish a bridge between the learning laboratory and the classroom was initiated during the 1950s and is still actively flourishing (Ericksen, 1973). Glaser (1972, 1973) points out the advantages of operating in an environment in which scientist, concerned with relatively basic questions regarding human learning and development, and educational practitioners concerned with problems of curriculum development and application in the public schools, live in fruitful interaction with one another. The existence of many laboratories throughout the country concerned with cognitive development in children, development of learning materials, and the like attests to the fact that Glaser's views are widely shared.

Compared to the fertile developments in the area of instruction, educational psychologists' concern with anxiety has not profited from similar interdisciplinary activity. In three recent comprehensive reviews of research in education and instruction (Kerlinger, 1973; Kerlinger & Carroll, 1974; Travers, 1973) anxiety is indexed only once in all three sources. In a cummulative index of the last four years of the *Review of Educational Research* (1973), anxiety is not indexed at all.

It is instructive to compare the infrequency with which anxiety was mentioned in the educational sources mentioned to the data reported by Spielberger (1972a), regarding the indexing of anxiety in *Psychological Abstracts*. Spielberger reports that under the heading of anxiety over 2500 articles and books have been indexed in the *Abstracts*. Furthermore, Spielberger estimates that during that same period over 4000 studies on anxiety and similar topics have appeared in medical journals. Even though research reports dealing with anxiety are frequently published in educational psychology and symposia devoted to anxiety are frequently given at conferences, as are research reports dealing with this topic, nevertheless it is also clear that compared with other topics in educational psychology, the area of anxiety is at present in a somewhat undernourished state.

Anxiety, Prevention, and Instruction

The relative lack of activity concerning anxiety in educational psychology is a pity. Education offers an ideal arena for the fruitful interrelationship of a number of disciplines. One can hardly imagine a more appropriate source of subjects for the study of the effects of anxiety than the use of students at all branches of the educational ladder. Since all individuals attend educational institutions of some kind at some point in their lives, if anxiety has any important effects those effects must be evident during these periods and in these institutions. Opportunities are thus provided for *in vivo* studies of the effects of anxiety on acquisition of different kinds of subject matter, attitudes, skills, and the like.

The point is often made that the greatest advances in medicine were not open heart surgery, or other exciting treatment breakthroughs, but the development of vaccinations. Treatment always implies restoring individuals from sickness to health. Vaccinations, on the other hand, imply that individuals will be maintained in a state of good health, not requiring treatment. Vaccination for polio, for example, has rendered the expensive, painful, and time consuming treatment for polio victims largely unnecessary. Similarly, of course, smallpox vaccinations have made this illness a relative rarity.

Education offers an ideal arena for the development of similar preventative models. Applying the example of vaccination to anxiety, the development of educational programs which would either reduce anxiety or adapt instruction to anxiety levels would do much more for society's mental health than any number of breakthroughs in the behavioral or psychoanalytic treatment of anxiety. Unfortunately, compared to medicine, education does not have a comparable body of knowledge that would permit such developments at present. It is this area that this chapter addresses, specifically, how instruction can be adapted to students' anxiety states so that learning would be maximized?

Individualized Instruction

The movement to adapt instruction to individual differences among students goes under the fashionable name of "individualized instruction." While that term has been very much in vogue with the advent of teaching machines in the late 1950s, and maintained its popularity when teaching machines went out of fashion to be replaced by the use of computers for instruction in the late 1960s and the 1970s, nevertheless, individualizing instruction has a hallowed educational tradition of its own.

Plato's classic dialogue with the slave boy, Meno, is a clear-cut example of adapting instruction to the student's prior knowledge of subject matter. Cohen (1963) recast this example into a linear program, neatly relating the ancient and modern interests in adapting instruction to the student.

There have been numerous exhortations among educators to individualize instruction. Countless books and articles devoted to this subject have been published. Typically, the type of individualization was based on the teacher's experiences, or the experiences of teachers of teachers. As the subsequent reviews of the literature reveal, there are painfully few empirical data in support of any of these practices.

As one would expect, individualized instructional practices vary substantially. Baker (1972) described a number of individualized instructional systems, and others are described in Atkinson and Wilson's (1969) book of readings. Some contemporary computer-based instructional systems are described by Atkinson (1974) and Bunderson (1973). It may be helpful to describe some of the common elements of most individualized instructional systems at this point in order to acquaint the reader unfamiliar with these, and so as to be able to refer back to them in the subsequent discussion.

In individualized instruction students are typically provided with a highly specific objective, often expressed in behavioral terms specifying what is to be learned. For example, the objective may be to enable students to compute the square root of four-digit numbers. An instructional sequence is then provided to attain this objective. The instruction may occur by carefully sequenced workbooks, by programed instruction, by computer-assisted instruction, or by audio- or videotapes specifically designed to teach this objective. The student then studies these instructional materials independently at a comfortable rate.

When the student feels the objective has been mastered, there is an evaluation in order to determine whether the skill has, in fact, been learned. If the evaluation results indicate that a student has failed to attain mastery at a satisfactory criterion level, the student is typically asked to go back and restudy the same set of materials used previously, and upon completing them the student gets an alternate form of the test. Different instructional systems vary with respect to the criterion for competence, though achievement in the range of 75–90% is generally considered necessary in order for a student to attain competence in a skill. Instructional systems also vary with regard to the availability of pretests which allow students familiar with a skill to branch around a unit, they may also vary with regard to the length of the instructional sequence, the number of objectives given, as well as a number of other variables. After passing the posttest on a particular objective the student is generally routed to the next objective in the instructional sequence which is contended with in pretty much the same fashion as the prior one.

Individualization such as that described here only varies the rate of instruction to suit student needs. Truly individualized instruction implies that different instructional methods would be employed for students with different characteristics. For example, students high in anxiety could be assigned to an easy programed instructional sequence to teach square-root skills. This sequence may require the student to calculate a number of examples of gradually increasing difficulty so that the high ratio of reinforcement, and low level of uncertainty would be ideally suited to such students. Students with lower anxiety, however, may be assigned to a preselected printed text, or a lecture which might be more difficult than the programed sequence. Such individualization would vary not only the rate of instruction, but the method as well. In turn, such individualization demands that there are well-established research findings documenting an interaction between the instructional methods and anxiety. Presence of such interactions is, of course, the cornerstone for individualizing the method of instruction. Theories about such interactions and the research findings pertaining to anxiety and different instructional treatments will be reviewed in detail in this section of this book.

ATTRIBUTE–TREATMENT INTERACTIONS

The field of research concerned with adapting method of instruction to individual differences among students has come to be known as aptitude treatment interaction (ATI). Aptitude has generally been defined as "any characteristic of the individual that increases (or impairs) his probability of success in the given treatment" (Cronbach & Snow, 1969, p. 7) and again following Cronbach and Snow, treatment has generally been defined as "variations in the pace and style of instruction" (p. 7). While it may seem somewhat grotesque, anxiety qualifies as an aptitude, in terms of this definition. Furthermore, different instructional strategies described in the previous example, such as programed instruction, workbooks, computer-based instruction, and so on qualify as the different instructional treatments. Problems addressed by this area of research can then be phrased succinctly. Do individuals differing in anxiety learn optimally from different instructional treatments?

Definition and Background

Since aptitude–treatment-interaction research has individual differences as one of its bases, it is not surprising that there are individual differences among writers in this general area with respect to their preferred labels for it. Berliner and Cahen (1973) prefer the term "trait–treatment interaction." Hunt (1975) suggests that this general area applies to problems larger than those exclusively in the instructional domain and prefers to refer to it as "person–environment interactions." Hunt relates this area of research to Kurt Lewin's (1951) formulation that behavior is a joint function of personological and environmental variables ($B = f(P, E)$). In my own work (Tobias, 1969, 1973b, c,) the ATI abbreviation has been retained, though the "attribute" has been substituted for aptitude.

The labels attached to this area of research are important only in so far as they shape researchers' thinking. Aptitude has so traditionally been associated with the cognitive domain that it may well predispose investigators to concern themselves primarily with variables such as scholastic aptitude or intelligence. Measures of intelligence were developed in order to predict which students were likely to profit most from instruction. In other words, intelligence measures, and measures of othe cognitive variables were designed to predict the outcomes of instruction. As Glaser (1972) has pointed out, there is no reason to expect that the same cognitive measures would predict with equal accuracy which strategy or instructional method is optimal for the attainment of instructional outcome.

"Trait," in trait–treatment interactions has different connotations which may be equally dysfunctional. "Trait" usually suggests a stable predisposition, not infrequently in the personality domain, relatively unchanging over short periods of time. The trait term implies that interactions should be sought with trait, as distinguished from state measures. The latter are less consistent over time, more responsive to situational content and other characteristics of the subject matter. The state–trait distinction with respect to anxiety is discussed in greater detail elsewhere in this book, (Chapters 3, 8–11) and is reviewed with respect to interactions with instructional method in Chapter 6.

The research in this area (Berliner & Cahen, 1973; Cronbach & Snow, 1977) does not justify such restrictions, unintentional though they may be. In principle, these concerns do not apply to Hunt's (1975) person–environment inter-action, though communication may be impaired by the introduction of a more varied terminology. "Attribute," in attribute–treatment-interaction research appears most attractive since it both retains the most widely used abbreviation for this body of work, and does not limit, intentionally or unintentionally, the range of variables studied.

Attribute–treatment-interaction research is of relatively recent origin. Cron-bach's (1957) appeal for a rapprochement between the fields of correlational and experimental psychology was perhaps the first contemporary call for such research. The 1965 conference on "learning and individual differences," the proceedings of which were subsequently published (Gagné, 1967), was another important milestone. In that volume, Cronbach (1967) specifically formulates the rationale for attribute–treatment-interaction investigations, and Glaser (1967) reviews some of the research alluding to this problem, though not specifically designed to investigate it, in the learning area. Bracht (1970) reviews research studies in which two treatments are employed and individual difference measures are available. These studies, generally not conceptualized from an attribute–treatment-interaction viewpoint, are, nevertheless, relevant to the attribute treatment interaction problem. Cronbach and Snow's (1977) compre-hensive review of method, theory, and findings in ATI research, and Berliner and Cahen's (1973) review the important sources in this area. Much of the prior work is reviewed by Cronbach and Snow (1969).

A reasonable general conclusion to be drawn from these reviews of research is that there are few replicated interactions which permit prescriptions such as: "This kind of student should be instructed with this method, whereas that kind of student should be instructed by an alternative approach." There are some interesting findings, some worthwhile clues, leading some reviewers to conclude that there are grounds for "cautious optimism" (Berliner & Cahen, 1973). Nevertheless, the bulk of the work in this field remains to be done. It has yet to be demonstrated that attribute–treatment- interaction research can illuminate our understanding of instructional events, or advance practice to a point where instructional prescriptions can be made.

Interactions

If instruction were to be adapted to students' anxiety levels, an interaction between the instructional treatment and anxiety level is presupposed. One such possible interaction is depicted in Figure 5.1. Anxiety level, as determined by some test score or anxiety induction procedure is represented on the x axis, and achievement on the y axis. The outcome of two different instructional treat-ments, A and $B,$ as shown by the lines in Figure 5.1, form a *disordinal* inter-action. A disordinal interaction is one in which the two regression lines (the line graphs drawn by connecting cell means derived from analysis of variance) cross

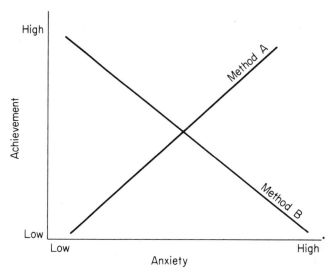

FIG. 5.1   Example of disordinal interaction between anxiety and instructional method.

one another such that one treatment is superior for students along one point of the anxiety continuum and an alternate treatment superior at a different point. In Figure 5.1, Treatment A yields high achievement for high-anxiety students and low achievement for low-anxiety students. Conversely, Treatment B yields high achievement for individuals low in anxiety and lower achievement for high-anxiety students. The presence of such replicated disordinal interactions is presupposed whenever it is anticipated that students varying in anxiety will be assigned to different instructional treatments in order to maximize their accomplishments.

There are, of course, other types of interactions. Figure 5.2 illustrates an *ordinal* interaction. The x and y axis, as in Figure 5.1, represent anxiety and achievement respectively, and the two functions Treatments A and B. In Figure 5.2, it can be seen that Treatment A leads to higher achievement at all points of the anxiety continuum than Treatment B, though the difference between treatments is not uniform. That is, in Figure 5.2 the superiority of Treatment A over Treatment B increases as anxiety goes up. At low-anxiety levels the differences appear small. Figure 5.2 defines an ordinal interaction in which the regression lines for different functions do not intersect at any point, though the lines are of different slopes.

A disordinal interaction indicates that assigning high-anxiety students to Treatment A and low-anxiety students to Treatment B allows each to attain maximal achievement. Disordinal interactions also suggest ideas about the relationships between the processes required by Treatments A and B and the effects of anxiety. Ordinal interactions such as those depicted in Figure 5.2 would typi-

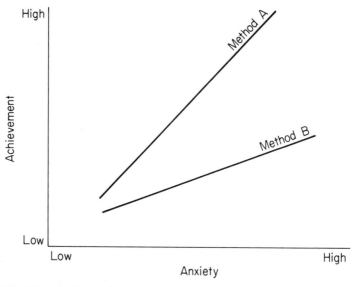

FIG. 5.2   Example of an ordinal interaction between anxiety and instructional method.

cally suggest that all students be assigned to Treatment A since it uniformly results in higher achievement. If Treatment A, however, is twice as expensive as Treatment B, with respect to the amount of time required or the cost of instruction, one would think twice about assigning students to treatment A at the lower end of the anxiety continuum, where there is little difference between the treatments, and probably assign students to the less expensive treatment, Treatment B in this example. Ordinal interactions are also of considerable theoretical interest. They may reveal, for example, that while the interaction between the instructional treatments is ordinal within the range of anxiety observed in a particular experiment, disordinality (a crossing of regression lines) is implied for anxiety levels below these utilized in the particular experiment. Thus, hypotheses arising from an ordinal interaction may be that with students of anxiety levels considerably below that utilized in this experiment the observed differences in slopes are such that Treatment B might be superior. This can be observed by extrapolating from the data in Figure 5.2, as shown in Figure 5.3. The solid lines in Figure 5.3 represent obtained data. The dashes represent extrapolations to data that might have been obtained if students with lower anxiety had been available. If the extrapolation were correct, then the disordinal interaction shown in Figure 5.3 would exist, as predicted.

Ordinal interactions are of further importance when the problem of the statistical significance of interactions is considered. When the interaction in an analysis of variance, or a multiple linear regression analysis is significant, such significance applies to the overall slope of the two lines. It does not, however, mean that, in the case of a disordinal interaction, those students close to the

FIG. 5.3   Example of an ordinal interaction between anxiety and instructional method with hypothetical extrapolation shown by dotted line.

crossover points should automatically be assigned to treatment above the cross-over point. In order to make such an assignment it must be assumed that the differences in slope are equally significant at all points along the functions. Such an assumption would be unwarranted since techniques such as the Johnson and Neyman (1936) procedure have to be invoked to determine significance regions. That is, it remains to be determined *at what point* there is a significant difference among the treatments warranting differential assignment of students to one instructional treatment or another. In terms of attribute treatment interactions, then, this discussion suggests that assignment to different instructional methods is warranted only when there is a significant difference between the two treatments *at that point* on the *x* and *y* coordinates. This is of some significance for ordinal interactions as well, since it implies that at the point where regression lines of the treatments are fairly close, there are unlikely to be significant differences among them. Therefore, assigning students to the treatment that appears to yield high achievement may actually not result in any significant achievement differences.

It should be noted that techniques such as the Johnson and Neyman (1936) procedure should be invoked when there is sufficient data available to make the jump from research to application. This would suggest that, at a minimum, the attribute–treatment interactions have been replicated in a number of research studies on populations similar to those for which practical applications are envisaged. At that point, regions of significance are crucial in determining which

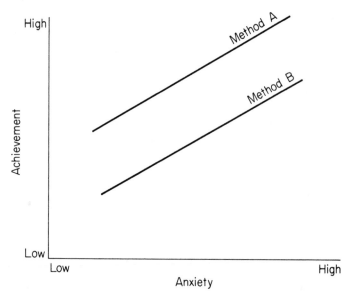

FIG. 5.4   Example of anxiety and instructional method main effect *without* interaction.

of several instructional strategies a student should be assigned to. Unfortunately, aptitude–treatment–interaction research has not yet provided a data base of interactions to make it possible to apply the available statistical techniques for assessing the regions of significance.

For purposes of comparison it is useful to look at a graph in which there is an anxiety main effect, and a treatment main effect, but the two do not interact. Such hypothetical data are displayed in Figure 5.4. In order to facilitate comparison with the other figures, the x and y axes are the same as those in the prior figures. As can be seen by an inspection of Figure 5.4 achievement is higher for Treatment A than it is for Treatment B all along the x axis. Achievement appears to increase, for both treatments as anxiety increases (a result expected only on very easy tasks). Absence of interaction between anxiety and instructional treatment is demonstrated by the equal distance between lines for Treatments A and B. That is, the slope of the two lines is very similar, indicating that the effect of anxiety on achievement is about the same in both groups. Evidence of interaction is implied whenever the slope of the lines differ, as indicated in Figures 5.1 and 5.2.

REGRESSION ANALYSIS

Many of the attribute–treatment-interaction anxiety studies, reviewed in detail in Chapters 6, 8, 9, 10 and 11 employed a design such as the following. Some form of anxiety scale was administered to students, and on the basis of these scores two or three groups were typically formed: a high- and low-anxiety group, or a high-, medium-, and low-anxiety group. Such division into groups is accomplished by separating the anxiety scores into two groups at the median, or by dividing the distribution into equal thirds. The students are randomly assigned to different instructional treatments, and the interaction between the anxiety groups and treatment then studied. A logical analysis reveals that the research design described here is inefficient. If, for example, the median score is 15, students with scores of 14 could end up in the "low" group and students with 16 and above in the "high" group. Then, students with anxiety scores of 4 and 5 would be in the same group as those with scores of 14, but students with a score of 16 end up in a different group. Clearly such a data-analytic procedure is inefficient, since near the breaking points students in different groups are more similar to one another than they are to many others ending up in their group. This logic is behind Cohen's (1968) estimate that dichotomizing continuous anxiety data costs experimenters 36% of the available variance.

In order to cope with this loss of power, it is generally recommended (Cohen, 1968; Cronbach & Snow, 1969, 1977) that multiple-linear-regression analysis be employed in attribute–treatment-interaction research. In such an analysis the students anxiety score is used in its continuous form, and dividing students into different groups is not necessary. In regression analysis the instructional treatments are coded as dichotomous variables, sometimes also referred to as "dummy" variables. In effect, the treatment variable is represented as a score which signifies a subject's group membership. The interaction between anxiety and treatment is, then, ascertained by cross-multiplying the anxiety and treatment variables.

The rationale and procedures for the use of multiple-linear regression analysis, as a powerful data analytic tool in psychological contexts in general, is discussed in detail by Cohen (1968); and Cronbach and Snow (1969, 1977) discuss its use in attribute–treatment-interaction research. Books and computer programs devoted to this subject have been published by Kerlinger and Pedhazur (1973), and by Kelly et al. (1971), among others. A detailed discussion of regression is beyond the scope of this presentation. It should be noted, however, that multiple-linear-regression procedures are not as well standardized as other techniques and the investigator should consult Cronbach and Snow's (1977) treatment of the subject matter with care before designing attribute–treatment-interaction studies.

6
Anxiety-Treatment Interactions: A Review of Research

This review of research is limited largely to studies of an interaction between anxiety and treatments that have clear-cut relevance to instruction. Specifically excluded from this review are investigations of anxiety using such experimental tasks as paired associates, digit span, or other essentially laboratory-based research techniques. While studies such as these are clearly important in enlarging our understanding of the various effects of anxiety, a legitimate case can be made (Ausubel, 1968) that meaningful learning in classroom contexts may well follow principles and laws different from those revealed in laboratory-based experimentation since there are many uncontrolled variables in the content learned, the instructional method and the social milieu.

The studies reviewed here are organized into the following categories: studies using programmed or computer-assisted instruction (CAI); studies using different versions of a program dealing with heart disease; and studies comparing individualized versus classroom techniques, or comparing different classroom techniques. Within each section the research will be reported in chronological order.

RATIONALE

A comparison of the distinguishing characteristics of individualized and conventional instructional practices suggests a compelling rationale for an interaction between anxiety and these two instructional strategies.

Organization

Typically, in individualized instructional contexts the materials are developed to attain specific instructional objectives, and tangential materials are systemati-

86

cally eliminated from course content. Not infrequently, the objectives of a course are provided to students. In conventional instruction, such as classroom lecture, recitations, assigned readings of different types, film presentations, and so on, objectives are generally not as specific as they are in individualized instruction; nor is it typical for objectives to be given to the students. The clear organization, specific instructions, and elimination of extraneous material evident in individualized instruction should be especially helpful to anxious students due to the elimination of uncertainty.

Rate

The rate at which instruction proceeds is another variable suggesting that individualized instruction should be optimal for anxious students. In individualized instructional contexts students typically may take as much or as little time as they feel necessary in order to complete a unit. This is one of the hallmarks of individualized instruction. In conventional instruction, on the other hand, students often have only a single opportunity to listen to a lecture or demonstration. Furthermore, the rate at which material is presented during lectures is *not* determined by a particular student's needs, but generally paced by the teacher's ideas of what an average group pace should be. In individualized contexts, on the other hand, if a criterion test indicates that the student has not attained adequate mastery, the student is generally able to reinspect the instructional materials and obtain a second evaluation. If success is achieved the second time, the failure to attain criterion at first is ignored, and not averaged into a grade. In conventional instruction, of course, the student does not have the opportunities for repeated study, control of the rate of instruction, or opportunity for multiple evaluation without penalty. Clearly these considerations would lead one to expect an interaction between anxiety and these two instructional methods.

Evaluative Stress

Another major difference between individual and classroom instructional practices is in the degree to which they involve evaluative stress. In the conventional classroom environment a fair amount of evaluative stress is likely to be present. Such stress may be related to concerns regarding the student's achievement compared to other class members, fears of being asked to respond orally in class, and so on. In individualized instructional contexts there is considerably less stress on students' relative standing, and, of course, there are no grounds for fears regarding oral questioning. The reduction of opportunities for negative self-evaluation in individualized instruction, then, would also suggest the presence of an interaction between these instructional modes and anxiety.

PROGRAMMED INSTRUCTION
AND COMPUTER-ASSISTED INSTRUCTION

A large number of studies investigating the interactions between anxiety and instructional methods have used instructional materials presented via programmed instruction, or computer-assisted instruction. Undoubtedly, one of the reasons for the popularity of such investigations is that such materials tend to be self-instructional. Teachers or experimenters do not intervene once the material is given to the student, yet the content taught by such programs is quite similar to subject matter covered in schools. Use of such programs for research, then, appears to offer an avenue for the investigation of the effects of anxiety on meaningful learning similar to that occurring in schools; yet it is free from the potentially confounding effects of classroom environment, teacher personality, and the like.

In this section studies pertinent to anxiety that utilize programmed instruction, or computer-based instruction are reviewed. A large number of investigations, using both a programmed and a computer-based instructional format, used different versions of an instructional program dealing with the area of heart disease. For convenience in comparing the results of different experiments, these are discussed together in a succeeding section.

Statistical Significance and Description

Cronbach and Snow (1977) generously have made prepublication copies of their new and comprehensive review of the attribute treatment literature available to researchers. In that work, they argue that it may be dangerous to overestimate the importance of statistical significance in attribute treatment interaction research. While acknowledging the danger or errors, they suggest that the cumulative descriptive significance of a number of studies, which in themselves may be nonsignificant, may be missed if the descriptive data are ignored due to lack of significance. Therefore, these writers interpret descriptive results even though they may not be significant. Consequently, their interpretation of anxiety studies, including those conducted by this writer, tends to differ from that offered here.

It is, of course, quite clear that much can be learned from nonsignificant results. Often these are and have been of major importance to investigators formulating a program of research. Furthermore, nonsignificant results from a number of experiments, run by different investigators, with different instructional methods and subjects which generate similar though nonsignificant data do, as Cronbach and Snow (1977) indicate, generate a good deal of food for thought. Whether such results should, then, be interpreted raises something of a philosophical problem. On the one hand, there is a danger that important trends may be obscured by noting only data which are statistically significant and failing to interpret other relationships. On the other hand, interpretations of nonsignificant relationships run the danger of raising unconfirmed speculation to the level of theory. That such results are not significant suggests that they may be attributable purely to sampling errors. Therefore, a more conservative course is taken here than advocated by Cronbach and Snow (1977). Nonsignificant results will not be interpreted.

There are three principle reasons for this cautious position. Interpretation of nonsignificant findings may be of importance in areas where hypotheses and theory are scarce, as they are in much of attribute–treatment-interaction research in general. In such cases, interpretation of nonsignificant results may provide the guidelines for future research. This is decidedly not the case with anxiety. As indicated previously, anxiety is perhaps one of the most thoroughly investigated topics in psychology, if not educational psychology. The vast anxiety literature, composed of rigorous experimentation, numerous descriptive studies, and equally numerous clinical case studies is hardly bereft of hypotheses. In such an area, then, where numerous generalizations from related research are available for testing, it would seem more prudent to follow a cautious course.

A second reason for erring in the direction of conservatism has to do with the frequent failure to replicate phenomena in anxiety treatment interaction research. For example, it is pointed out subsequently that relatively minor alterations in the mode with which a program is presented can account for marked inconsistencies in the results. The lack of robustness of these phenomena, then, is such that the interpretation of nonsignificant findings may lead investigators to search for patterns having not only the distinctive outlines of castles in the sand, but also sharing their durability.

Finally, the discussion regarding the degree to which nonsignificant results should be interpretated resolves itself to a decision regarding the relative seriousness of different types of error in the inferences drawn from statistical results. A Type 1 error may occur when the null hypothesis is rejected even though it is true; and a Type 2 error can happen when the null hypothesis is *not* rejected even though it is false. When trends in the results are not discussed because the overall analysis was not statistically significant a Type 1 error is viewed as being most serious; the possibility that nonsignificant results might lead to erroneous conclusions, and futile further research are viewed as being the gravest risks. Interpreting the trends in nonsignificant results suggests, on the other hand, that the danger of discarding fruitful hypotheses is considered most serious.

There are no guide posts permitting a clear choice between these twin dangers. It would appear from our viewpoint that a Type 2 error is most serious in those situations in which a failure to reject the null hypothesis seriously impedes the conduct of further research. In such situations the danger that an error will not be corrected by future research is great indeed, since the error itself discourages such further experimental ventures. The popularity of anxiety as a research topic should reduce the probability of such an occurrence. The danger of a Type 1 error, on the other hand, in the anxiety area may cause considerable misdirected energies in the conduct of investigations which may be based on faulty research precedents. These considerations lead to the greater concern with Type 1 errors in this discussion, and hence the decision not to interpret such results.

Correlational Studies

A number of studies appearing in the early 1960s utilized an instructional program, and then correlated performance on that program and achievement from it with a number of individual difference variables including anxiety. Strictly speaking, these were not anxiety–treatment-interaction studies since instructional mode was not varied. These studies, however, were influential in suggesting that anxiety might be a useful variable in the understanding of the outcomes of such self-instructional devices, and are therefore reviewed here.

Traweek (1964) administered a program on arithmetic fractions to a fourth-grade group of students in order to determine whether those who were successful differed from the unsuccessful ones with respect to test anxiety, general anxiety, and a variety of personality variables. The results indicated that successful students were significantly more test anxious than unsuccessful ones, although there were no differences on general anxiety.

Kight and Sassenrath (1966) also used one version of a constructed response instructional program dealing with test construction. These investigators used a college-student population and found that anxious students, defined by scores on the test-anxiety questionnaire (Mandler & Sarason, 1952), worked faster and made fewer program errors than less anxious individuals. There were, however, no achievement differences between the anxiety groups.

A program dealing with latitudes and longitudes was employed by O'Reilly and Ripple (1967) with nine sixth-grade classes. The program was organized into ten daily lessons with approximately 40 frames per lesson. Posttest results were correlated with a battery of tests including the test-anxiety scale for children (Sarason *et al.,* 1960) which had a correlation of $-.53$ with achievement. In a stepwise regression analysis, this impressive correlation dropped to a much less impressive beta of $-.125$, which, while still significant, accounted for a fairly small percentage of the achievement variance.

Shrable and Sassenrath (1970) studied the interactive effects of achievement motivation, assessed by an achievement-imagery measure, test anxiety, determined by the test-anxiety questionnaire, and prior achievement, as determined by pretest, on a number of variables. (Since only one instructional mode was used in this study, it is discussed here.) The program employed was identical to that used by Kight and Sassenrath (1966). The only significant effect on posttest was pretest score; not surprisingly, students with higher prior knowledge achieved more than those with less prior knowledge. Test anxiety and achievement motivation had no effect on retention, not were any of the interactions significant.

There were two significant effects on program errors. Anxious students made fewer errors than a less anxious group. There was also a significant disordinal interaction between achievement motivation and anxiety on number of errors. High- and low-anxiety students who were also low in achievement motivation made pretty much the same number of errors. Among students high in achievement motivation, however, those high in anxiety made fewer errors than the less anxious students. The posttest was an alternate form of the pretest. Pretest means for the sample employed in this study were 20.5, and the posttest grand mean equaled 24.6, yielding a total achievement of only about 4 points. These data suggest that, on the average, students learned very little from this program, making even those effects which appeared difficult to interpret.

The only consistency in these descriptive studies appears to be the finding that test-anxious students made fewer errors than their less anxious counterparts. The two studies dealing with the relationships between anxiety and achievement yielded contradictory findings. In one case, anxiety was positively associated with achievement, and in another negatively. The Kight and Sassenrath (1966) study was cited by a number of investigators as evidence for the likelihood that programed instruction might be especially advantageous for high-anxious students. In retrospect, it may be noted that these relationships occurred only on acquisition data, that is, number of errors on the program, as distinguished from achievement data (posttest). The difficulty of interpreting relationships between anxiety and acquisition indices in programed instruction are discussed subsequently.

Response Mode Studies and Other Program Variables

In addition to being self-instructional, as indicated above, instructional material prepared in a programed-instruction format or for presentation by a computer-based instructional system has a number of other distinctive characteristics. Generally, the instructional content is presented in a series of tightly organized units, called frames. A program with small steps generally contains relatively little material in each frame; and the amount of new material per frame is substantially larger, making such programs generally more difficult and causing a higher incidence of student error.

The types of responses required of students in such instructional programs also varies. *Constructed-response* programs require students to construct an answer to each frame, or fill in a blank. In multiple-choice programs, as the name implies, the student has to choose an answer from a number of alternatives. Feedback regarding the accuracy of students' responses is generally provided in one of a number of ways. In the programed format students often make an answer to a frame, either on the program booklet itself or on an accompanying answer sheet while the correct answer is not in view, then check the answer by flipping the page to reveal the right response printed adjacent to the next frame. In computer-based instructional systems, students enter an answer on a typewriter terminal, connected to a computer, and feedback regarding the response accuracy is provided by the computer system.

The constructed response mode is generally considered to be the condition in which the student receives maximal instructional support. Surprisingly, however, this mode has not consistently resulted in superior achievement (Anderson, 1967). Recent research has suggested that constructed responding yields higher achievement in situations where the subject matter is relatively novel to the student (Tobias, 1973a).

In order to study interactions with anxiety constructed response programs are typically altered in one of several ways:

1. Program blanks are filled in and questions answered creating a reading mode in which the program is read by students without requiring responses, or offering specific feedback of any kind.

2. The feedback portion of the program is eliminated, creating what is generally called a *no-feedback version.*

3. The constructed response program is sometimes altered to require multiple-choice answers.

Such alterations have generally been assumed to reduce instructional support provided by the program.

In response-mode studies it was typically expected that the condition of maximal support, constructed responding would be especially beneficial for anxious students. Reducing the instructional support was expected to interfere most with anxious students, and least with individuals low in anxiety. The careful organization of the subject matter, reduced amount of uncertainty, and provision of feedback were considered to be features which should reduce the debilitating effects of anxiety for anxious students.

Lache (1967) studied the interaction between four response modes to programed instructions and three levels of test anxiety. A program on vocabulary was presented in four different ways: constructed response; optional constructed response; covert response, in which students were asked to "think" an answer rather than actually make it; and a reading mode. Analysis of variance of this 4 X 3 X 2 design revealed no significant main effects or interactions.

Tobias and Williamson (1968) used a program dealing with binary numbers in a study with college students. High- and low-anxiety groups were created on the basis of the Taylor Manifest Anxiety Scale (Taylor, 1953), and students were then randomly assigned to three response modes: constructed response, constructed response without feedback, and a reading group. A 2 X 3 analysis of covariance of posttest scores, with pretest as the covariate, indicated that there were no differences between anxiety groups or among response modes, nor was there any interaction between them.

Campeau (1968) used a constructed-response program with a sample of fifth-grade students. Half the students did not receive feedback concerning the accuracy of their responses. Campeau reported a significant interaction between anxiety and feedback for girls, but not for boys. High-anxiety girls achieved more than the low-anxiety group in the standard constructed response with feedback condition. When feedback was removed, however, the achievement of the low-anxiety students exceeded that of the high anxiety group.

Morris, Blank, McKie, and Rankin (1970) studied the interaction among anxiety, different types of motivational feedback, and size of step in programed instruction. In large-step programs, each frame contains a lot of information, and hence yields higher error rates than small-step programs. Motivational instructions were manipulated by informing a group of students that they had done well on pretests; the second group received pretests but was not informed about them, and a third group did not receive pretests. Intelligence formed a third independent variable in this 2 X 3 X 3 design. It was found that the small-step program produced higher posttest scores, took more time to complete, and yielded lower error rates than the large-step program. The succeeding analyses were conducted within each step size separately. On four dependent variables there were no significant main effects or interactions with anxiety, measured by the Test Anxiety Scale for Children (Sarason *et al.,* 1960), on the more difficult large-step program where they might have been expected.

On the small-step program, high-anxiety students made more errors than low-anxiety students, and the interaction between anxiety and motivational treatment was significant. This disordinal interaction indicated that low-anxiety students performed best under conditions of positive feedback, and most poorly without any pretest. High-anxiety students, on the other hand, performed best without pretest, and most poorly under conditions of positive feedback. It should be remembered that this interaction was the only one of 12 interactions (three on each of four dependent variables) in which anxiety was a factor which achieved significance. It should also be remembered that no interactions to which anxiety contributed reached significance in the large-step program.

In a complex experiment, Hall (1970) studied the interactive effects of stress, level of test anxiety (low, medium, and high), and task difficulty. An easy portion of the program used, divided into two parts, had error rates of 25 and 22%, respectively. The difficult program had error rates of 55 and 57%, respectively. Dependent measures consisted of errors, posttest score, and state anxiety measures administered at four points in the instructional sequence. Data analysis consisted of different analyses of variance for which subjects were randomly discarded so as to equalize cell sizes.

The results indicated that difficult material produced higher levels of state anxiety than the easy; stress did not yield significant increases in state anxiety compared to nonstress. Indeed, the results indicated an effect approaching significance such that nonstress had higher state anxiety scores than the stress condition. The predicted anxiety X stress X difficulty interactions on the achievement and error indices were *not* supported by the results. Hall (1970) raises questions regarding the degree to which anxiety was actually engaged in his experimental situation. Even though the differences between state anxiety measures on the easy and difficult part of the program were statistically significant, the magnitude of this difference consisted of less than two points out of a possible score of 80.

Summary

In these studies two interactions between anxiety and instructional treatments were found. Campeau's (1968) finding that, among females, high-anxiety students did better than low-anxiety students when feedback was provided, and the opposite occurred under conditions of no feedback. Morris *et al.* (1970) found that on an easy, small-step program, students high on anxiety achieved more when they were not given the program relevant pretests than low-anxiety students; when students were given positive feedback regarding pretest scores, those low in anxiety outperformed the high-anxiety students. Campeau's (1968) findings, on the face of it, appear consonant with expectations from the anxiety literature. Providing feedback reduces program difficulty; hence, high-anxiety students could be expected to outperform those low in anxiety under such conditions. The opposite results would be expected—and were obtained—when feedback is removed, since the program is substantially more difficult under such conditions.

The Morris *et al.* (1970) finding that low-anxiety students achieve more than those higher in anxiety with positive feedback, while the opposite occurred when neither feedback nor relevant pretests were administered is hard to interpret. Being given positive feedback should have reduced the uncertainty and tensions of high-anxiety students, facilitating their performance rather than interfering with it. These studies, then, can best be described as confusing, regarding the interaction between anxiety and different programed instructional formats.

STUDIES USING THE HEART-DISEASE INSTRUCTIONAL PROGRAM

A number of studies used different versions of a program dealing with heart disease (Tobias, 1968). Since program content, and format are important in understanding some of the findings reported in different studies, a detailed description of the program may be helpful.

Program Content and Format

The program deals with heart dieseae in general, and can be divided into two parts. The first part contains material dealing with the prevalence and incidence of heart disease: risk factors that increase the probability of contracting heart disease, such as smoking, tension, lack of exercise, and so on; and the relationship between cholesterol and coronary insufficiency. The average adult has encountered some of this material in the public media, although not with the thoroughness and detail covered by the program.

The second two-thirds of the program, Frames 55–144, deal in technical detail with the diagnosis of heart disease from the fifth precordial lead of the electro-cardiograph. Medical terminology regarding heart disease is employed. Also discussed are the different types of tracings by which different levels of heart disease may be diagnosed, the reversibility of the various types of heart disease, and the tracings characteristic of different stages in the healing cycle after a heart attack.

In the first study using this program (Tobias, 1969), first-year college students obtained pretest scores of 34% on the familiar part of the program. Pretests for the technical program were not administered because during tryout the pretest revealed that college students had no prior experience with this part of the content. Initially the program was prepared in a constructed-response format with feedback provided regarding response accuracy.

A Study of Response Mode, Stress, and Two Types of Anxiety

This program was employed in a study (Tobias & Abramson, 1971) in which the independent variables were response mode and stress, as well as facilitating and debilitating anxiety (Alpert & Haber, 1960). Students were randomly assigned to a neutral, or a stress condition in which they were informed that program achievement was highly related to intelligence. Students were also assigned to one of three response modes: constructed response with, and without feedback, and a reading condition.

Interactions had been expected among response mode, stress, and debilitating anxiety on the more difficult technical program. It had been anticipated that a combination of stress, and overt responding without feedback would be espe-cially disadvantageous on the difficult, technical program for students high in debilitating anxiety. Instead, an interaction between debilitating anxiety and stress was found for the easy familiar section of this program and *not* for the technical part. This interaction, depicted in Figure 6.1, indicated that in the stress condition anxiety was negatively related to achievement; whereas under neutral conditions the relationship was positive. It should be pointed out that in this experiment the major instructional manipulations consisted of different response modes, which do not affect the relationships depicted in Figure 6.1.

Preliminary analysis had indicated that there were differential sex effects for the facilitating anxiety; correlations between achievement and facilitating anxi-ety were .50 for females and −.03 for males. Facilitating anxiety effects were, therefore, examined in interaction with sex.

On the technical part of the program, facilitating anxiety was positively related to achievement; and a high-order interaction among facilitating anxiety, response mode, stress, and sex was also found. This relationship is depicted in Figure 6.2.

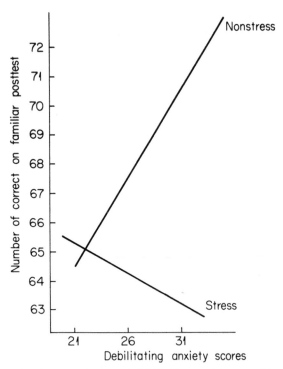

FIG. 6.1 Interaction between stress and debilitation anxiety on achievement from the familiar part of the heart-disease program.

Analysis of that figure indicates that the greatest differences in slope are accounted for by the differences in relationship between stress and debilitating anxiety for males and females. Under stress, achievement and facilitating anxiety appear to have been negatively related to achievement for males, whereas for females the relationship was positive. By and large, the regression slopes for different response modes are essentially similar. Again, then, this high-order interaction was not supportive of the anticipated interaction among the different instructional methods, represented by the response modes, and anxiety. There were no relationships or interactions between anxiety measures and number of errors committed on the program.

Facilitating anxiety. It will be recalled that, on the complex material, interactions had been expected with debilitating anxiety. These were not found, but interactions with facilitating anxiety were found. This raises some questions regarding the nature of the facilitating anxiety construct as indicated in Chapter 3. Alpert and Haber (1960) conceptualized the facilitating-anxiety scale as a measure of the type of tension which tends to improve students' performance in achievement situations. This scale contains items such as the following: "The more important the exam or test, the better I seem to do"; "I enjoy taking a

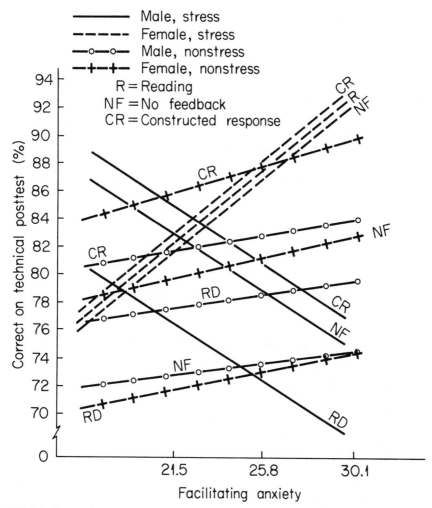

FIG. 6.2   Interaction among stress, response modes, facilitating anxiety, and sex on achievement from the technical part of the heart disease program. (From Tobias & Abramson, 1971.)

difficult test more than an easy one"; "Nervousness while taking a test helps me to do better," [Alpert & Haber, 1960, p. 211] and the like. The contents of these items suggests that something very different from the usual conceptions of anxiety—featured by fearfulness, tension, lack of psychological well-being, and similar phenomenal descriptions—is measured by this scale.

It is not surprising to note that researchers such as McKeachie (1969) have suggested that the facilitating-anxiety scale may be more closely related to achievement motivation than to traditional conceptions of anxiety. Datta (1967) reported that students with high debilitating-anxiety scores tended also to have high scores on other measures of general anxiety, while high facilitating-anxiety scorers did not. In a factor analysis of 46 other personality scales, Datta found that debilitating anxiety and other scales had factor loadings of −.4 on a psychological-well-being factor. Facilitating anxiety, on the other hand, had a loading of only .05 on this factor, and no higher saturations on any other factor except that defined by the two achievement anxiety scales.

The facilitating-anxiety findings in the Tobias and Abramson (1971) study make sense when viewed in terms of motivation for academic achievement. From this perspective it is not surprising that students with high motivation should achieve more than low scorers, thus accounting for the facilitating-anxiety main effect. Again, in accord with McKeachie's (1969) finding, this scale appears to be especially useful for females. In this study the facilitating anxiety scale correlated .5 with achievement from the technical program for females, compared to −.03 for males, yielding the interaction previously described. These data suggest that the facilitating anxiety scale of the achievement-anxiety test may be fruitful to apply in investigations studying academic motivation among females. The degree to which the facilitating-anxiety scale illuminates our understanding of anxiety as conventionally understood, however, remains in doubt.

A Study of Sequence, Scholastic Aptitude, and State and Trait Anxiety

The failure to find anxiety–treatment interactions involving debilitating anxiety in the Tobias and Abramson (1971) study was attributed, at first, to the possibility that, despite the stress manipulations, anxiety may well not have been engaged during the research situation. This possibility was strengthened since the main effect for stress in that study was not significant. Furthermore, O'Neil, Spielberger, and Hansen (1969), and O'Neil, Hansen, and Spielberger (1969) had found that trait anxiety was unrelated to performance; state anxiety, however, assessed while subjects were working on the experimental tasks, was related to performance indices in both investigations. Since Alpert and Haber's (1960) achievement-anxiety test was essentially a trait-anxiety measure, it was hypothesized that in future research the sought-after attribute–treatment interactions would emerge with state-anxiety measures.

The next investigation (Tobias, 1973b) using the programed version of the heart-disease materials investigated anxiety–treatment interactions among sequence, scholastic aptitude, state, and trait anxiety. On the sequence variable, half of the students were assigned to take both the familiar, and technical program with frame sequence arranged by a table of random numbers. State-anxiety measures, determined by the short form of the State–Trait Anxiety Inventory, which had been used successfully in the two investigations referred to above by O'Neil et al. (1969a, b) were administered at four points in the instructional sequence: before the beginning of instruction, at program mid-point, and prior to the beginning of the posttest for both the familiar and technical parts of the program.

Regression analysis of this study indicated that students receiving the logical sequence achieved more than those using the random version. With respect to anxiety, however, the results were again disappointing. On the achievement test for the familiar part of the program, an interaction among sequence, scholastic aptitude, and A state did achieve significance and accounted for 6% of the variance. This interaction shown in Figure 6.3, plotted by holding scholastic aptitude constant and varying state anxiety, shows a negative relationship between A state and achievement for students receiving the regular sequence. For the scrambled sequence, on the other hand, there was no relationship between achievement and state anxiety. A possible interpretation of this relationship suggests that in order for anxiety to affect performance, a person must attribute performance to personal inadequacy. The scrambled sequence was so obviously disorganized, however, that it would take a rare individual to attribute

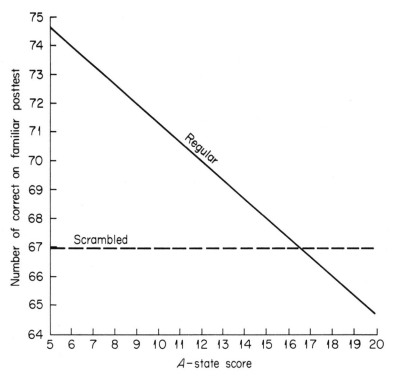

FIG. 6.3 Interaction among A-state, sequence and Scholastic Aptitude Test scores (held constant) on percentage correct on achievement for familiar program. (From Tobias, 1973b.)

poor performance to himself, rather than the chaotic organization of the material. This interpretation of the interaction, however, fails to explain why similar interactions were *not* obtained on the more difficult technical material. A state had a significant main effect that indicated that as A state increased achievement from the technical posttest decreased.

Errors on the program. There were several significant interactions on the number of errors made on the program in the sequence study (Tobias, 1973b). One interaction occurred among sequence, scholastic aptitude, and state anxiety on number of errors on the familiar program. This interaction indicated that as A state score increased, the percentage correct on the regular program tends to decrease for students taking the regular sequence, whereas the opposite occurred, though the regression was not as steep, for the scrambled sequence. A similar interaction occurred among sequence, scholastic aptitude, and A trait. There was little relationship between A trait and percentage correct on the familiar program, whereas on the regular sequence there was a slight tendency for students with high A trait scores to achieve a slightly higher percentage correct on this program.   •

It may be tempting to interpret these interactions, however, two cautions are in order:

1. Anxiety treatment interactions are concerned mainly with optimizing instructional outcome, as determined by posttest score in this experiment, as distinguished from acquisition data, such as errors on a program.

2. When programmed instructional materials are administered in booklet format, as they were in this experiment, there is a large potential for cheating.

Even though they are instructed not to, students can check their responses prior to making them, and thus apparently reduce the number of errors.

Anderson, Kulhavy, and André (1970) demonstrated, using a modification of the same heart-disease program administered by computer, that when students have the opportunity to peek ahead, the percentage of errors decreased, compared to those occasions when no such peeking was possible. It is safe to assume, therefore, that data based on program errors are not as solid as they might be. No peeking was possible on the posttest, hence, such data are more rigorous tests of hypotheses.

The failure to find interactions on posttests for the technical material in the sequence study was unexpected. One possible interpretation of the results was that the sequence variable had such a strong effect on outcome, accounting for 31% of the total variance, as to obscure the operation of other variables.

Computer-Assisted Instruction Studies

The programed instructional format of the heart-disease material was modified for presentation on an IBM 1500-computer-assisted instructional system at

Florida State University. Two studies utilizing this computer assisted instruction adaptation, reported by Leherissey, O'Neil, Heinrich, and Hansen, 1973, are discussed in greater detail in Chapter 11. In the first study, an interaction on achievement from the familiar program was found between trait anxiety and the four response modes used in that experiment. The two groups making overt responses to the program, a constructed response and a modified multiple-choice group, had roughly similar slopes; indicating that as trait anxiety increased, achievement decreased for the groups not making overt responses, whereas the opposite occurred for the multiple-choice group. For the constructed-response group, however, students low and high in state anxiety performed well, whereas the medium-anxiety group did relatively poorly.

In the second study Leherissey *et al.* (1973) used a long and short form of the program, in addition to constructed-response and reading modes. Again an interaction between response mode and trait anxiety was obtained. However, when the response-mode data, which were the same in both studies, were compared, reverse relationships appeared. Achievement from constructed responding decreased as trait anxiety increased. For the reading group, on the other hand, students of medium trait-anxiety achieved more than the high- and low-anxious students. In this study an interaction between response mode and state anxiety was also found.

Neither of the two Leherissey *et al.* (1971, 1973) studies reported any interaction on the more difficult posttest. Of further concern was that these computer-assisted-instruction studies failed to replicate the superiority of constructed responding previously reported on the programed-instructional format of this material (Tobias, 1969; Tobias & Abramson, 1971).

The inconsistencies of the interactions, and failure to replicate response-mode data previously reported with the use of the programed instructional version of this program led to a thorough revision cycle of the instructional material (Tobias, 1972). In an attempt to replicate the programed-instruction version of this course, Leherissey *et al.* (1973) had transferred the frame-by-frame structure of the program to a computer-assisted instructional system. Part of the program, it will be recalled, involved instructing students regarding the type of electrocardiograph tracings characteristic of different degrees of heart disease. Since such drawing could not occur on the terminal, different segments of the tracings were keyed to different numbers. In order to "draw" a normal tracing on the terminal, the student had to punch in Numbers 1, 6, 3, 4, 2. The posttest, however, was administered in paper-and-pencil format. Since students had to draw tracings on the posttest, rather than to punch numbers on the terminal, they were engaging in a task for which the instruction had not prepared them. The inconsistency of the anxiety interactions, and the failure to replicate the superiority for constructed responding may well have been attributable to this crucial procedural difference.

In a succeeding study, conducted by Leherissey (1971), the program and posttest were both administered on the computer system. Previous findings regarding the superiority of constructed responding were replicated when this modification was made. Apparently the procedural change made a difference in the results.

Analysis of the computer-assisted instructional-program format revealed another major source of difference. In the computer version, the feedback provided after the student constructed a response was identical to that offered in the programed format. Often, therefore, after the student constructed an answer, the system provided feedback with an equivalent synonym. When the materials were administered in paper-and-pencil format it seemed likely that students were able to understand that the preprinted feedback synonym indicated that their answers were correct. The lifelike character of computer-assisted instruction, however, suggested that frequently students may have been in doubt as to whether a particular response had been evaluated as being correct or incorrect, since the system only provided feedback without evaluating the accuracy of the student's response.

A second revision cycle was instituted in which, in addition to providing the text book answer, the student was given feedback regarding the accuracy of responses. Three types of evaluative feedback were provided:

1. The student was informed that the answer was identical to the textbook response, and the textbook response was then provided.

2. The student was informed that the answer was similar to the textbook response, and the textbook response was then provided.

3. The student was informed that the answer was incorrect in comparison to the textbook response which was then provided.

Succeeding studies using the heart-disease program used this last modification to the heart-disease instructional materials.

Studies Using the Revised Heart-Disease Program

In the next study (Tobias, 1973c), only the technical portion of the revised heart-disease program was employed. The interaction among distraction, response mode, and test anxiety was examined. Students were randomly assigned to a regular, or a distraction condition in which they were required to memorize consonant–vowel–consonant nonsense trigrams at the same time that they worked on the program. These syllables were flashed on the screen of the computer terminal and recall for the syllable was requested every one, two, or three succeeding frames. In addition, students were randomly assigned to a constructed-response or reading condition. Prior to the beginning of the instructional sequence, students took Sarason's (1972) test-anxiety questionnaire. State-anxiety scales were administered at four points during the instructional sequence and were considered an independent variable in this investigation. The A state data is subsequently discussed separately.

An interaction between test anxiety and the instructional conditions had been expected in this experiment. Specifically, it had been expected that the distracting condition should be especially debilitating to the achievement of students high in test anxiety, since there is a substantial body of evidence (Sarason, 1972; Wine, 1971b) that such students have a good deal of difficulty attending to the task, even under conditions where there is no experimentally induced distraction. Furthermore, an interaction among distraction, response mode, and test anxiety had also been expected. Making responses and receiving feedback concerning them appeared to be an instructional manipulation designed to redirect the attention of students who had been diverted, either by their own preoccupations relating to test anxiety, or by the experimental manipulation of distracting conditions.

The results of this experiment failed to support any of the expected interactions. Test anxiety did not interact with distracting conditions, nor was there any interaction between test anxiety, distraction, and response mode. Equally surprising was the fact that, in contradiction to prior research which had reported that students high in test anxiety tended to perform more poorly than students with low test anxiety, in this study anxiety appeared to have no effect on achievement from the program or on the amount of time taken to complete it.

A succeeding experiment, Tobias and Duchastel (1974), also investigated the interaction between test anxiety and a number of instructional manipulations. A set of behavioral objectives, referenced to posttest questions, were developed and presented to half of this group while the other half of the group studied the program in the usual manner. Students to whom objectives were given were assigned to working the program in a random sequence, similar to that used in the previous sequence study (Tobias, 1973b), or in a regular sequence. All students used the constructed-response mode, and worked on the modified form of the technical portion of this program. In addition to the test-anxiety questionnaire (Sarason, 1972) given prior to the beginning of the program, the brief state-anxiety scale was administered at four points during the instructional sequence. In this experiment A state was also used as an independent variable.

An interaction among anxiety, objectives, and sequence had been expected. It was reasoned that presenting objectives would enable high-anxiety students to organize the instructional content more efficiently than they could in the absence of such objectives. Furthermore, the objectives had been considered to be especially advantageous in the scrambled condition in which availability of objectives should have led to higher achievement for all students, but especially for those high in anxiety who otherwise would have no conceptual structure to organize this disordered input.

The results again failed to confirm expectations. As in previous investigations, sequence was highly significant and accounted for 13% of the variance. Test anxiety did not interact with either objectives, or sequence; nor was there a triple interaction among these variables. The only significant result involving test anxiety occurred on number of program errors, in which test anxiety accounted for 4% of the variance. There were no other significant effects regarding test anxiety.

Research dealing with the interaction between anxiety and provision of objectives to students, and between anxiety and giving the learner control of the instructional sequence is reviewed in some detail in Chapter 9, and is, therefore, not discussed here. Also, research dealing with anxiety and computer-managed instruction is reviewed in Chapter 11 and hence is not taken up here.

Summary

The results of the preceding studies of anxiety–treatment interactions indicated few such interactions. In the majority of these investigations, interactions between anxiety and instructional manipulations were nonsignificant. Where interactions were found, they were inconsistent, sometimes even on different variations of one program. Equally disturbing was that when interactions of any kind were reported, these were often very small effects. Furthermore, in every one of the studies conducted by this investigator, the main effects for response mode, or program organization, were generally highly significant; anxiety interactions, on the other hand, rarely were.

These results suggest that such highly structured instructional methodology as programed instruction and computer-based instructional systems are less than desirable techniques for research on anxiety–treatment interaction. It is not clear which characteristics of programed and computer-based instructional systems contribute to these negative findings. In Chapter 12 an attempt is made to develop a model that specifies which characteristics of instructional systems are most likely to interact with variations in instructional programs.

STATE ANXIETY AND ANXIETY-TREATMENT INTERACTIONS: SOME PROBLEMS

Interpretation of the state-anxiety data reported in the prior section is difficult for a number of reasons. The results are quite inconsistent, permitting few generalizations to be made regarding the interactions of state anxiety with instructional treatments on performance and achievement. In several of the investigations previously described (Tobias, 1973b, c; Tobias & Duchastel, 1974), state anxiety measures were administered at several points in the instructional sequence. Typically, an A state scale was administered prior to the beginning of instruction, at one, or several points during instruction, and immediately at the end of the program, prior to the posttest.

If a purpose of the research is to examine the effects of different conditions on state anxiety, as is the case in the investigations reported by O'Neil and his colleagues in other sections of this book (Chapters 9 and 10), there are few problems of interpretation. The state-anxiety indices are simply treated as dependent variables, and the instructional or test manipulation as independent variables, and their effects assessed by analysis of variance or regression analysis. But if state anxiety is seen as an independent variable, a number of problems regarding analysis and interpretations of such data are raised, especially when the interactive effects of A state with different instructional modes is of major interest. These problems concern:

1. Which state anxiety index is used for analyzing achievement data?
2. How can one separate the "cause" and "effect" character of state-anxiety sequences?

Selecting the Appropriate State-Anxiety Measure

Discussion of these questions is clarified by briefly reviewing the procedures of one of the experiments in which state-anxiety measures were employed. In the distraction study (Tobias, 1973c) the brief A-state scale was administered at four points: (1) immediately before the program; (2) in the middle; (3) at the end of the program; and (4) after completion of the posttest. If state anxiety were used as an independent variable in that investigation, which A-state measure would be employed to analyze posttest data? An obvious candidate, of course, would be the A state in which students were instructed to indicate how they felt during posttest. On the other hand, how well students did on posttest was obviously affected by their performance on the program. In turn, performance on the program may have been affected by state anxiety during the program. This reasoning would suggest that both the posttest state-anxiety measure and the A-state measure administered during the program should be used in the analysis of achievement data. Which of the two A-state scales administered during the program should be employed? Since there is probably no logical way of choosing between the two, both of these would have to be employed as independent variables. Logically the A state administered prior to the program may also enter this analysis since students' affective state at that point probably helps to determine how they reacted to the onset of instruction. Therefore, all four A-state measures should be employed as independent variables in the analysis of achievement.

Multiple linear regression is ideally suited for the testing of interactions between continuous measures, such as the A-state scores described here, and instructional conditions. In the distraction experiment the experimental variables consisted of distraction and nondistraction, and response mode. Each of these could be coded as 1 or 0. That is, a score is generated for each student representing the condition in which he participated. A student in the regular condition might be assigned a score of 1 and a student in the distraction condition a score of 0, similarly, constructed responding may be coded 1, and reading 0. In order to examine the interaction between distraction and response mode, an interaction vector is generated for each student simply by cross-multiplying the scores on the distraction and response mode conditions. Then, in order to ascertain the interactions among state anxiety and either or both instructional conditions, the state-anxiety scores would have to be cross multiplied with the scores on the instructional condition, or with their interaction.

In order, then, to assess the interactive effects of the four A-state measures with the instructional treatments in the distraction studies, the four A-state scales would have to be cross-multiplied with each treatment vector. Thus far, then, four A-state measures, and four interaction vectors have to be included as independent variables in the equation in order to do complete justice to the effects of A state on achievement, yielding a total of 12 effects that have to be included: four main effects, four interactions between the A-state and distraction, and four interactions between the A-state and response mode. Since a high-order interaction among the A states, the two experimental conditions, distraction and response modes, is also possible, four more effects have to be scrutinized: the triple interaction between each A state, distraction and response mode. Sixteen additional terms would, then, have to be introduced into a regression equation in order to fully assess the effects of A state on achievement in this particular experiment.

While the preceding example might be considered extreme in order to make the point, a sound rationale can be advanced for including the two within program A states, and the posttest A state together with the interaction in any analysis of the effects of A state on achievement. In that case only 12 terms are introduced into the regression equation. Such a procedure introduces two formidable problems. Determining the meaning of interactions, even low-order interactions, is not an easy matter as readers of this chapter can easily attest to, and adding nine interaction terms, three of which involve three-way interactions, poses formidable interpretative and conceptual problems which may completely swamp even the experienced investigator.

In the distraction study which was used as an example, several variables were of major concern: distraction, response modes, test anxiety, and their interactive effects. The state-anxiety research reported in Chapters 9 and 10, has repeatedly confirmed that state anxiety is modified by the student's trait anxiety. In this instance, test anxiety, which can be considered a trait-anxiety measure, may then have modified the A state. A rationale can then be established for ascertaining the interactive effects between test anxiety and the four A states obtained in this experiment. Once this rationale is accepted, the investigator has to ascertain the interactive effects among test anxiety, state anxiety, distractions, and so on, and so on.

It seems clear that not only are the investigator's interpretative talents challenged by such expansion of regression models, but the degrees of freedom available for a sufficiently powerful analysis pose a challenge as well. In the study which has been used as an example, 121 students were employed as subjects, and the regression analysis of the effect of distraction, response mode, test anxiety, and their interactions was based on a full model with 113 degrees of freedom. Looking only at the effects of state anxiety in interaction with distraction and response modes, and ignoring the equally plausible interactive effects with test anxiety, reduces that analysis to a total of 101 degrees of freedom. Including the effects of test anxiety in interaction with A states would reduce it by another 12 degrees of freedom, leaving a total of only 89 degrees of freedom. Clearly, a point is reached where the thoroughness with which state anxiety deserves to be analyzed in order to ascertain its effects on achievement prejudices the total data analysis. For that reason, state anxiety was analyzed as a dependent variable in the particular investigation described. On the other hand, in the sequence study reported here (Tobias, 1973b) state anxiety was coded as an independent variable. In order to avoid the interpretive problems discussed, only the state-anxiety measure obtained during the posttest was employed in analyzing posttest effects.

The problems ennumerated here which befall the investigator employing state-anxiety measures as independent variables in anxiety-treatment-interaction (ATI) investigations can be solved by practical means. A greater number of subjects could be recruited, and experiments with small numbers of variables conducted. Needless to say, both of these restrictions reduce the probability of much research being done. Recruiting subject pools of 200–300 is no mean chore, as any investigator can readily attest. Furthermore, reducing the number of variables in experiments addressed to instructional issues is a dangerous matter, since it is widely known that such instruction is complexly affected by many variables; and any reduction of these thus threatens the external validity of such an experiment. Conceptually, however, it is possible to deal with the problems raised above. There are some other difficulties in the interpretation of A-state data that are not so easily disposed of.

"Cause and Effect" Problems

To return again to the example of the four A-state measures in the distraction experiment. If the within-task A-state measures were used in the analysis of acquisition data, such as error rates, time on program, attitudes towards program, and so on, several conceptual problems result. The A state administered at midprogram was presumably affected by errors the student committed on the program up to that point, the student's attitude toward the program, and the time taken to reach that point, not to mention other variables concerning which no measures may be available. *That is, the A-state measure itself was affected by the very same variables it is assumed to affect.* Matters are made more complex by the probability that, in turn, the succeeding number of errors, attitudes, and time taken were affected not only by the state anxiety experienced by the student at that point, but obviously also by the prior errors, attitudes, and time.

It is also likely that the state anxiety may have affected succeeding indices in some complex interactive way with the preceding indices. The problem, then, is that the use of state anxiety in anxiety–treatment-interaction studies as *either* a dependent, or an independent variable obscures both the meaningfulness and complexity of the effect. It is, of course, easy to separate the effect of the instructional treatment on A state by regression. One could simply partial out these effects, and compute a residual score free of the effects of these variables. Once could also eliminate the effects of A state on the succeeding treatment. In this situation the residual error, time, or attitude scores would have the effects of A state removed from them. What do such residual scores, however, represent? In one case we have an estimate of A state unaffected by the preceeding instructional treatment, and in the other case within task-instructional data free from the effects of anxiety. In neither case are such results especially useful in understanding the interactive effects of anxiety and instructional manipulations. Perhaps path-analytic techniques (Land, 1969) may be needed to capture this ambiguity regarding the effects of state anxiety. It remains to be seen whether such techniques circumvent the effects of complexity of interpretation and reducing the degrees of freedom of the total analysis alluded to here.

Instructional Support and State Anxiety

It maybe recalled that researchers have typically assumed that those instructional strategies which provide maximal support to the student would be especially advantageous to those high in anxiety. In the studies previously reviewed, the condition of maximal support has generally been constructed responding. In that mode, students construct their answers, and immediately check the accuracy of their responses before proceeding to the next frame. It was anticipated that the high incidence of reinforcement, averaging upward of 80% in most programs, and the reduced uncertainty (by virtue of immediately getting the right answer) would reduce the anxiety level of anxious students and hence enable them to function more effectively.

Surprisingly, most response-mode studies in which state-anxiety indices were collected while students worked on the material, have indicated that constructed responding typically yields *higher* levels of state anxiety than comparable response modes. Thus, for example, Leherissey *et al.,* (1973) found that constructed responding quite consistently yielded higher levels of state anxiety compared to the other response modes. Similarly, in the distraction study (Tobias, 1973c), A-state data were collected at two points in the instructional sequence. The grand means for constructed responding during instruction were 10.5, whereas those for the groups reading the program were .9.3. This presents something of a contradiction as the condition which was presumed to be maximally advantageous for anxious students in fact results in higher levels of state anxiety than comparable conditions.

A hypothesis regarding this apparent contradiction emerges from a detailed inspection of the state-anxiety data from the distraction study. These data are depicted in Figure 6.4.

In this figure the within-task A-state measures for the group reading the material under neutral, nondistraction conditions was markedly lower than that of any of the other groups. This is also the only group that was not required to make any overt response at any time during instruction, nor was any specific feedback provided. In the group reading the program under conditions of distraction, students were required to memorize trigrams and then asked to recall these, one, two, or three frames after their presentation the student entering an incorrect response was informed that the answer was wrong and asked to try again. Students reading the program, therefore, made no responses

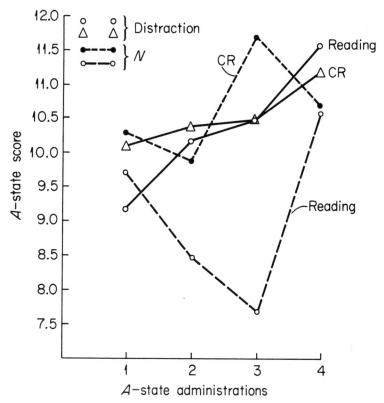

FIG. 6.4 Mean A-state scores for different groups during instruction. (From Tobias, 1973c.)

to the program but had their responses to the nonsense syllables evaluated. The large difference in state anxiety between the reading-distraction group and the regular-reading group, and the difference in state anxiety between the reading group and those in the three other groups strongly suggests that the variable accounting for this difference is that in all the other conditions the responses of students were evaluated and, therefore, sometimes considered inaccurate. This hypothesis suggests, then, that any instructional conditions in which students are required to make answers that might be found incorrect is likely to evoke higher levels of state anxiety than conditions where responses are not so evaluated.

Some phenomenological evidence supports this hypothesis. In this, and similar studies, students frequently referred to the constructed-response instructional mode as "the test." Initially this was quite confusing to experimenters who presumed that students were referring to the posttest administered at program conclusion. It rapidly became clear, however, that the constructed-response mode was so viewed by students. Consequently, one can then assume that the heightened evaluative stress represented by having answers evaluated would generally lead to heightened levels of state anxiety. (Further evidence supporting these conclusions is presented in Chapter 9.)

State Anxiety and Optimal Instructional Strategy

Problems in the interpretation of state-anxiety research data have been discussed at length in this chapter. If one can assume for the moment that these problems may be solved, in some as yet undetermined manner, a number of additional questions regarding the practical applications for interactions with state anxiety remain. Recall that the ultimate aim of anxiety–treatment-interaction research is to assign students to an instructional method assumed to be optimal for them in terms of their anxiety status. By definition, state anxiety is highly responsive to stimulation and temporal factors, and is expected to fluctuate over time. How could state anxiety, then, be used to assign students to the appropriate instructional method, if it can change so rapidly? Reports of changes in state anxiety in the preceeding pages have indicated, that in some instances, marked shifts occur in a 10- or 15-min period. This analysis suggests that the fluctuating character of state-anxiety measures severely restricts the range of instructional events where A state could be fruitfully employed as a variable for the assignment of students to an optimal instructional method.

For state anxiety to be employed as a differential assignment variable, the instructional system would have to have the following characteristics:

1. Frequent measures of state anxiety would have to be administered.
2. The state-anxiety scales would have to be rapidly scored, and analyzed prior to assigning the student to the next step in the instructional sequence.

3. A decision rule or algorithm would have to be available, permitting rapid decisions regarding which of a set of instructional strategies the student should be assigned to, in view of the state-anxiety index at the specific time.

4. Alternate instructional strategies would have to be instantly available to cover identical instructional objectives in ways differentially susceptible to the effects of anxiety.

These four requirements would be invoked every time a state-anxiety measure was obtained. In order for the measure to be maximally useful, frequent state-anxiety administrations could be foreseen and in fact should be obtained.

The preceding analysis would suggest that using state anxiety, or any fluctuating index for assigning optimal instructional strategies to students is practical in only an enormously reactive and dynamic instructional system. Practically, then, this suggests that only computer-based instructional systems possess both the flexibility, capacity to alter instructional tracks, and ability to make frequent rapid decisions required for the use of state-anxiety indices in particular, and any state index in general. It seems clear that this is indeed an exciting possibility.

One can imagine, sometime in the future, a situation in which the continually changing cognitive and affective state of the student is matched by an instructional system that monitors these changes and reacts to them in a dynamic way equal to the ever-changing state of the student. As indicated in Chapter 5, the field of instruction has been the subject of an enormous scientific ferment in the last decade. It is conceivable that some time in the distant future such systems as those alluded to here will be created. For the foreseeable future, however, it would appear that lacking the requirements outlined above, trait-anxiety measures are most likely to be productive with respect to suggesting instructional strategy.

The pessimism regarding use of state indices sounds somewhat discouraging with respect to the possibility of using dynamic instructional systems. An analogy is appropriate here. In the late nineteenth and early twentieth centuries, automobiles were beginning to make their appearance. Invariably, the owner of the new horseless carriages was asked to race against a horse and buggy. It may well be inconceivable in this age of overpowered, high-speed automobiles that invariably, in these early races, the horse and buggy won. It is tempting to apply this analogy to the advent of automation in education. The use of computers in education have been seriously entertained for little more than a decade. In that decade development has been slow, and painful. It is also clear that the problems faced by early automobile technology may well have been much less complex than those faced by computer technology in education. The types of variables involved, and the knowledge base required were quite different for automobiles than they are for instruction. On the other hand, knowledge is accumulating at a much faster rate today than it did at the turn of the century. It is conceivable, therefore, that such dynamic systems which could profitably utilize reactive-state measures may not be as far away as one thinks.

STUDIES OF CLASSROOM AND OTHER MODES OF INSTRUCTION

In the research described here, students working an individualized instructional mode were compared to others assigned to traditional classroom organizations such as lecture, recitation, and the like. The individualized mode sometimes consisted of programed or computer-based instruction. Comparisons between different classroom organizations are also reported here. Research is reviewed in a chronological sequence. The interaction between these instructional strategies and anxiety was ascertained by administering one of a number of anxiety scales.

In a widely quoted study, Grimes and Allinsmith (1961) investigated the interaction among anxiety, compulsivity, and amount of structure in reading instruction. A phonic instructional method was considered by Grimes and Allensmith (1961) to be representative of a high degree of structure compared to a whole-word approach which was described as "relatively unstructured because of its lack of discipline in word attack, and its encouragement of 'intelligent guessing' on the basis of loosely defined clues" (p. 251). Furthermore, "objective categorizing of the data confirmed the classification of each school as structured or unstructures [254]." Anxiety was assessed by the revision of Castaneda *et al.* (1956) of the Taylor (1953) anxiety scale for use with children. The dependent measure in this investigation was a discrepancy score between the expected achievement, based on the regression of intelligence on achievement, and actual achievement obtained from a composite score of the Stanford Achievement Test.

An ordinal interaction between anxiety and instructional method was found. The structured phonic treatment (N = 72) resulted in superior achievement in all anxiety levels, and showed a slight tendency for achievement to increase with anxiety status. In the unstructured whole-word method (N = 156) a marked tendency for achievement to decrease with anxiety was noted. Post hoc analyses indicated that in the structured treatment, high-compulsive, high-anxious subjects outperformed all others. In the unstructured treatment, however, the high-compulsive, low-anxious group outperformed all the others.

Flynn and Morgan (1966, p. 260) investigated the effects of test anxiety on achievement in an introductory unit in vector geometry. Elementary-school students were separated into low-, medium-, and high-anxiety groups. One set of students learned the material from an instructional program, while another group was instructed by teachers. Flynn and Morgan made provisions to insure uniformity of the subject-matter content for all six classes. A 3 X 2 analysis of variance revealed no significant main effects or interactions.

Ripple, Millman, and Glock (1969) conducted a study using 44 classes selected from 22 junior high schools. Classes were of average and slightly-above-average intelligence. In each school one class was randomly assigned to a programed-instruction condition, the other to conventional instruction. A vocabulary-development program was used which had been divided into 10 lessons, each containing approximately 30 pages. Constructed responses were required. Analyses of variance in which sex, intelligence, instructional methods, and anxiety were independent variables in a four-way design revealed no interactions among any of these characteristics and anxiety on four criterion measures. (No interactions among these variables with compulsivity, exhibitionism, or convergent—divergent thinking were revealed either.) There were some significant main effects for anxiety in which high anxiety was associated with low criterion scores in all instances. Students receiving conventional instruction in this experiment outperformed those receiving programed-instruction on each of the four criterion measures. It was noted that students in the programed treatment spent less time working on the instructional material than students receiving conventional instruction.

Schultz and Dangel (1972) studied the interaction among frequency of response, whether students knew when they had to respond, and facilitating and debilitating anxiety in a laboratory analogue of classroom recitation. Students were told that they were required to respond 35% of the time, 15% of the time, or to make no responses. In the second variable, some of the students were told that they would be required to respond, and others were not informed when they would be called to respond. Of a total of 164 high-school students, 36 facilitators and 36 debilitators were selected on the basis of scores on the Achievement Anxiety Test (Alpert & Haber, 1960). On one of the dependent measures, amount of tension experienced, determined by a single multiple-choice question, an interaction between anxiety status and response rate was found. The interaction indicated that there were no differences between facilitators and debilitators in reported tension when they were not required to make any responses, while students high on debilitating anxiety reported more tension than facilitators when responses for 15 and 35%, respectively, of the questions were required. Facilitators acquired more information than debilitators on a measure of retention of material covered by the recitation. No other effects involving anxiety were significant, nor were there any significant anxiety-by-treatment interactions.

Goldberg (1972) conducted a massive exploratory study comparing traditional lecture instruction to a self-study format. A large battery of tests were administered to the sample, including Sarason's (1966) Test Anxiety Scale, the Minnesota Multiphasic Personality Inventory, and the California Personality Inventory, among a number of others which yielded 350 test scores for each individual. The number of significant interactions was only slightly greater than one would have expected by chance with preestablished scales. New scales were developed empirically and were then cross validated on a different course. Little difference between these new scales and the preestablished ones were found. Of those significant interactions reported, none involved traditional anxiety measures.

Spielberger, O'Neil, and Hansen (1972) reported a study comparing the proportion of errors, number of avoidance responses, and state-anxiety scores of sixteen seventh-grade students working on a science curriculum in both a laboratory setting and on computer-assisted instruction. The results indicated that the laboratory evoked more avoidance responses, higher state anxiety, and a greater proportion of errors. Of further interest was the finding that high- and low-anxiety groups differed on the mean number of avoidance responses in the laboratory setting, but not in computer assisted instruction. Finally, while high-anxiety students made more errors than those lower in anxiety, in both computer and laboratory settings, the effect was larger in the latter group. These data suggested an interaction between anxiety and the instructional setting which, due to the small sample is only suggestive.

Dowaliby and Schumer (1973) studied the interaction between anxiety and teacher-centered as opposed to student-centered classroom organizations. In the teacher-centered group the class was conducted in a lecture format, and student-initiated responses were discouraged beyond a brief 5-min question—answer period at the close of each class. Finally, the instructor summarized the material covered in each class. In the student-centered group, the class was conducted according to a discussion format. Student questions were welcomed any time during the class period, and the instructor elaborated upon student questions, and used them to convey the subject matter covered. The summary of the lesson was given by a student in the class, rather than the instructor.

Junior-college students registered for two psychology classes participated in this experiment. The course lasted for a whole semester, and one instructor taught both sections. The Taylor (1953) Manifest Anxiety Scale was administered to the sample. Dependent measures consisted of two multiple-choice exams covering the topics of basic conditioning and psychological measurement. The results indicated disordinal interactions between instructional modes and manifest anxiety for both topics. The student-centered mode resulted in higher achievement than the teacher-centered mode for students low in manifest anxiety, and the opposite occurred for those high in manifest anxiety.

In a pilot study following this investigation, Dowaliby and Schumer (1973) asked students halfway through a semester to rate the structure of a course on a 1—7 rating scale; in which a 1 indicated a discussion-type course, and a 7 a lecture course; students scoring at the extreme points of the scale were used for data analyses. The manifest-anxiety scale was administered at the same time. Dowaliby and Schumer (1973) report that, in general, "the results were consistent with those evidenced when classroom structure was actually manipulated [p. 130]."

Marantz and Dowaliby (1973) studied the interaction between anxiety, as determined by the Taylor scale, field dependence, and two instructional modes. In one of these modes, students viewed a film, Milgram's *Obedience* (1965), and in the other condition a 20-min videotape lecture based on this film was viewed. College students enrolled in an educational-psychology course were randomly assigned to these conditions. The results indicated that students low on manifest anxiety obtained slightly higher posttest scores than high-anxiety students. Other than this effect, no interactions involving anxiety were significant, nor were there any significant effects on a constructed response fill-in-type posttest.

Oosthoek and Ackers (1973) studied differences in achievement between conventional lectures, and a lecture mediated via audiotape in interaction with a number of personality variables, including facilitating and debilitating anxiety. The tape presentation was better organized than the lecture, and encouraged students to take posttests to determine their degree of mastery of lectures. These tests were also available to a lecture group, who were, however, not induced to avail themselves of them. A *t* test computed on students above the mean in debilitating anxiety found that among this group the tape respentation resulted in significantly higher achievement than the lecture method; there were no differences for the low-anxiety group. Students in the tape methodology were asked to record the number of times they rewound each tape in order to listen to it again. For each of seven lectures, the correlation between debilitating anxiety and rewinding of the tape was low but significant. A marginally significant interaction between ability, debilitating anxiety, and instructional method was also found indicating that for high-anxiety high-ability students the tape was significantly superior to the lecture. The other subgroup comparisons were not significant.

Domino (1974) essentially replicated the Dowaliby and Schumer (1973) findings. A total of 83 students were randomly assigned to a teacher- or student-centered section in English literature, taught by the same instructor. The Taylor (1953) Manifest Anxiety Scale was administered to students. Four tests, given throughout the term, dealing with material exclusive of class sessions, were used as criteria. Consistent with the prior findings, a significant interaction indicated that the student-centered group yielded higher achievement for students low in manifest anxiety whereas the opposite was found for students high in manifest anxiety.

Summary

These classroom anxiety–treatment-interaction studies appear to be the most encouraging, and most consistent with respect to interactions with anxiety. Despite the fact that a number of studies inexplicably reported no interaction or main effects with anxiety, a fairly consistent theme can be perceived in these investigations. Generally, students high in anxiety achieve more with those instructional methods that can be characterized by either a high degree of structure and organization, or by opportunities for student-initiated repetition of selected parts of the content. All of the studies reporting anxiety—treatment interactions on achievement utilized instructional methods varying either degree of organization or the opportunity for the student to go back and inquire about subject matter not yet mastered, and generally, varied both of these simultaneously.

Another characteristic of studies reporting significant interactions was that they tended to be of long duration, ranging from seven lectures (Oosthoek & Ackers, 1973) to a school year (Grimes & Allinsmith, 1961). It is frequently recommended that studies pretending to have pertinence to education be conducted over periods similar to those actually occurring in educational institutions. Hence, what is gained by the tighter control over variables in the laboratory may well be lost by the shorter duration of such studies. While it is possible to prolong laboratory studies, any investigator who has to rely on large numbers of subjects to return for succeeding experimental sessions is well aware of the difficulties of such a procedure, and the enormous amounts of time needed to collect such data. For many investigators, as for this one, one such experience is enough to abandon this line of investigation (Tobias, 1960).

The comparison between the guardedly optimistic state of affairs in the studies discussed in this section compared to the inconsistent and confusing results from individualized instructional environments are an interesting contrast. In programed and computer-based instruction a good deal of control over the instructional process has occurred. In the conventional classroom, of course, the opposite is the case. Apparently this contrast may be of some importance. Chapter 12 attempts to specify which aspects of this contrast between high and low control may be of importance in attempting to establish interactions between anxiety and instructional treatments.

Part III

ANXIETY AND COMPUTER-BASED INSTRUCTION

In this part, the role of anxiety in computer-based learning environments is discussed.

Computer-based learning provides a context for studying anxiety and learning under carefully controlled conditions, and yet it closely resembles a school learning environment in many respects. Consequently, computer-based instruction provides a unique opportunity to experiment with the effects of anxiety on student performance with as much rigor as can be obtained in the laboratory, coupled with the meaningfulness and realism of actual school learning.

Chapter 7 provides an overview and critique of this program of computer-based research on anxiety, instruction, and learning. Chapter 8 provides a discussion of the key concepts and methods of computer-assisted instruction and computer-managed instruction that are used in the remaining chapters. Chapter 9 focuses on the role of instructional design considerations (such as the use of behavioral objectives) in the reduction of state anxiety. Results are discussed in terms of state–trait anxiety theory and a systems model for instructional design. Chapter 10 delineates a clinical approach to the reduction of state and trait test anxiety in a computer-managed instructional setting. Three studies are reported that document the importance of personalization in the automated program. In Chapter 11, the relation of state anxiety to learning and performance is discussed. Studies performed in various settings ranging from basic to applied research are reviewed.

7
Computer-Based Research on Anxiety and Learning: An Overview and Critique

Charles D. Spielberger

University of Southern Florida

Since the turn of the century, clinical studies of anxiety have appeared in the psychiatric literature with increasing regularity. Prior to 1950, however, there were relatively few experimental investigations of human anxiety. The complexity of anxiety phenomena, the lack of appropriate instruments for assessing anxiety, and ethical problems associated with inducing anxiety in the laboratory all contributed to this paucity of research. With the development of self-report procedures for the measurement of anxiety in the early 1950s, experimental research on human anxiety has rapidly accelerated, and more than 5000 articles or books on anxiety have been published during the past two decades (Spielberger, 1972a).

In the introductory chapter to this volume, McKeachie notes a number of major advances in theory and research on anxiety and learning, and correctly attributes these advances to improvements in methods for measuring anxiety, and to greater sophistication with regard to experimental design and research methodology. McKeachie also points out that current theoretical conceptions concerning the relationship between stress, anxiety and performance, such as the classic Yerkes–Dodson law, appear to be oversimplifications. It is now apparent that early studies failed to take into account the complex interactions of state and trait anxiety with task variables, learning strategies, and situational factors that influence anxiety level.

On the basis of his review of the chapters that appear in the first half of this volume, McKeachie identified a number of general theoretical and methodological issues that are important in research on anxiety and complex learning. In this chapter, I endeavor to provide an overview and critique of the five chapters in the second half of the volume. While the main concern in these chapters is with research on anxiety and computer-based learning, it is apparent that many of the same issues highlighted by McKeachie are again encountered.

AN OVERVIEW OF COMPUTER-BASED RESEARCH
ON ANXIETY AND LEARNING

In Chapter 8, O'Neil and Richardson describe the unique characteristics of computer-based learning environments, and the instructional strategies and technical procedures that are used in presenting learning materials and processing subjects' responses. They also describe and distinguish between computer-assisted instruction (CAI) and computer-managed instruction (CMI), discussing the advantages and limitations of each of these instructional strategies. In addition to the important advantages of truly individualized, self-paced instruction and more optimal utilization of students' and instructors' time, CAI and CMI are ideally suited for research on the learning process.

Computer-based instructional procedures provide the researcher with enormous flexibility in the presentation of learning materials, while permitting observations of the step-by-step performance of students as they respond to these materials. Computer-based instruction also permits input of timely information about performance and feedback that can be designed to influence the students' motivational state. In addition, the use of computers facilitates the measurement of *process* variables such as the anxiety experienced while the subject performs on a learning task. In the research reported by O'Neil and his colleagues in Chapters 9, 10, and 11, brief anxiety scales interspersed among the learning materials permit the investigators to assess changes in anxiety level as learning progresses. The availability of these A-state measures also permits evaluation of the influence of anxiety on performance at different stages of learning.

The findings reported by O'Neil and his colleagues in Chapters 9–11 are examined within the context of the theories that have guided much of the computer-based research on anxiety and learning. Comments on the model for research on anxiety and instruction proposed by Tobias in Chapter 12 are offered at the conclusion of this chapter, along with suggestions for the further development and elaboration of this model.

DRIVE THEORY AND TRAIT–STATE ANXIETY THEORY

Early research on anxiety and learning was guided by drive theory (Spence, 1958; Spence & Spence, 1966; Taylor, 1956). Although this theory is reviewed by O'Neil, Judd, and Hedl in Chapter 11, a brief outline of the theory may facilitate the reader's understanding of the research on anxiety reduction and learning reported in Chapters 9 and 10.

Drive is conceptualized as the capacity to energize or activate the behavior of a learner. The theory assumes that noxious or aversive stimuli arouse a hypothetical emotional response (r_e), with properties that are similar to the clinical concept of anxiety (Taylor, 1956). This emotional state combines with other need states to determine an individual's total effective drive level, D, at a given time. Drive theory further proposes that the strength of a given response, R, in any learning situation is a multiplicative function of habit strength, H, and drive level, that is, $R = f(H \times D)$. Habit strength refers to the tendency to make a particular response to a specific stimulus or stimulus pattern. In research on human learning, habit strength is typically defined, empirically or intuitively, in terms of the strength of "correct" responses, that is, specific responses that reflect mastery of the learning task, relative to competing error tendencies.

In early research on anxiety and learning, individual differences in drive level were typically inferred from scores obtained on self-report personality inventories such as the Taylor (1953) manifest-anxiety scale (MAS). It was assumed that persons with high MAS scores were higher in anxiety, or drive level, D, than persons with low MAS scores. More recent research findings suggest that the MAS measures individual differences in anxiety proneness, that is, the disposition to respond with elevations in anxiety to stressful situations that involve threats to self-esteem (Spielberger, 1966a), not the anxiety *actually experienced* by an individual at a particular moment.

While drive theory specifies the effects of anxiety or drive level on performance in learning experiments, it does not articulate the relationship between anxiety as a transitory emotional state (A state) and as a relatively stable personality trait (A trait), nor does it deal with the process through which anxiety states are evoked by stressful stimuli. Trait–state anxiety theory (Spielberger, 1966a, 1972b, 1975) was developed to account for the arousal of anxiety states in persons who differ in trait anxiety. This theory is briefly described by O'Neil and Richardson in Chapter 8, and elaborated by O'Neil and co-workers in Chapter 11.

Since trait–state anxiety theory provides a convenient conceptual framework for evaluating the research on anxiety reduction reported in Chapters 9 and 10, the principle assumptions of this theory are briefly summarized:

1. In situations that are appraised by an individual as threatening, an A-state reaction will be evoked. Through sensory and cognitive feedback mechanisms, high levels of A state will be experienced as unpleasant.

2. The intensity of an A-state reaction will be proportional to the amount of threat that the situation poses for the individual.

3. The duration of an A-state reaction will depend upon the persistence of the individual's interpretation of the situation as threatening.

4. High A-trait individuals will perceive situations or circumstances that involve failure or threats to self-esteem as more threatening than will persons who are low in A trait.

5. Elevations in A state have stimulus and drive properties that may be expressed directly in behavior, or that may serve to initiate psychological defenses that have been effective in reducing a states in the past.

6. Stressful situations that are encountered frequently may cause an individual to develop specific coping responses or psychological defense mechanisms which are designed to reduce or minimize A state. (Spielberger, 1972b, p. 44)

Early experimental work on anxiety and learning was largely concerned with investigating learning differences for groups of subjects who were presumed to be consistently high or low in anxiety or drive level. Subjects were assigned to high- and low-drive groups on the basis of extreme scores on self-report measures of trait anxiety such as the trait MAS, and the performance of these subjects was then compared on a variety of learning tasks (e.g., see Spence & Spence, 1966; Spielberger, 1966b). It is now apparent that state anxiety is more closely related to drive level than is trait anxiety. The development of measures of state anxiety has greatly facilitated progress in experimental research on anxiety and learning.

The construction, psychometric characteristics, and construct validity of the A-state scale of the state–trait anxiety inventory (STAI) (Spielberger, Gorsuch, & Lushene, 1970) are described by O'Neil and Richardson in Chapter 8. They also discuss a brief A-state measure, consisting of five items selected from the STAI A-state scale, that was used to measure state anxiety in most of the research reported in Chapters 9–11 of this volume. The research discussed in Chapters 9 and 10 is concerned primarily with the amount of state anxiety that is aroused by different instructional strategies, whereas the studies that are described in Chapter 11 evaluate the effects of A state on learning.

THE EFFECTS OF INSTRUCTIONAL STRATEGIES ON STATE ANXIETY

A series of studies designed to evaluate the effects of specific computer-based instructional procedures on the level of state anxiety is described by Hedl and O'Neil in Chapter 9. A unique and innovative feature of this research is that repeated measures of state anxiety are obtained at different stages of the learning process. It should be noted that these measures were taken by the computer without disrupting the subject's performance.

The relationship between instructional strategy and state anxiety is examined by Hedl and O'Neil within the context of an instructional-design-systems model for computer-based learning. This model helps to identify the multiple points at which relevant components of a particular instructional strategy may influence level of state anxiety. The three aspects of instructional strategy that were investigated in the studies that are described were: (1) behavioral objectives; (2) response modes; and (3) the effects of learner control. Hedl and O'Neil also discuss the results of several studies in which the impact of computers on state anxiety was evaluated in intelligence testing and computer-managed instruction.

Behavioral Objectives and State Anxiety

Two major functions of behavioral objectives are to facilitate the integration and organization of subject matter, and to specify goals for the learner that provide an objective framework for self-evaluation. It would seem reasonable to expect that structuring a learning task through the specification of behavioral objectives would reduce state anxiety and facilitate performance; but clearly this is not the case. The impact of behavioral objectives on level of state anxiety seems to depend upon the complexity of the objectives that are specified, and the difficulty of the learning task.

The research on behavioral objectives reviewed by Hedl and O'Neil indicates that state anxiety varies as a function of task difficulty, and that the specification of behavioral objectives can modify the perceived difficulty of a computer-based learning task. In general, simple or easy behavioral objectives appear to reduce A state, but only for relatively easy learning tasks, whereas complex or difficult behavioral objectives induce higher levels of state anxiety. Once the student has obtained some experience with a learning task, however, the perceived difficulty of the task appears to have greater influence on A state than prior specification of behavioral objectives.

The findings that the specification of complex objectives increases state anxiety relative to control groups for which no objectives are specified is especially interesting. These results suggest that the students' perception of the learning environment as more or less threatening is the critical variable in evoking A-state reactions. Clarification of the learning problem through behavioral objectives can contribute to the reduction of state anxiety, but only when the learning task is perceived as relatively easy and the learning situation as nonthreatening.

From the limited information provided by Hedl and O'Neil, it would appear that behavioral objectives tend to facilitate performance. Paradoxically, however, behavioral objectives appear to be least helpful for difficult learning tasks for which one might expect the clarification of what must be learned would be most facilitative. The potentially facilitative effects on performance of the specification of complex behavioral objectives are apparently mitigated by elevations in state anxiety that are evoked by students' reactions to the statement of the objective. Since trait anxiety also seems to be a determinant of the influence of behavioral objectives on state anxiety and performance, future investigations of the impact of behavioral objectives on cognitive tasks should take individual differences in A trait into account.

Response Mode and State Anxiety

The research reviewed by Hedl and O'Neil provides evidence that the mode of responding to a learning task influences both state anxiety and performance. Higher levels of A state are typically found during CAI and CMI for more difficult modes of responding, such as the constructed response option that was employed in the four studies described in Chapter 9. Apparently, students view constructive responses as more threatening than reading or multiple-choice responses because the former may more clearly reveal the students' limitations than less demanding response modes.

In general, the mode of responding to a learning task appears to influence the perceived difficulty of the task, and more demanding response modes cause students to perceive the learning task itself as more difficult, resulting in higher levels of state anxiety. The results of investigations of the effects of response mode on state anxiety provide further evidence that individual differences in trait anxiety interact with situational variables to influence level of state anxiety and performance. Here again, it would seem that persons who are high in trait anxiety perceive learning tasks as more threatening when a more demanding response mode is required. Indeed, high- A-trait individuals may initially perceive tasks with easy response modes as more threatening than do low-A-trait individuals.

The Effects of Learner Control on State Anxiety

It has been suggested that the more control a student has over a learning task, the better will be the performance. Furthermore, it would seem reasonable to expect that level of state anxiety would decrease as the student's control over learning materials increases. The results of the studies described by Hedl and O'Neil indicate that lower levels of state anxiety were consistently found under conditions of greater learner control, especially for low-trait-anxious students, but the findings were inconsistent with regard to the effects of learner control on performance.

If learner control reduces state anxiety, the question may be raised as to why it does not facilitate performance. A possible answer to this question requires consideration of the interactive effects of task difficulty and state anxiety on performance. Reduction in state anxiety will generally lead to improved performance on a difficult task for which error tendencies are stronger than correct responses, especially for persons who are high in trait anxiety. But reduction in state anxiety may lead to poorer performance on easy tasks, especially for low-A-trait persons who may not exert the effort required to obtain high performance scores on such tasks. Thus, trait anxiety and task difficulty should be taken into account in the design of future investigations of the effects of learner control on state anxiety and performance, and in the interpretation of the results of such experiments.

State Anxiety Reactions to Computers

With the increasing use of computers for testing and instructional purposes, it is important to evaluate student reactions to computers compared with traditional testing and classroom procedures. The results of the experiments summarized by Hedl and O'Neil suggest that the level of state anxiety that is initially evoked by a computer may be somewhat higher than when the same task or test is presented in a conventional manner. However, greater initial elevations in A-state reactions to computer-presented tests and learning materials seem to be related to lack of familiarity with the computer terminal or ambiguity in instructions, rather than negative reactions to the computer itself.

The finding that students show lower levels of state anxiety as a function of prior experience with similar computer tasks suggests that careful attention be given to instructions and practice in CAI and CMI. In gereral, the nature and the difficulty of computer-presented learning tasks appears to determine the level of A state that is induced, and A-state reactions to computer-presented tasks are similar to reactions to tasks of comparable difficulty presented in a traditional manner. Nonthreatening, gamelike situations and easy instructional programs result in lower levels of state anxiety than do intelligence tests or difficult instructional programs when presented by computer.

It should be noted that Hedl and O'Neil implicitly assume that low levels of state anxiety are desirable, and that curricular and instructional systems should be designed to minimize A state. While extremely high levels of A state are likely to be detrimental to performance, low levels of A state may also contribute to poor performance. For most persons, performance on learning tasks is facilitated by low to moderate amounts of state anxiety that stimulates the alertness and attention of the learner. Low levels of situational stress are generally more optimal for high-A-trait individuals, whereas moderate levels of stress tend to facilitate the performance of low-A-trait persons.

In summary, the level of state anxiety that is induced by computer-presented materials appears to be a function of the difficulty of the task and the amount of evaluative threat perceived by the student. Whether behavioral objectives or different response modes results in higher or lower levels of state anxiety seems to depend upon the extent to which these variables contribute to subjects' perceiving the learning task or the computer environment as threatening. Greater control of a learning situation generally reduces state anxiety, and leads to better performance under conditions of learning that evoke high levels of state anxiety.

COPING WITH ANXIETY IN TEST SITUATIONS

Richardson, O'Neil and Grant describe a promising automated program for the reduction of test anxiety in Chapter 10. One particular advantage of this program is that the student can complete it independently; no contact with a therapist or counselor is required. The anxiety reduction program makes use of a manual providing information about the nature and sources of test anxiety, relaxation techniques, and written exercises that help students to develop behavioral strategies for coping with anxiety in test situations. This program also provides the student with the opportunity to view video tapes demonstrating effective and ineffective responses for the management of test anxiety, and a modified desensitization procedure that involves deep muscle relaxation and the visualization of a graded series of test-taking scenes. Finally, the automated test-anxiety-reduction program gives students an opportunity to practice responding to test questions at a computer terminal.

The automated test-anxiety-reduction program was evaluated in the context of a course, Introduction to Educational Psychology, which included instructional modules presented via computer-managed instruction. Students with high levels of test anxiety who were enrolled in this course were identified early in the term and invited to take part in the anxiety-reduction program. Measures of test anxiety, state anxiety, and performance on the instructional modules were obtained periodically to monitor the students' progress in the course.

Significant reductions in self-reported test anxiety were found for students who participated in the anxiety-reduction program as compared to an untreated control group that was equally high in test anxiety. The test-anxiety level of students in the control group remained relatively stable throughout the course. While some improvement in the performance of the students who participated in the anxiety-reduction program was observed, the performance of these students was not significantly different from that of the control group.

When the study was repeated with a larger sample of test-anxious students, the results were disappointing. Reduction in state anxiety and in test anxiety (as measured by scores on Sarason's, 1972 test-anxiety scale, TAS) were no greater for students who participated in the program than for the control group. Significant reductions in scores on the Liebert and Morris (1967) worry and emotionality scales, and on the Alpert–Haber (1960) debilitating-anxiety scale, were found, but follow-up testing indicated that the anxiety scores for the control group also dropped. By the end of the term, there were no differences between students who participated in the anxiety-reduction program and the controls. Also, as in the previous study, the performance of students who participated in the anxiety-reduction program did not improve when compared with the control group.

On the basis of interviews with students, Richardson and co-workers speculate that the failure to confirm the promising findings in their first study resulted primarily from the "depersonalizing" of the anxiety-reduction program. Students in the first study had greater contact with the investigators, creating the feeling that they were members of a small group in whom the investigators were keenly interested.

While depersonalization might have resulted in the anxiety-reduction program being less effective in the second study, an equally plausible interpretation is that the positive findings obtained in the initial study reflected efforts on the part of the paid participants to please the investigators, rather than any real reduction in test anxiety. Since no improvement in performance resulted from the anxiety-reduction program, it would seem that the latter explanation is at least as plausible as the former.

Increased contact with students was provided by Richardson and co-workers in a third study in which a graduate student was assigned to monitor the progress of students who participated in the test-anxiety-reduction program. The monitor had personal contact with each student before and after the program, and scheduled office hours for consultation. Students were encouraged to consult with the monitor if any problems or questions arose. Otherwise, the treatment procedures were about the same as in the two earlier studies. The results of this study confirmed the finding in the initial study in which the anxiety reduction program was successful in reducing test anxiety for students who participated as compared with the control group. While there was also some improvement in the performance of the treatment group on the modules test, the amount of improvement was not significantly greater for the treatment group than for the controls.

The results in the anxiety reduction studies reported by Richardson and co-workers are similar to the findings that have been reported in a large number of investigations of the treatment of test anxiety. Systematic desensitization procedures were successful in reducing test anxiety in 29 of 33 investigations reviewed by Spielberger, Anton, and Bedell (1976). In contrast, the effectiveness of systematic desensitization in improving academic achievement has yet to be clearly demonstrated. Improvement in grades are most often found in studies in which a combination of desensitization and some form of study skills training are employed (e.g., Allen, 1971; McManus, 1971; Mitchell & Ng, 1972).

It has been recently demonstrated that study habits may be a critical variable in determining whether or not desensitization leads to improvement in grades for test anxious persons. Gonzalez (1976) has shown that desensitization facilitates the academic achievement of test-anxious students with good study habits, but has little or no effect on students with poor study habits.

The test-anxiety-reduction program developed by Richardson and co-workers is certainly deserving of further study. It may be that the program is effective for test-anxious students with relatively good study habits, but does not influence the performance of students with poor study habits. Many test-anxious persons typically have poor study habits and attitudes that contribute to their performance decrements on cognitive–intellectual tasks. More detailed attention needs to be given to the evaluation of study habits in text-anxiety-treatment programs concerned with helping students to improve their grades.

STATE ANXIETY AND PERFORMANCE
IN COMPUTER-BASED LEARNING ENVIRONMENTS

In Chapter 11, O'Neil and co-workers report the results of a series of studies on the effects of state anxiety on performance in computer-based learning tasks. These studies were conducted in the context of drive theory which predicts that effects of differences in drive level will depend upon the relative strengths of correct and competing response tendencies that are evoked by a learning task. In general, more errors are activated on difficult tasks, and at earlier stages in learning, by high anxiety or drive level.

In the studies reported by O'Neil and co-workers in Chapter 11, measures of state anxiety were obtained as subjects performed on various learning tasks. A clear and consistent finding in the five studies that examined the effects of state anxiety on a mathematics task was that performance decrements were associated with high levels of A state. In general, high-anxious students made significantly more errors than low-anxious students on the more difficult mathematics problems. While these results are consistent with drive theory in some respects, it is apparent that the theory, as initially formulated by Spence and Taylor (Spence, 1958; Spence & Spence, 1966; Taylor, 1956), requires considerable elaboration and extension to account for the complexity of the empirical findings. It has been demonstrated, for example, that the sex of the subject is a critical variable in research on anxiety and computer-based learning, and that situational stress interacts with trait anxiety to influence the effects of state anxiety on performance (e.g., Spielberger, 1966b; Spielberger & Smith, 1966). It has also been observed (Spielberger, O'Neil, & Hansen, 1972) that the effects of high levels of state anxiety on performance in computer-assisted learning may depend upon whether state- and trait-anxiety levels are congruent (high A state, high A trait) or incongruent (high A state, low A trait).

Recent research indicates that intelligence and stages of learning must be taken into account in making predictions from drive theory since these variables influence the relative strength of the correct responses and competing error tendencies that are evoked by a learning task. Spielberger has extended the Spence–Taylor (Spence & Spence, 1966) drive theory to specify the interactive effects of trait anxiety and individual differences in intelligence or learning ability on performance at different stages of learning. The following theoretical statements, with regard to the effects of anxiety (A state) on learning, are derived from Spielberger's (1966b, 1971a) extension of drive theory:

1. For subjects with superior intelligence, high anxiety will facilitate performance on most learning tasks. While high anxiety may produce initial performance decrements on difficult tasks, correct responses will become dominant more quickly as bright subjects progress through the task, and high anxiety will eventually have facilitative effects. For tasks of moderate or low difficulty, high anxiety will generally facilitate performance at all stages of learning.

2. For subjects of average intelligence, high anxiety will facilitate performance on simple tasks, and, later in learning, on tasks of moderate difficulty. On difficult tasks, high anxiety will generally lead to performance decrements at all stages of learning.

3. For low-intelligence subjects, high anxiety may facilitate performance on simple tasks that have been mastered. For tasks of greater difficulty, however, performance decrements will generally be associated with high anxiety, especially in the early stages of learning.

The research reported by O'Neil and co-workers on the relationship between worry and emotionality scores and various cognitive performance measures suggests another important area in which theories of anxiety and learning must be expanded. High levels of worry consistently appear to be more detrimental to performance than do elevations in emotionality, providing impressive support for the distinction first proposed by Morris and Liebert (1969). In future research on anxiety and computer-based instruction, it would seem important to obtain measures of both worry and emotionality during the course of learning.

TOBIAS' INFORMATION-PROCESSING MODEL
FOR RESEARCH ON ANXIETY AND LEARNING

Tobias' information—processing model for attribute—treatment interactions is a useful conceptual framework for conducting and evaluating research on anxiety and complex learning. It is certainly reasonable to investigate the impact of state and trait anxiety on performance at different stages of the learning process. Instructional manipulations of input, individual differences in processing, storing and retrieving information, and the nature of the output requirements associated with particular instructional strategies may all interact with anxiety to influence learning outcomes.

The schematic presentation of Tobias' model in Figure 12.2 properly calls attention to important stages in learning at which anxiety and other individual difference variables may influence the learning process. This model also suggests that initial deficiencies in the assimilation of input materials may have a cumulative impact on information processing, and on the demonstration of what has been learned as reflected in output-performance measures. For example, in several studies reported in this volume, persons who scored high in trait anxiety tended to perceive certain instructional strategies as more threatening or difficult than others, and responded to such strategies with greater elevations in state anxiety. It has also been repeatedly observed that elevations in state anxiety are frequently associated with decrements in performance on learning tasks.

While Tobias' model tells the investigator where to look, a comprehensive theory of anxiety and learning must specify how state and trait anxiety will influence the perception of learning materials and the processing, storage and retrieval operations of the learner. Drive theory has typically not been applied to the complex processes that are central to Tobias' model, but an extension of this theory could provide a useful first approximation in making predictions with regard to the effects of anxiety on the learning process. A combination of drive theory and Tobias' model would, indeed, facilitate specification of the type of effects one might expect, and thus focus the attention of researchers on the useful kinds of behavioral measures.

In his discussion of the arousal and maintenance of anxiety in instructional situations (Chapter 12), Tobias emphasizes the importance of obtaining measures of state anxiety. In early investigation of anxiety and learning, it was typically assumed that students with high scores on trait-anxiety measures such as the Taylor (1953) MAS were chronically higher in drive level. It has now been convincingly demonstrated that the MAS and other A-trait scales do not measure drive level directly, but reflect instead individual differences in anxiety proneness, that is, the disposition to respond with differential elevations in state anxiety in situations that pose threats to self-esteem (ego threats). Thus, it is state anxiety, not trait anxiety, that appears to provide the most meaningful index of drive level.

In research on anxiety and learning, it has been demonstrated that the arousal of state anxiety is a function of anxiety proneness and task and situational factors, such as the difficulty of learning materials and the kind of feedback given to the learner (e.g., Spielberger *et al.,* 1972). Therefore, in investigations of the effects of anxiety on learning, there is no substitute for the actual measurement of state anxiety in the instructional situation. Furthermore, repeated measures of A state should be obtained as learning progresses. In the context of Tobias' model, it would seem important to obtain measures of A state following input, at one or more times during acquistion, and immediately before and after output.

Trait–state anxiety theory specifies the effects of different kinds of stress on the arousal of A states in persons who differ in anxiety proneness (Spielberger, 1966a, 1972a). According to this theory, the critical factor in the arousal of an anxiety state is an individual's perception of a particular situation as personally dangerous or threatening. The theory also notes that high A-trait persons will experience greater elevations in state anxiety than low-A-trait individuals in situations that pose threats to self-esteem, but not in response to physical dangers. This aspect of trait–state anxiety theory is especially germane to Tobias' observation that research on instructional strategies may not pose ego threats for test-wise college students. Consequently, laboratory studies may not be appropriate analogues for classroom situations in which there are genuine evaluations of each student's performance usually having important consequences in terms of the student's future educational and vocational goals.

The results of the study by B. Hall (1970) that are cited by Tobias clearly indicate that an investigator's definition of an instructional situation as more or less stressful is not necessarily reflected in students' reactions to the situation. It may be recalled that Hall found that the "nonstressful" control condition proved to be more stressful than his experimental (ego-threat) condition as reflected in higher mean A-state scores for the students assigned to the control conditions. Tobias' discussion of the types of experimental manipulations that are most likely to yield achievement differences for high- and low-anxiety students is also very illuminating, and provides further evidence of the utility of his model.

Accumulating evidence that the level of state anxiety changes as students perform on a learning task, and that such changes are often directly related to instructional strategies (such as feedback about performance), requires investigators to be constantly alert to potential interactions between level of A state and instructional strategy. In discussing applications of his model to research on anxiety and learning, Tobias describes several excellent examples of such interactions at different stages of learning. Research on each stage of learning will contribute to developing instructional strategies for eliminating or reducing the interfering effects of state anxiety and, thereby, facilitating learning.

One final general comment about Tobias' model is required. In focusing upon the processes that take place at different stages of learning, this model calls attention to the fact that gross outcome measures reveal very little useful information regarding how anxiety influences the learning process. Tobias' model calls attention to the complexity of the learning process, and helps to identify important situational, task, and individual difference variables that must be taken into account in research on anxiety and learning. A meaningful intergration of the insights provided by Tobias' model, drive theory, and trait–state anxiety theory should provide a useful framework for future research on anxiety and complex learning.

SUMMARY AND CONCLUSION

In this chapter, I have endeavored to provide an overview and critique of the five chapters on anxiety and complex learning that comprise the second half of this volume. The research findings reported in these chapters reflect the major theoretical advances and improvements in experimental design and methods for measuring anxiety that were noted by McKeachie in his introductory chapter to this volume. The utilization of computers in this research provided the investigators with a great deal of flexibility in the presentation of learning materials, and with the capability of measuring changes in both state anxiety and performance at different stages of the learning process.

Much of the research described in this volume was carried out within the context of Spence–Taylor (Spence & Spence, 1966) drive theory and Spielberger's (1966b, 1971a) trait–state anxiety theory. While these theories provide useful first approximations for organizing the findings in investigations of anxiety and learning, it is apparent that both theories require revision and extension. Spence–Taylor drive theory must be extended to account for the interactions of anxiety and individual differences in aptitude or ability at different stages of learning. Trait–state anxiety theory must be expanded to incorporate growing evidence of the importance of distinguishing between worry and emotionality, both conceptually and empirically.

From the research findings reported in this volume, it is apparent that instructional strategies involving specification of behavioral objectives, the manipulation of learner control, and utilization of different response modes can influence level of state anxiety and performance on complex learning tasks. It was also demonstrated in these studies that students can be helped to cope more effectively with anxiety in learning situations, and that reductions in state anxiety facilitates performance on learning tasks. The most consistent finding in this research is that decrements in performance on computer-assisted learning tasks are generally associated with higher levels of state anxiety. It was also repeatedly shown in research on anxiety and computer-based learning that situational stress interacts with trait anxiety to influence the effects of state anxiety on performance, and that the sex of the subject is a critical variable. Intelligence and stages of learning must also be taken into account in making predictions regarding the effects of anxiety on the learning process.

In the final chapter of this volume, Tobias presents an information-processing model that calls attention to the processes that take place at different stages of learning. This model provides a useful conceptual framework for conducting and evaluating research on anxiety and complex learning, and helps identify important situational, task, and individual-difference variables that must be taken into account in future research on anxiety and learning. Integration of the insights provided by Tobias' model with extensions of drive theory and trait–state anxiety theory should provide a useful theoretical framework for future research on anxiety and complex learning.

8
Anxiety and Learning in Computer-Based Learning Environments: An Overview

In recent years there has been increased emphasis on individualized instruction and computer technology to facilitate learning at all levels of education. Anecdotal experience with these innovative instructional methods indicates that they may have important affective benefits for the learner. However, there has been as yet little systematic research in this area. The chapters in this part of the book focus on some affective considerations within computer-based learning environments. The purpose of this chapter is to provide a focus and overview for the remaining chapters in Part III. Thus, computer-based learning environments are discussed, followed by a discussion of trait–state anxiety theory. Finally, an interpretive summary of the role of anxiety in computer-based learning environments is provided.

COMPUTER-BASED LEARNING ENVIRONMENTS

Computer-based learning environments were chosen for this research partly because they represent a promising educational technology for the future. They also present a promising vehicle for educational research, as this section of the book indicates. The learning tasks administered to students in this research, some of which are actual coursework in the students' academic specialization, almost certainly engage their real-life motivations and interests to a much greater degree than is possible with traditional laboratory learning tasks. In addition, learning materials may be presented in a much more carefully controlled manner via computer than is possible in most educational settings. The context of most of this research represents a compromise between relevance and rigor, but may preserve some of the advantages of each.

As the field of computer-based education has progressed, empirical data have accumulated to suggest that computer-based education has several advantages over other instructional methods. One of these advantages is the potential to individualize instruction. The computer can be programmed to adapt the learning environment to each individual's strengths and weaknesses. Thus, a computer potentially allows for true individualization of learning. A second advantage is a savings in instructional time. In general, these approaches require less time than traditional methods to teach the same amount of material. This is particularly important in environments in which the students are paid, such as military and industrial training systems.

Compared with traditional instruction, the major disadvantages of computer-based instruction include the greater time and cost required for course development, greater personnel requirements, higher initial outlay of funds, and higher total costs. The advantages and disadvantages of computer-based instruction with respect to cognitive performance are reviewed elsewhere (e.g., Atkinson & Wilson, 1969; Holtzman, 1970; Levien, 1972). Two major types of computer-based instruction investigated in the following chapters are computer-assisted instruction and computer-managed instruction.

COMPUTER-ASSISTED INSTRUCTION

Computer-assisted instruction can be defined as a form of human–computer interaction designed to make the learning of instructional materials more efficient. The nature of this interaction has been defined in various ways. For example, Judd (1972) defined computer-assisted instruction as a general name for a number of methods of instruction in which a computer is programmed to accomplish the teaching functions of conveying information to the student, evaluating the student's understanding of this information, and providing feedback. Classification of computer-assisted instruction programs depends on the instructional role of the program and, to some extent, on the program's complexity and sophistication. Drill and practice, and tutorial are two types of computer-assisted programs.

Drill and practice. In general, drill and practice programs are designed to supplement regular instruction received elsewhere. They provide a means by which concepts presented and developed in the classroom can be practiced and refined at the computer terminal. In the use of such a program, each student might spend a limited amount of time at the computer terminal each day practicing and reviewing the skills developed in the classroom. Such practice can be individualized by assigning to different students problems of different difficulty levels. This assignment could be made on the basis of the student's work at the terminal or could be preassigned by the classroom teacher. Drill-and-practice programs have the advantage over classroom work of providing a gradual progression through the material and immediate, corrective feedback for a number of students, while relieving the teacher for more complex and personalized teaching activities.

Tutorial. It is difficult to draw a clear distinction between drill-and-practice and tutorial programs. In general, however, a tutorial program is intended to stand alone as an instructional entity; it is not used as a supplement to classroom teaching, as is drill and practice. This requires that the program teach the rules and concepts embodied by the subject matter and evaluate the student's comprehension of these concepts, in addition to providing practice in specific skills. A well-designed tutorial program leads the student through the subject matter by presenting concepts of ever-increasing complexity. It responds to the subtleties of the errors in the student's incorrect responses by diagnosing and correcting these errors. The program ideally has available alternative representations of the concepts which can be selected and presented on the basis of the error diagnosis.

As the name implies, programs of this type attempt to duplicate the idealized instructional interaction between a single student and tutor. Obviously, this is a problem of greater magnitude than the design of a drill-and-practice program. The record keeping and branching capabilities necessary for tutorial instruction are more complex than those required for drill and practice. In general, this requires more sophisticated computer-system equipment and places greater demands on the language by which the computer is programmed.

Computer-assisted instruction systems are organized so that the instructional treatment received by each subject may be achieved independently of other subjects who are interacting with the system. For research purposes, an experimental event paradigm for computer-assisted instruction is given in Figure 8.1, in which each event represents a discrete computer function. The learning session is started by assigning the subject to a particular experimental treatment, and the computer then determines which instructional item to present. Immediately after the item is presented, a response is requested by the computer. The subject's response is evaluated by the computer via either a prestored set of answers or a symbolic matching algorithm. After the response is evaluated, it is recorded, and the learning history of the subject is updated. The system then branches back to the decision rule (for example, mastery or not) which governs the instructional unit to be presented next. When mastery has been achieved, the system presents new instruction in the same manner until the end of the course.

In a computer-assisted instruction system, the instructional items and the correctional feedback can be intermeshed according to the design characteristics prescribed by the instructional psychologist. It is also possible to intersperse personality measures, such as brief anxiety scales, within the learning materials so that changes in personality states can be assessed as the student progresses through the task. In essence, a computer-assisted instruction system allows the psychologist to program an array of differential treatments, and to pursue the execution of an experiment according to specified contingent rules which determine each event or sequence of events for each student.

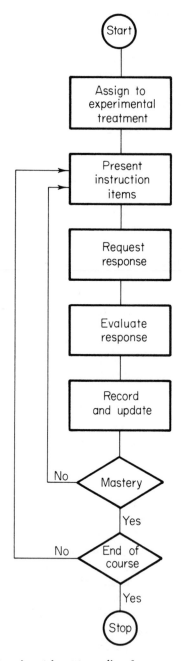

FIG. 8.1 Experimental event paradigm for computer-assisted instruction.

COMPUTER-MANAGED INSTRUCTION

Computer-based instructional applications such as computer-assisted instruction involve intensive interactions between the student and the computer. Due to the amount of effort required to carefully specify these interactions, the design, development, implementation, and evaluation of computer-assisted instructional programs is a very expensive and time-consuming process. As a result, most of the computer-assisted instruction programs which are currently available are fairly short and cover only a small part of a total course. Thus, one sometimes finds short segments of highly individualized computer-assisted instruction embedded in a course which is otherwise taught in a traditional, nonindividualized way.

An alternative, less expensive, approach is to use a computer to manage the instructional process. In a computer-managed instruction program the instruction itself is not presented by means of the computer. Rather, instructional materials consist of conventional printed or audiovisual materials. The student sets the pace, and the computer is used to monitor, and to some extent to direct progress through the use of noncomputerized instructional materials. This is done by testing the student at frequent points in the program in order to diagnose strengths and weaknesses, providing prescriptions for remedial work, and scheduling the student's use of the available instructional resources. Short segments of computer-assisted instruction might, of course, be one of the resources available for assignment by the computer-managed instruction system. While individualized instruction could be (and has been) conducted without relying on a computer, the amount of record keeping and management activity required becomes a serious problem when large numbers of students are involved (Holtzman, 1970).

The terminal equipment (hardware) needed to implement computer-assisted– computer-managed instruction systems varies with respect to: (1) the type of terminal (such as typewriters, cathode ray tubes, film projectors, audiotape players, and combinations of these); (2) the response devices (such as keyboards, light pens, and touch sensitive surfaces); and (3) the number of terminals (typically 1–60). The instructional materials and response recordings are usually stored on random-access disks or magnetic tapes. The control of each student's program is implemented in the central processing unit. This unit is the "brain" of the system and controls the remaining elements of it. While other devices may also be found in computer-based instructional systems, the above units of equipment are essential.

The majority of the studies that are described in the following chapters were conducted either at the Florida State University Computer-Assisted Instruction Center or at The University of Texas at Austin Computer-Assisted Instruction Laboratory. Each location used an IBM 1500 computer-assisted instruction system to support computer-assisted—computer-managed instruction activities. The 1500 system has a 32K central processor; 5,000,000 characters of disk storage; 2 9-inch magnetic-tape drives; and the usual input—output devices such as a card reader and a printer. The stimulus materials for this system are presented on individually controlled cathode ray tube (CRT) terminals with 7 × 9-inch screens. The stimulus-presentation rate may be extremely fast (up to 400 characters per second). For each problem, the student enters a response either on an attached typewriter keyboard, or with a light pen. The terminals were located in an air-conditioned room and separated by sound-insulated walls. A computer-data management system recorded all pertinent data.

TRAIT—STATE ANXIETY THEORY

A number of researchers have found it useful (following Spielberger, 1966a) to differentiate conceptually between anxiety as a transitory state and as a relatively permanent trait. According to Spielberger (1966a), "anxiety states are characterized by subjective, consciously perceived feelings of apprehension and tension accompanied by or associated with activation or arousal of the autonomic nervous system" (pp. 16—17). Anxiety as a personality trait implies a motive or acquired behavioral disposition to perceive a wide range of objectively nondangerous circumstances as threatening, and to respond with a state of anxiety that is disproportionate in intensity to the magnitude of the objective danger. In general, higher levels of trait anxiety are usually associated with higher levels of state anxiety.

However, while difficult instructional tasks may evoke high levels of state anxiety, a high trait-anxious individual who has the prerequisite skills and abilities to perform well on the task will probably not appraise the situation as threatening and thus not respond with high levels of state anxiety. Conversely, a task that most people perceive as nonthreatening might be regarded as extremely threatening for a low trait-anxious individual based on prior negative experiences. Thus, while measures of trait anxiety provide useful information regarding the probability that higher levels of state anxiety will be aroused, the stressful impact of any given instructional situation can be determined only by obtaining actual state anxiety measures in the situation. A number of studies have supported this approach and have shown that measures of state anxiety are more closely related to performance and instructional strategies in computer-assisted instruction than are measures of trait anxiety (e.g., Spielberger, O'Neil, & Hansen, 1972).

It should be noted that since few studies in this section investigated state anxiety as a joint function of level of trait anxiety and instructional treatments, the results are not evaluated within the context of trait—state anxiety theory. The reader is referred to Chapter 3 and to Spielberger (1972c) for a more extended discussion of trait—state anxiety theory.

VALIDITY AND RELIABILITY
OF THE STATE-ANXIETY SCALE

The research in Part III of this volume deals predominantly with anxiety as a state (either as an independent or dependant variable). The reliability and validity of measures of states of anxiety then becomes important. Spielberger (1972c) discussed three important requirements of state-anxiety measures, which determined the procedures used to construct the 20-item state-anxiety scale: brevity, reliability, and ability to reflect stress. Spielberger recommended brevity for state measures since long, involved scales would be unsuitable for experimental tasks in which administration of an extensive measure could interfere with performance on the task.

The type of reliability assumed suitable for state-anxiety measures was internal consistency, since anxiety states vary in intensity and fluctuate over time. Thus, it was assumed and later demonstrated that test—retest correlations would be nonsignificant. Only in the case in which a person is placed in the same situation on retest would one expect a high degree of relationship between two state-anxiety measures, taken at two different times. This expectation was also confirmed by O'Neil (1972).

With respect to the reflection of stress, the mean of each item was expected to increase when measured during a sequence of increasingly stressful situations. Validation data of this type can be found in the test manual for the state—trait anxiety inventory (Spielberger, Gorsuch, & Lushene, 1970). To cite one example, a study reported in the manual assigned undergraduate students to four different experimental conditions which, on an *a priori* basis, were assumed to represent different points on a stress continuum. This ranged from a procedure designed to induce a relaxed state, to a motion picture used to induce states of extreme fear and panic. The first administration of the state scale occurred at the beginning of the testing session (normal condition). The second administration followed a 10-minute period of relaxation training (relaxed condition). The third occurred following a very difficult timed intelligence test (exam condition). The final administration followed a film developed by Lazarus and Opton (1966), illustrating a number of shop accidents (movie condition).

The full, 20-item scale means, standard deviations and alpha-reliability coefficients for each of these four conditions are reproduced in Table 8.1. As may be noted, the requirement that the scale have a high degree of internal consistency was met. Alpha-reliability coefficients ranged from .83 to .94. Further, the state-anxiety scores reflected the *a priori* stress continuum since the lowest levels of state anxiety were observed during relaxation and the highest during the motion picture. Data reported in the test manual reflect a general increase in mean item scores as a function of the four stress conditions.

Males and females had equivalent levels of state anxiety in the normal and exam conditions. In contrast, the movie condition was particularly stressful for

TABLE 8.1
Means, Standard Deviations and Alpha Reliabilities for the State-Anxiety Scale under
Stressful and Nonstressful Conditions[a]

	Males (N = 109)			Females (N = 88)		
Conditions	Mean	SD	Alpha	Mean	SD	Alpha
Movie	50.03	12.48	.94	60.94	11.99	.93
Exam	43.01	11.23	.92	43.69	11.59	.93
Normal	36.99	9.57	.89	37.24	10.27	.91
Relaxed	32.70	9.02	.89	29.60	6.91	.83

[a]Adapted from Spielberger, Gorsuch, and Lushene (1970).

females and the relaxation condition seemed to be more effective in reducing state anxiety for females than for males. Spielberger, Gorsuch, and Lushene (1970) suggest that females may either be more emotionally labile than males or more willing to report their feelings.

DEVELOPMENT OF A BRIEF MEASURE
OF STATE ANXIETY

Since the state anxiety scale was to be employed in the context of computer-based learning tasks, it was feared that the 20-item scale could, by its length, interfere with performance on the task itself. It was hoped that a briefer state-anxiety measure, which could be administered in less than a minute, would still provide reliable and valid information. Preliminary pilot data indicated that a scale of 5 items would meet those requirements.

Items were selected from the 20-item state-anxiety scale on the basis of the following criteria:

1. The mean score for each item was to increase with increasing levels of stress.
2. In particular, each item was to discriminate significantly between the relaxation condition and the exam condition.
3. Excluding the relaxation condition, item-remainder correlations with the entire scale were to remain high (for example, $r > .52$).
4. The items chosen were to be equally reliable for females and males.

Ten items were selected from the 20-item scale on the basis of these criteria. From these ten, five items, both positively and negatively worded, were chosen on an intuitive basis. The five items are shown in Table 8.2. The means for these items have been abstracted from the table in the test manual and are shown in Table 8.3 for both males and females. All items increased as a function of stress.

TABLE 8.2
The Five-Item State-Anxiety Scale

Items	Student Responds:			
	1 Not at all	2 Somewhat	3 Moderately so	4 Very much so
I feel calm[a]				
I feel tense				
I feel at ease[a]				
I feel jittery				
I feel relaxed[a]				

[a]Scoring is reversed.

As with the 20-item scale, the means for males and females are roughly equivalent for the normal and exam situations but are lower for the females than for the males in relaxation and higher for females under the stress (movie) condition. Additional evidence of the construct validity of this scale has been provided by a number of studies (Leherissey, O'Neil, Heinrich, & Hansen, 1973; O'Neil, Spielberger, & Hansen, 1969; Spielberger, O'Neil, & Hansen, 1972). In all of these studies state anxiety varied as a function of task difficulty, that is, higher state anxiety occurred during more difficult materials.

Reliability for the five-item scale has been reported by several authors for subjects involved in computer-assisted learning tasks and computer-based intelligence tests. Leherissey, O'Neil, and Hansen (1971) reported alpha-reliability coefficients for five state-anxiety scales in a computer-assisted learning task of .87, .83, .87, .86, and .93. O'Neil (1972) reported alpha reliabilities for the three

TABLE 8.3
Mean Scores for Individual Items on the Five-item State-Anxiety
Scale under Stressful and Nonstressful Experimental Conditions[a]

Item	College males				College females			
	Relaxed	Norm	Exam	Movie	Relaxed	Norm	Exam	Movie
Calm[b]	1.54	1.74	2.39	2.85	1.32	1.74	2.35	3.51
Tense	1.30	1.57	2.11	2.53	1.14	1.51	2.08	3.16
At Ease[b]	1.56	1.82	2.44	2.83	1.51	1.76	2.54	3.48
Jittery	1.2	1.35	1.58	2.21	1.13	1.34	1.58	2.87
Relaxed[b]	1.7	1.81	2.42	2.89	1.50	2.10	2.60	3.56
Scale	7.30	8.29	10.94	13.21	6.60	8.45	11.15	16.58

[a]Adapted from Spielberger, Gorsuch, and Lushene (1970).
[b]Scale items are reversed.

five-item state anxiety scales given during a computer-assisted instruction-learning task of .86, .88, and .89. Leherissey, O'Neil, Heinrich, and Hansen reported alpha reliabilities of .87, .89, and .92 for the 3 short-form scales given during a computer-assisted instruction-learning task. Hedl (1971) reported alpha reliabilities of .91 and .92 before and after a computer-based intelligence test. Further research by Hedl, reported in Chapter 9, found alpha reliabilities of .87 and .89. In another study by Hedl (1973), alpha reliabilities of .83 and .93 were reported for the five-item state-anxiety scale before and after the computer-based intelligence test. In summary, reported alpha reliabilities ranged from .83 to .93 in 17 comparisons. These values indicate that the five-item state-anxiety scale has high internal consistency.

OVERVIEW OF REMAINING CHAPTERS

The research reviewed in the remainder of this overview deals with attempts to reduce debilitating anxiety and with the relationship between anxiety and performance in computer-based learning environments. Some of the authors' tentative conclusions concerning what these results have to say about anxiety, performance, and what to do about it in an educational environment are presented.

Some of the studies reviewed and discussed in these chapters investigated the effects of a number of different instructional strategies on state anxiety that might reasonably be expected to lower state anxiety and facilitate performance on the learning tasks involved. Another series of studies explored the effectiveness of a brief, semiautomated treatment or training program to teach highly test-anxious students new skills of coping with anxiety about tests in a computer-managed instructional context. Finally, the debilitating effects of state anxiety on performance in various computer-based environments are reviewed.

State Anxiety and Instructional Design

Chapter 9 of this section reviews a number of studies which investigated the effects of several promising instructional design procedures on reduction of state anxiety in computer-based learning. Generally, the results offered very little support for the hypothesis that these procedures would result in lower levels of state anxiety on learning tasks. Several studies found that presenting behavioral objectives to students for instruction did not result in facilitated learning or reduced state anxiety. Several other studies found that the widely recommended procedure of providing active, constructed responding by students with immediate and appropriate feedback actually led to higher levels of state anxiety than in a comparison reading condition. Mixed results were found with several studies focusing on the effects of learner control on state anxiety. There was evidence that learner-control strategies may somewhat reduce state anxiety in the *absence* of a facilitating cognitive treatment.

One plausible interpretation of these rather unexpected findings was suggested by a cognitive-attentional view of test anxiety (Meichenbaum 1972; Wine 1971b). From this perspective test anxiety is predominantly self-oriented cognitive worry. The test-anxiety is predominantly self-oriented cognitive worry. The test-anxious individual typically responds to an evaluative situation with panicky, irrational, distracting, and self-defeating worry. Characteristically unaware of engaging in these behaviors, the individual is generally very anxious or tense, and is not aware of alternative, more adaptive modes of coping with the stress of the evaluative situation.

Presenting behavioral objectives to the test-anxious student simply does not provide any of the specific awareness or training the student requires. It might be compared with presenting someone with an irrational plane phobia statistics concerning the relative safety of airplanes as compared to automobile travel— that is not where the solution lies. Constructed responding with feedback may simply provide the anxious student with additional, repeated cues, in effect defining an evaluative situation. It may work to repeatedly trigger cognitive worry about performance without providing any additional tools to cope with it. Learner-control procedures may have a modest impact on anxiety because they tend to guide the student in the making of certain kinds of deliberate, task-oriented choices.

One implication of this view is that any future consideration of instructional procedures designed to lower anxiety in a learning or test situation must address the question of whether these procedures can reasonably be expected to reduce cognitive worry in the anxious student. Will they provide an awareness of how the student is cognitively self-generating anxiety and harming performance and of possible alternative coping strategies? Do they provide any kind of training or specific guidance in the execution of adaptive approaches that minimize worry and focus attention and thinking on the task at hand? Improved instructional procedures characteristically facilitate the exercise of task-oriented thinking on learning tasks, but cannot supply the proper attentional focus or cognitive approach if it is lacking or blocked at the outset.

A Semiautomated Test-Anxiety Reduction Program

Chapter 10 describes the development and validation of a media-based, semi-automated program designed to reduce test- and state-anxiety and to improve performance in a computer-based learning environment. Devised partly in response to the difficulties related to reducing anxiety through modifications in instructional procedures, the program, based on a cognitive-attentional view of test anxiety, provides students with highly specific information about: (1) the cognitive, emotional, and behavioral dynamics of test anxiety; and (2) alternative strategies for coping with anxiety. This information is provided largely through the media of written materials and videotape modeling of anxious and adaptive approaches to test taking. The program also provides several kinds of experiences designed to assist the student in working new and more adaptive approaches into the actual behavior in the test-taking situation. It is highly economical regarding professional time and energies, and it is suggested that a program of this type could be utilized to impart valuable skills in coping with anxiety to large numbers of interested students in a very efficient manner.

The studies reviewed in Chapter 10 indicate that the program was highly successful in reducing self-reported test and state anxiety, but produced only a slight, nonsignificant improvement in test scores in a computer-managed instructional sequence. If the program reduces cognitive worry about performance, one would expect performance differences to occur. However, for at least some students, a reduction in cognitive worry may be a necessary but not sufficient condition of improved academic performance. Chapter 10 concludes with suggestions for revision and modification of the program that might result in a greater impact on test performance. These include the addition of a brief study-skills and test-taking-skills component focusing on some of the characteristic maladaptive study and test-taking habits of anxious students.

The apparent success of this program in reducing test and state anxiety and its considerable efficiency suggest to the authors the possibility of generalizing the program format to inform, educate, or train students in a variety of skills and approaches necessary for academic survival or enrichment. Hops and Cobb (1974) have reported some interesting data on the success of "academic-survival-skill" training in increasing academic achievement in first-grade children. Perhaps the college and university educational environment stands in need of a kind of "affective curriculum" designed to teach educational and life enhancing skills such as, for example, coping with anxiety (see Chapter 10), creativity-engendering cognitive behaviors (Meichenbaum, 1974), tolerating subjective uncertainty (see Chapter 4), or rational problem-solving approaches to academic and social problems in living (D'Zurilla & Goldfried, 1973). The prospect seems an exciting one.

Anxiety and Performance

Sarason (1972) has stated that "what distinguishes the high-test-anxious individual are (1) the manner in which he attends to the events of his environment; and (2) how he interprets and utilizes the information provided by these events" (p. 382). Wine (1971b) pointed out that studies in the test anxiety literature show generally "an interaction between level of test anxiety and evaluation emphasis." That is, high-test-anxious persons perform on these tasks more poorly, following highly evaluative "ego-involving" instructions than following nonevaluative "anonymous" instructions; while low-test-anxious persons do just the reverse and perform better following evaluative than nonevaluative instructions. The majority of these studies explored performance differences on various types of laboratory learning tasks.

Only very few studies have investigated the relationship between test anxiety and academic performance in realistic learning situations. For example, the results of behavior-therapy treatment programs for test anxiety, which sometimes show improvement in course grades following reduced test anxiety (Allen, 1972), strongly suggest that some of the relationships determined in the laboratory are tenable in educational settings. Direct tests, however, are generally lacking. Part of the significance of the studies reviewed in Chapter 11, which investigated the relationship between state anxiety and performance in several types of computer-based instructional settings, is that they provide empirical support for some of these relationships. They show that in situations in which the learning materials are more complex and the stress either greater or more closely related to real-life concerns than on laboratory tasks, high-state-anxious students often perform poorly as compared to students who report low state anxiety. Several exceptions and some unexpected sex differences are noted and discussed.

Generally, these studies provide what Bowers (1973) has called "ecological validity" for previous laboratory findings concerning test anxiety and performance. One implication of this research may be that now, rather than demonstrate these general relationships between anxiety and performance, there is need to investigate the specific and differing effects of anxiety on performance across different learning tasks and types of students.

Examples of these studies reported in Chapter 11 investigated the relationship between anxiety and performance in a large-scale computer-managed instruction curriculum dealing with various topics in educational psychology. The correlation between state anxiety and performance on module tests was lower than in previous studies. But much more substantial correlations (ranging in one study from −.33 to −.54) were found between test performance and scores on a scale of "state worry." State worry is a measure of cognitive worry about oneself and about one's performance and its outcomes as distinguished from "emotionality," or reported autonomic arousal per se.

Data from several studies in this computer-managed instruction context indicate that state anxiety correlates more highly with emotionality than with worry, and that cognitive worry is a materially or educationally significant factor in test performance, whereas state anxiety probably is not. These results offer strong support, in a real-life educational setting, for a cognitive-attentional interpretation of test anxiety and its debilitating effects on performance.

It would appear profitable for future research concerning anxiety and educational performance to focus on and assess more precisely the specific kinds of anticipatory and performance-disruptive cognitive worry processes that impede learning and test taking in different tasks and learning environments. While the cognitive-attentional view of test anxiety has empirical support and has suggested apparently successful intervention strategies of several types, the research review in this section indicates that there may be substantial variations across persons, the sexes, learning tasks and settings, and types of tests in terms of how worry disrupts performance. Additional specific information of this kind may be necessary for programming for the reduction of anxiety in computer-based learning situations, and may further clarify the impact of anxiety and worry upon performance.

9
Reduction of State Anxiety Via Instructional Design in Computer-Based Learning Environments

Although it has been recognized that anxiety can interfere with the learning process (Sarason, 1960; Spielberger, 1966b, 1972c), there has been relatively little research concerned with reducing anxiety per se in realistic learning situations. The purpose of this chapter is to review a number of studies in computer-based learning environments in which instructional procedures were modified in attempts to reduce anxiety directly.

Each experiment is designed to examine the effect of a designated aspect of instructional procedure on level of state anxiety. The aim of this research is primarily pragmatic: to discover whether certain changes in instructional procedure reduce state anxiety. The relationship between anxiety and performance is presented in Chapter 11. The innovative features of the research are its use of well-controlled treatments in real learning settings, and its use of in situ monitoring of state anxiety throughout the process of learning. As discussed in Chapter 8, computer-assisted—computer-managed instruction makes possible the presentation of well-controlled treatments and the acquisition of detailed response data, while trait—state anxiety theory and related measurement techniques provides the conceptual and methodological tools for monitoring momentary changes in level of anxiety. For a more detailed discussion of the trait—state distinction and its measurement, the reader is refered to Chapter 8.

By measuring changes in level of state anxiety in the course of learning, we can determine whether anxiety has, in fact, been reduced instead of inferring this reduction from performance data. Most prior research employing treatments designed to reduce the disruptive effects of anxiety on performance have not assessed change in level of anxiety directly. A few examples will serve to distinguish this research approach from related efforts by other researchers.

Sieber (1969) argues that if high anxiety is disruptive to the functioning of cognitive processes that are required for performance of given tasks, then this disruption is one way in which anxiety causes poor overall performance (see Chapter 4). Experimental manipulations designed to supplement the affected cognitive processes (like provision of external memory support) were shown to reduce the debilitating effects of anxiety on intellectual functioning. Overall performance improvements were assumed to have come about either through a reduction of the level of anxiety or through alteration of the task such that performance requirements were more congruent with the abilities of high-anxious students. In Sieber's (1969) paradigm, the exact causal relationships cannot be directly determined.

Smith and Rockett (1958) found that if students were allowed to comment on ambiguous or misleading test items while taking a multiple-choice examination, the performance of high-test-anxious students was improved. These authors inferred that commenting allowed the high-test-anxious students to discharge their tensions over the exam. In other words, they assumed that lower levels of state anxiety were operative in the situation.

Other techniques which have improved the performance of high anxious students include: (1) the provision of feedback in programed instruction (Campeau, 1968); (2) reassurance instructions to students that their performance will not be used in evaluation (I. Sarason, 1972); and (3) relaxation instructions prior to a paired-associate learning task (Straughan & Dufort, 1969). Many of the treatments which have been employed have been shown to improve the performance of high-anxious students, and thus suggest anxiety reduction techniques. However, in all of these studies, anxiety reduction has been inferred from behavioral and performance indices rather than directly measured.

In this chapter we review a number of studies in which measures of state anxiety were employed directly to evaluate the impact of instructional procedures on the reduction of state anxiety. To provide a frame of reference for discussion of these instructional procedures, an instructional design model is introduced. Traditionally, instructional models have focused on this relation between instructional events and cognitive responses. This model incorporates affective as well as cognitive response data to more fully evaluate the learning process.

AN INSTRUCTIONAL-DESIGN MODEL

Although some researchers in instructional technology have recognized the importance of including affective components in the design and evaluation of instructional systems (e.g., Gagne, 1970; Krathwohl, Bloom, & Masia, 1964), the majority of systems models have not explicitly included this component. McCombs, Eschenbrenner, and O'Neil (1973) have, however, considered affective variables within a cybernetic model for the optimization of instruction, a model adapted from previous research by Dick and Gallagher (1972). This model

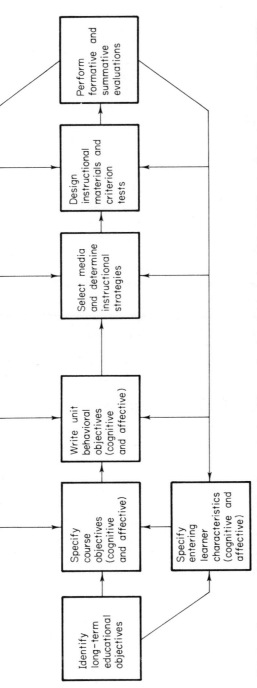

FIG. 9.1 Systems model for the design of computer-based instructional materials. (Adapted from McCombs, Eschenbrenner & O'Neil, 1973).

is described briefly as it provides a context for reviewing the research on state anxiety in computer-based learning environments.

This systems model (see Figure 9.1) starts with the identification of long-term educational objectives. Cognitive, psychomotor, and affective instructional objectives are specified on the basis of course-content analysis and an examination of entering learner characteristics. Next, unit behavioral objectives are stated in terms of the types of required terminal performances. At this stage, these authors recommend that careful consideration be given to the affective or motivational component of the objectives.

Instructional sequencing is then accomplished by task-analysis techniques that determine the learning-task hierarchy of superordinate and subordinate skills (e.g., Gagne, 1968). Measurement instruments are constructed to evaluate the intended cognitive, affective, and psychomotor outcomes. Ideally, media are selected in terms of the types of learning involved (e.g., Briggs, Campeau, Gagne, & May, 1966), cost effectiveness, and the differential motivational effects of various ability–media matches.

The instructional strategies employed are the ones considered most likely to facilitate achievement of the stated terminal objectives. The instructional materials and procedures are then designed with careful attention to the novelty and meaningfulness of such events. Criterion tests are placed at appropriate intervals within the instructional sequence. Formative and summative evaluation of the instructional system is based on indices of cognitive performance as well as affective values. These evaluations, in turn, serve as feedback to the entire system. In Figure 9.1, this feedback is indicated by arrows.

For our purposes, the three major components of this systems model are the behavioral objectives, instructional strategies (like response modes or learner control) and the evaluation component. We use these three components as a framework for organizing our review of the effects of instructional procedures on state anxiety.

First, the effects of behavioral objectives on state anxiety are discussed in the context of both computer-assisted and computer-managed instruction. Next, the effects of response modes on state anxiety in computer-assisted instruction are reviewed. Then, the effects of learner control of a variety of instructional treatments on state anxiety are examined. Last, studies relating to the use of state anxiety as a measure of value in evaluations of both computer intelligence testing and computer-managed instruction are discussed.

BEHAVIORAL OBJECTIVES AND STATE ANXIETY

The use of specific behavioral objectives has increased in popularity since the publication of the classic book on objectives by Mager (1962). Behavioral objectives are an anchor point in the majority of instructional systems and curriculum development models (e.g., Dick & Gallagher, 1972; Gagne & Briggs, 1974; Glaser, 1962; McCombs et al., 1973). Although various rationales can be expressed for specifying behavioral objectives, it seems reasonable to conceptualize behavioral objectives as serving three major instructional functions: direction for curriculum development, guidance in the evaluation process, and facilitation of the learning process (Duchastel & Merrill, 1973). If behavioral objectives do serve these instructional functions, then one would expect that their use would result in a reduction of the level of stress inherent in an instructional situation, and thus the level of state anxiety would be lower. In this section we focus on their impact in reducing state anxiety.

Gagne and Briggs (1974) suggest that the facilitation of learning via objectives may be based on their function of providing direction for learning; facilitating subject-matter organization and integration; stimulating increased self-management toward the achievement of specific learning goals; and introducing a mechanism for nonthreatening self-evaluation. However, a recent review of research concerning the effects of behavioral objectives on performance indicated limited experimental support with respect to their facilitation of learning (Duchastel & Merrill, 1973). In this context, four studies are reviewed in which the effects of behavioral objectives on state anxiety in computer-assisted and computer-managed instruction have been examined.

Computer-Assisted Instruction Tasks

Merrill and Towle (1971) investigated the effects of presenting behavioral objectives and test items in a computer-assisted instruction task on imaginary science. The terminal objective of the ten-module program required that the students predict the state of the system at successive time intervals given information of the previous state of the system.

The results of this study indicated that neither objectives nor test items facilitated cognitive posttest scores. The analysis of the state-anxiety data indicated a significant triple interaction between objectives, test items, and task periods. The interaction was related to minor fluctuations of various groups' mean state-anxiety levels. Contrary to the hypothesis, the lowest state-anxiety levels were observed on the posttest for students who received neither objectives nor test items, but only examples.

In a similar study, Merrill, Steve, Kalish, and Towle (1972) investigated the effects of behavioral objectives and/or rules on performance and state anxiety in computer-assisted instruction. The instructional program consisted of eight modules on programming rules for a programming language (APL) (McMurchie, Krueger, & Lippert, 1970) ordered in a subjectively determined easy-to-hard sequence. The results of this study indicated that both the presentation of rules and/or objectives reduced the number of examples required to learn the task and increased cognitive posttest performance.

It was also found that level of state anxiety increased significantly across the task periods. The pretask mean state-anxiety score was 9.8; midtask was 9.5; and posttask was 11.8. This finding was consistent with the performance data since all students achieved criterion on the first four modules, but only about two-thirds achieved criterion on the remaining modules. Thus, level of state-anxiety tracked task difficulty. A significant rule by period interaction was also found. Students in the rule groups had higher pretask state anxiety, lower state anxiety during the first four modules, and similar anxiety levels to the no-rule groups during the last four modules, which were the most difficult. The effects of rules on state anxiety washed out with the difficult materials, although one might predict the effect to be most striking in this instance.

Tobias and Duchastel (1974) reasoned that objectives would facilitate achievement and reduce state anxiety in a difficult, scrambled instructional sequence in computer-assisted instruction, since objectives would help to provide organization and integration which would otherwise be lacking in the scrambled version. The hypothesis that behavioral objectives would facilitate achievement in less structured instructional environments was not supported.

Analysis of the state-anxiety data indicated that an objective X sequence interaction approached significance ($p < .10$). There were minimal state anxiety differences in the behavioral objective logical-sequence groups. However, in the scrambled condition, the students given behavioral objectives showed somewhat higher state anxiety ($\bar{X} = 9.63$) than did the students who were not given behavioral objectives ($\bar{X} = 8.36$). These findings, of course, were contrary to expectation. Perhaps the addition of 25 objectives to the 80-frame sequence may have served to increase the difficulty of the task, especially in the scrambled version, which, in turn, increased state anxiety.

Computer-Managed Instruction Tasks

Merrill and Towle (1972) investigated the effects of behavioral objectives on performance and state anxiety in a graduate level computer-managed instruction course. This course, originally developed by Dick and Gallager (1972), basically taught the necessary skills, identified through hierarchical task-analysis techniques (Gagne, 1970), which a student must acquire to design, implement, and evaluate a programmed unit of instruction using a systems model. The course contained both cognitive productive modules with a maximum of three objectives per module. The cognitive modules consisted of specific content mastery, and the productive modules focused on project development skills (like writing behavioral objectives).

The term "module" refers to a complete package of self-instructional programmed material in written form covering prespecified behavioral objectives, and adaptable for presentation via various types of media (including textbooks or

TABLE 9.1
Adjusted Means for State-Anxiety Scores for Modules 1–6

Group	Modules						Average mean
	1	2	3	4	5	6	
No-objective group	12.90	12.20	10.64	12.04	11.37	11.59	11.81
Objective group	10.16	9.61	8.36	11.33	10.81	9.78	9.86

workbooks, tape–slide presentations, or television and film, as well as computers). The term usually includes the following components:

1. The specific behavioral objectives to be attained through the module.
2. Criterion measures to assess whether or not the student has mastered the specific objectives for the module.
3. Instructions for the use of the module when these are not self-evident.
4. The instruction itself.

For the first six modules, the experimental group received objectives, and the control group no objectives. The students completed the series of assignments in an individualized, self-paced manner. After studying an assignment, the student took a module exam presented on computer terminals. The computer also presented five-item state-anxiety scales immediately after each module test. As students completed the test, they were given information about the correctness of their item responses.

The results indicated that the presence of behavioral objectives did not facilitate performance on the first six module tests. However, the results of an analysis holding trait anxiety and pretask state-anxiety constant indicated that the availability of objectives significantly decreased the level of state anxiety. The adjusted state anxiety means for the first six modules are reproduced in Table 9.1. A post hoc analysis of the differences in state anxiety between groups indicated that state anxiety was significantly lower for the group receiving behavioral objectives modules for Modules 1–3 but not for Modules 4–6, respectively.

Summary

The evidence reported here in terms of state anxiety and the review of performance results elsewhere (Duchastel & Merrill, 1973) demonstrate the relation between use of behavioral objectives and degree of state-anxiety reduction is quite complex. The results for cognitive measures have shown that objectives sometimes assist the student and rarely detract from the learning situation. Similarly, objectives sometimes reduce state anxiety and rarely increase it.

Only one study indicated that the statement of behavioral objectives reduces state anxiety, and this result held only in the earlier modules of a computer-managed instruction course (Merrill & Towle, 1972). Differences between the experimental groups with respect to state anxiety disappeared for the latter modules of the curriculum. Whether this effect is a function of task difficulty (earlier modules easier than later course modules) or whether the effects are related to task sequence is not interpretable from the research design. It is also possible that the effects disappeared as students adapted to the innovative computer-managed instruction course and were able to "psych out" the course (Merrill & Towle, 1972). Merrill et al. (1972) found that when easy rules were stated, state anxiety was reduced, but that when difficult rules were stated later in the instructional sequence, state anxiety again rose. In this study, it is quite possible that the extreme difficulty of the latter rules, as indicated by a number of students not reaching criterion on those rules, may have counteracted the earlier facilitative effects.

RESPONSE MODE AND STATE ANXIETY

One of the important instructional features of computer-assisted instruction is the provision for continuous, active responding with specific performance feedback for the student. However, a number of early investigations compared different response modes in order to establish the advantages of active responding plus feedback and found inconclusive performance results. The inconclusive results of these early studies, however, were attributed to the poor quality of the programmed instructional materials used (Holland, 1967).

The affective impact of various response modes has, with the exception of Tobias (1973c), not been investigated in previous studies of programmed instruction. It would be expected that if a particular response mode facilitated achievement, a reduction of state anxiety would also occur. Accordingly, four recent studies of computer-assisted instruction have examined this issue using a measure of state anxiety to assess the affective impact of response modes.

In the first of two studies reported by Leherissey, O'Neil, Heinrich, and Hansen (1973), the effects of trait- and state-anxiety levels and response modes on achievement for familiar and technical materials dealing with heart disease were investigated. Four versions of the learning materials were presented to students via an IBM 1500 computer-assisted instruction system as follows: (1) reading version, in which the students were required merely to read successive frames of material; (2) covert version, in which students were instructed merely to "think" their answer to themselves and then signal to obtain the correct answer; (3) modified multiple-choice version, which required overt responses on the verbal portions of the material, while on technical pictorial portions of the learning material, students were required to choose one of three or four multiple-choice answers before being shown the correct response; and (4) constructed response version, which was identical to the modified multiple-choice version on the verbal frames, but in which students were required to respond to the technical pictorial frames by constructing graphical representations of EKG tracings using various keyboard dictionary characters in succession prior to receiving the correct answer.

The content of the materials consisted of the program used by Tobias (1972), with minimal revisions for adaptation to the IBM 1500 system. Again, the content was divided into familiar materials dealing with such topics as the incidence and prevalence of heart disease and technical materials consisting of technical verbal materials that required verbal responses (words and phrases) and technical pictorial materials that required pictorial responses (simulated electrocardiogram, or EKG, drawings). Measures of trait anxiety were obtained and state anxiety scales were administered prior to the task, again at various points during and after the tasks, and immediately following the posttest. This procedure was followed in all four of the studies discussed here.

The results of this first study revealed that highest levels of state anxiety were evoked during the posttest for the students, whereas state anxiety levels were lower during the familiar materials than during the technical materials. Students who were high in trait anxiety were also found to respond with higher levels of state anxiety than were low trait anxious students. This is in accordance with Spielberger's (1966a) trait–state anxiety theory. A finding of particular interest here was that students in the constructed response groups, as compared to the reading group, had the highest levels of state anxiety during the technical learning materials and during the posttest. In addition, the constructed-response group had taken nearly twice as long as the reading group to complete the program.

In contrast to Tobias' (1968) findings that the constructed response mode led to superior performance compared to a reading mode on the technical posttest, this study indicated that these groups were equivalent in performance. The absence of a performance difference may have been due to this higher state anxiety exhibited by the constructed-response group.

In order to replicate these findings and to attempt to reduce state anxiety and improve performance, the amount of time students were required to spend on the learning task was reduced in the hope that this would reduce anxiety and improve performance. A study was undertaken using only the reading and constructed-response program versions. The reading and constructed response instructional programs described in the first study were labeled reading-long and constructed response-long. Two additional versions, reading-short and constructed response-short, were prepared containing the same subject matter and frame structure as their longer counterparts, but terminating following the first two frames containing EKG tracings. Female students who were grouped on level of trait anxiety (high, medium, low) were assigned randomly to the four experimental program versions.

Contrary to prediction, shortening this program did not reduce anxiety for the constructed-response group either during the learning task or the posttest. The other findings of this second study essentially replicated those of the first. High-trait-anxious students had higher levels of state anxiety throughout the task and posttest than either medium or low-trait-anxious students. Students in the constructed-response groups had higher state-anxiety scores than students in the reading groups both during the technical portion of the learning materials and during the posttest. Also, Tobias' (1969) findings in which the constructed-response group performed better than did the reading group on the technical materials were not replicated again. The possible reasons for this nonreplication are discussed in Chapter 11.

In the third study of the series, Leherissey (1971) sought to replicate the response mode and state-anxiety results of the first two studies in addition to investigating the effects of stimulating state epistemic curiosity on performance and state anxiety. For our purposes, only the results concerning anxiety are discussed; the findings on curiosity are reported elsewhere (Leherissey, 1971).

As in the previous studies, female undergraduate students were randomly assigned to conditions based on their levels of trait anxiety (low or high). Reading and constructed-response groups studied programs covering only the technical materials of the heart-disease program modified for the curiosity-stimulating condition by the insertion of special instructions. In addition, at the suggestion of Tobias (1972), the posttest was modified to be more congruent with the instructional objectives of the program.

High-trait-anxious students had significantly higher levels of state anxiety than the low-trait-anxious students, both during the program and posttest. In addition, there was a significant interaction between response modes, levels of trait anxiety, and periods. This interaction indicated that both high- and low-trait-anxious students in the constructed-response groups had relatively the same pattern of increases and decreases in state anxiety across the experimental task; however, the high- and low-trait-anxious students in the reading groups showed differential reactions. The high-trait-anxious students showed steady declines in state anxiety during the task, whereas the low-trait-anxious students remained at a relatively low level of state anxiety throughout.

Summary

The state-anxiety data for the learning task and posttest for these three studies are presented in Table 9.2. In addition, a related study by Tobias (1973c), using the same technical heart-disease materials, is also tabled. For purposes of this comparison, all in-task measures of state anxiety have been combined to yield an average measure of state anxiety during the learning task using a weighted-means approach where appropriate in each study. Only the constructed-response and reading versions are tabled.

TABLE 9.2
Mean State-Anxiety Scores for the Constructed-Response and Reading Modes

	Leherissey et al. (1973) Study 1: Periods		Leherissey et al. (1973) Study 2[a]: Periods		Leherissey (1971): Periods		Tobias (1973c)[b]: Periods	
Response mode	Task	Posttest	Task	Posttest	Task	Posttest	Task	Posttest
Constructed response	10.89	11.46	10.56	11.75	9.15	10.01	10.80	10.70
Reading	9.33	10.43	8.92	9.56	7.63	10.01	8.10	10.60

[a]Includes only the constructed-response and reading groups in the long versions.
[b]Includes only the constructed-response and reading groups in the no-distraction condition.

For all four studies the constructed-response groups had higher levels of state anxiety during instruction than did reading groups. Apparently, constructed responding is viewed by students as more evaluative and stressful.

In terms of reactions to the posttest, Studies 1 and 2 of Leherissey et al. (1973) indicated that the constructed-response groups had higher levels of state anxiety than did the reading group. However, there were no differences between these groups in the Leherissey (1971) and Tobias (1973c) studies. The discrepancies in the former two sets of findings with the latter two were apparently attributable to the modifications of the posttest in the latter two studies in order to more adequately reflect the behaviors taught in the program. In the prior two studies there were no significant differences between the constructured-response and reading groups on the technical posttest, whereas the constructed-response groups performed better than the reading groups on the latter two studies.

From an instructional-design viewpoint, the results of these studies are quite interesting, yet perplexing. A number of authors have cited the benefits of active responding and specific informative feedback during instruction. Eliciting responses with immediate confirmation (reinforcement) is generally viewed as a condition of good instructional methodology. However, these results suggest that such a procedure leads to high levels of state anxiety. Apparently the students view the evaluation of their constructed responses as a somewhat testlike situation. An interesting question for further research is whether students can be taught to view constructed responding more positively, rather than with implicit negative connotations of evaluation as suggested by these data.

LEARNER CONTROL AND STATE ANXIETY

Another instructional variable that has been considered to have affective consequences during the learning process is that of learner control. Learner control differs from conventional computer-based instruction in that the student is given some degree of control over the methods or materials by which the subject matter is learned. For example, the student in a learner-control situation would be allowed to alter the instructional sequence at his or her discretion, or be allowed to request information concerning the corrections of responses. This learner control, in turn, is assumed to possess both cognitive and affective advantages for the student.

The research evidence on the performance benefits of learner control has been inconclusive. For example, Mager (1961) and Mager and McCann (1961) have reported favorable performance results for learner control. However, Barnes (1970) and Thomas (1971) have reported nonsignificant findings.

These authors, as well as others (e.g., Judd, 1972) expected learner control to result in more positive student motivation and attitudes. However, few studies have actually measured these variables. In a review of the learner-control literature, Judd, O'Neil, and Spelt (1974a) indicated that while the variables of mastery and time to completion are sufficiently specific, the presumed affective advantages of learner control, perhaps its most promising aspect, have been ill-defined. The research reviewed in this section deals specifically with the effects of learner control on state anxiety during the learning process.

The general hypothesis of these studies was that a student's state anxiety would be elevated in a situation of no control over the instructional situation. Conversely, as the student's control is increased so as to allow manipulation of the learning material according to the student's perceived individual strengths and weaknesses, the level of state anxiety would be reduced.

In the majority of the learner-control research previously reviewed, the independent variables placed under learner control were not themselves shown to have any appreciable effect on learning. For example, in those studies concerning learner control of sequence, no evidence was presented that sequence variations led to differential learning outcomes. Therefore, it is not surprising that inconclusive performance results are obtained when these independent variables were placed under learner control. This research strategy was therefore designed that the instructional efficacy of the variable to be placed under learner control should be empirically determined.

As a check on the instructional efficacy of the variable that was to be placed under learner control, an experiment should ideally contain two control groups: one which always receives the facilitating treatment (treatment present), and one of which never receives the treatment (treatment absent). Subjects in the learner-control group would be given control over the instructional variable in question. With regard to performance, the independent variable under consideration would be considered a viable learner-control option only if the learner control group's performance exceeded those of the treatment-absent group and at least approached those of the treatment-present group. This particular research design has been used in several of the studies investigating both the performance and affective advantages of learner control.

Study 1

Collier, Poynor, O'Neil, and Judd (1973) studied the effects of learner control of memory support in a computer-assisted instruction learning task. The task consisted of three multicategory conjunctive concept-learning problems of increasing difficulty. On the basis of previous experience with such tasks these authors hypothesized that student performance on this task would be improved by providing memory support. In this study, memory support consisted of displaying the two previous stimuli and their correct classifications while the current stimulus was still present.

Students in the no-memory-support group did not have access to the previous stimuli during the task. In the memory-support group, students always received the two prior correct instances and classifications of the concept. In the learner-control condition, the students had the opportunity to request memory support at their discretion. With respect to the performance findings, there were no significant differences between the learner-control and memory-support groups, whereas both were superior to the no-memory-support group in terms of trials to criterion.

The mean state-anxiety data across the three problems were 10.6 for the no-memory-support group, 10.4 for the memory support group, and 8.3 for the learner-control group. These differences between the experimental and control groups were statistically significant. While memory support had a pronounced facilitative effect on performance, it did not by itself reduce the level of state anxiety. State anxiety was reduced only when the students had control over the availability of the memory support. These results provide suggestive evidence for the hypothesis that learner control of instructional variables may possess advantages in the affective domain.

Study 2

Judd, Daubek, and O'Neil (1975) further investigated the effects of learner control of visual materials on state anxiety and performance using a more realistic learning task concerning the identification of edible plants native to Texas. Research using a previous version of this computer-assisted instruction program (Judd, O'Neil, & Spelt, 1974a) suggested that photographs of the various plants facilitated the students' memory for the critical features and names of the plants. Students in the no-visual group did not have access to the plant pictures during the learning task. In the visual group, the students were always presented the pictures for each instructional frame. In the learner-control group, the students had the option to access the pictures at their discretion.

When task-specific memory ability was held constant, the results indicated that the no-visual group committed significantly more errors on both the critical features and identification components of the posttest than the visual group which always received the treatment. As in the Collier et al. (1973) study, the performance of the learner control group did not differ significantly from visual group.

The mean levels of state anxiety during the learning task were 10.8 for the no-visual group, 8.9 for the visuals group, and 9.6 for the learner-control group. Statistical analysis of these data indicated that the highest level of state anxiety was observed for the no-visual group in comparison to the 2 other experimental groups. In contrast to the Collier et al. (1973) study, the analysis also indicated that the learner-control group had similar levels of state anxiety to the visual group. Thus, in this study learner control over visual support did not lead to reductions in state anxiety.

Study 3

Hansen (1974) investigated the effects of learner control of information feedback on state anxiety and performance in a computer-assisted instruction task on imaginary science using the same research paradigm as the previous two studies. Students in a no-feedback group did not receive any information about the correctness of their test-item responses during the program. In a feedback group, the students always received the words "true" or "false" following each test item, plus a statement of the rule following the third test item for each rule. In the learner-control condition, the students could receive the true–false feedback at their individual request on any item. They also had the option of viewing the rule following the third test item for any example. However, presentation of the rule terminated the presentation on examples for that rule and resulted in the immediate presentation of the first example of the next rule. In essence, the student had the option of either terminating the instruction on a given rule, or of receiving test-item feedback.

The performance results of this study indicated that the learner-control group did not have control over a facilitative instructional variable. The three experimental groups were not found to differ significantly with regard to posttest performance. Analysis of the state-anxiety data indicated a significant interaction between the groups and the measurement periods. In general, both the learner-control and feedback groups showed decreases in state anxiety across the task whereas the no-feedback group remained at a relatively higher level during the task. The learner-control and feedback groups were not found to differ significantly from each other. In this study, the provision of feedback or learner control resulted in greater reductions in state anxiety than no feedback, although feedback by itself did not appear to facilitate posttest performance.

Study 4

The results of the first three studies were based on relatively well-controlled computer-assisted instruction tasks and indicated that learner control of various instructional variables may lead to reductions of state anxiety under certain conditions. In contrast, Gallagher, O'Neil, and Dick (1971) investigated the effects of learner control of module sequence on state anxiety and performance within a semester-long, graduate-level course conducted via computer-managed instruction.

As previously described in this chapter, this computer-managed course basically teaches the skills necessary for the development of programmed instruction. Approximately one-half of these students were required to complete the course in a prescribed sequence. The remaining students were allowed to determine their own sequence (learner control). Within these two groups, the students were further separated based on the type of evaluation of their term projects, either an instructor-evaluated or computer-evaluated group.

The results of this study indicated that the learner-control groups did not differ significantly from the fixed-sequence groups on the course midterm examination or the term-project grade. Thus, the learner-control groups were not found to have control over a facilitative-instructional variable. However, when the data were reanalyzed as a function of trait anxiety and experimental conditions on state anxiety, high-trait-anxious students had significantly higher levels of state anxiety than the low-trait-anxious students.

In addition, a significant triple interaction between learner control, trait anxiety, and module tasks indicated, as may be seen in Figure 9.2, that low-trait-anxious students in the learner-control groups reported the lowest levels of state anxiety. Learner control, as compared to the fixed sequence condition, did not appear to result in lower levels of state anxiety for the high-trait-anxious students. Later in the task, students in the learner control of sequence groups reported less state anxiety than students in the fixed-sequence

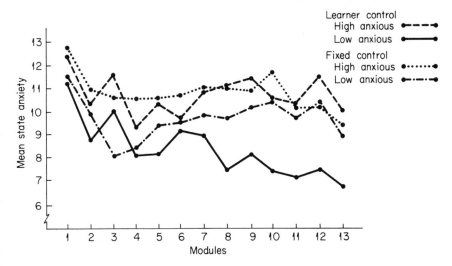

FIG. 9.2 Interaction between trait anxiety, learner control and modules on state anxiety.

groups. These results suggest that learner control of course sequence may result in reduction of state anxiety, particularly for low-trait-anxious students. However, the positive effects of learner control did not appear to generalize to the high-trait-anxious students.

Summary

In the studies reviewed in this section, state anxiety was used to measure the effects of learner control of various instructional variables on state anxiety. The results of these studies, although inconsistent with respect to performance, paradoxically are consistent in terms of state anxiety.

Collier et al. (1973) found that learner control of a facilitative treatment resulted in a greater reduction in state anxiety than always presenting the instructional treatment, while Judd et al. (1974a) found that these groups were equivalent but were less than the treatment-absent group. Hansen (1974) further indicated that learner control of a nonfacilitative treatment did not result in lower levels of state anxiety than those who always received the treatment. Both groups, however, had lower levels of state anxiety than the treatment-absent group. Gallagher et al. (1971) found that learner control of a nonfacilitative treatment (sequence) resulted in lower levels of state anxiety, especially for the low-trait-anxious students.

Viewed collectively, these studies suggest that when one has a generally facilitative instructional treatment that leads to relatively low overall levels of state anxiety (e.g., Judd et al., 1974a), the implementation of a learner-control option will not have additional affective advantages in terms of state-anxiety reduction. If in spite of a generally facilitative treatment, there appear to be high levels of state anxiety during the instruction (Collier et al., 1973), the implementation of a learner-control condition may reduce state anxiety. Further, when a facilitative treatment is not available (Hansen, 1974), learner control may allow the student to engage previously effective behavioral and cognitive strategies to cope with the situations, and therefore result in lower levels of state anxiety (Gallagher et al., 1971).

A larger question regarding learner control still remains. If the instructional treatment under investigation has a generally facilitative effect on performance for all students, why should one consider learner control? Why not administer the treatment to all students? With respect to performance in most situations, the answer involves costs for instructional resources or costs to the student in terms of time. For example, it is known that overlearning increases retention, but it is not generally assumed that all students should receive extensive doses of drill and practice.

With respect to state anxiety, the results indicated that although performance differences were not always found, the students generally reported either equivalent or less state anxiety. Thus, whether one considers the costs in terms of actual resources or in terms of affective feelings, it would appear that learner control is a promising instructional strategy.

PROGRAM EVALUATION AND STATE ANXIETY

The studies reported previously in this chapter dealt mainly with investigations of the effects of a number of instructional strategies (like behavioral objectives or learner control) on state anxiety. In this chapter section, state anxiety is viewed in a slightly different context; as an index or measure of the value of the various instructional settings. It was assumed that an effective instructional setting should in addition to leading to adequate performance outcomes, lead to moderate or low levels of state anxiety. Two settings are reviewed, computer-based testing and computer-managed instruction.

Computer-Based Testing and State Anxiety

Another aspect of the instructional-design process is the determination of a methodology for the evaluation of student achievement. Preliminary studies of automated testing systems suggested that they resulted in equivalent reliability and validity, compared to traditional examiner or paper-and-pencil administration (e.g., Elwood, 1969, 1972a, 1973; Lushene, O'Neil, & Dunn, 1974). It was also suggested that human–machine testing interactions were more objective and affectively neutral than typical interactions between examiner and student (e.g., Evans & Miller, 1969; Johnson & Mihal, 1973). The majority of these claims in the affective domain have not, however, been based upon experimental paradigms comparing computer-based interactive test administrations with traditional testing procedures.

A number of empirical studies have been reported that compared computer-based and traditional testing methodology using affective criteria. Lushene, O'Neil, and Dunn (1974) compared a computerized Minnesota Multiphasic Personality Inventory administration with a group booklet mode of administration. The computer-based Minnesota Multiphasic Personality Inventory scale scores were shown to correlate as highly with the booklet administration scores as correlations for comparisons between booklet and card administrations or booklet–booklet administrations. When compared to the booklet version, the computer mode initially produced relatively higher state-anxiety levels. By the end of the test, however, no difference in state-anxiety levels between the two modes of test administration was found.

Hedl, O'Neil, and Hansen (1973) investigated whether administering the Slosson (1973) intelligence test, an individually administered Binet-type scale, via computer would be a less stressful testing situation than examiner testing. Contrary to expectation, the computer testing situation led to higher levels of state anxiety in comparison to the two examiner testing situations. The state-anxiety scores were significantly higher in the computer-testing situation ($\bar{X}$ = 11.4) in comparison to either of the two examiner-testing conditions (WAIS $\bar{X}$ = 9.4; Slosson intelligence test $\bar{X}$ = 9.4), which did not differ from one another.

Student remarks during the debriefing session suggested that the ambiguity of instructions and unfamiliarity with the computer terminals and not the computer per se had caused the observed increase in state anxiety.

A series of studies then was designed to evaluate the nature of the stress stimuli in computer intelligence testing and investigate procedures for reducing state anxiety. The first study examined the effects of a number of program revisions on state anxiety within the computer test for students differing in trait anxiety (Hedl, 1973). The program was revised to begin at a difficult item and to present items in reverse order of difficulty until ten consecutive correct responses was reached. Then the more difficult items were presented until ten consecutive item failures occurred, or the entire array of test items was completed. The second revision also increased time limits for certain test questions.

Female students, selected on the basis of their upper- or lower-quartile scores from the state–trait anxiety inventory college norms participated in this experiment. The revised test was taken by each student on two occasions with a one-week time interval separating the two administrations. The high-trait-anxious students exhibited significantly higher levels of state anxiety than the low-trait-anxious students. State-anxiety levels decreased across the two testing sessions. As may be seen in Table 9.3, the revised program resulted in lower state anxiety than the earlier fixed item-sequence program. However, it still produced higher anxiety levels than those obtained by examiners giving the Slosson intelligence test.

In a second study, Hedl (1973) investigated the effects of prior terminal experience on subsequent state-anxiety levels within the computer-based testing situation. If nonfamiliarity with the terminal testing procedures operates as a stressor variable, state-anxiety levels should be differentially related to prior exposure and practice on the computer terminals. This hypothesis was examined

TABLE 9.3
Mean State-Anxiety Scores before and after a Computer-Based Intelligence Test

		Computerized Slosson Intelligence Test	
	Study	Pretest	Posttest
Initial computer program	Hedl (1971)	12.8	12.3
Revised computer program	Hedl (1973)	11.0	11.1
Examiner administered	Hedl (1971)	9.5	9.2

by varying type of terminal familiarity. In one condition, students played a computer game prior to taking the intelligence test. The second condition required students to interact with an easy constructed-response computer-assisted instruction program before testing.

The results indicated that students who had prior experience in the form of a computer-assisted instructional program showed significantly lower levels of state anxiety in the subsequent testing session than the students with prior game experience. Further, the state anxiety levels during the prior terminal experiences (Game = 7.73; CAI = 8.93) did not statistically differ. These data suggest that the effectiveness of prior experience for anxiety reduction within computer testing are a function of task similarity. No differences in intelligence-test scores were noted.

The effectiveness of prior terminal experience versus no prior experience for anxiety reduction within computer testing was not examined in this study. However, the state-anxiety data from this study may be compared with the data from the previous study. As may be seen in Table 9.4, anxiety scores for students with no prior computer-testing experience were comparable to those for students who had prior game experience.

In terms of comparisons with the previous examiner data, students with an easy computer-assisted instruction task had similar results. The pre- and post-intelligence-test state-anxiety levels for students who had the Slosson intelligence test administered via examiner were 9.5 and 9.2 compared with 8.6 and 9.8 for the CAI group. Thus, if adequate practice and familiarity with the task procedures were given in a nonstressful environment, computer intelligence testing appeared to yield state anxiety scores that are essentially equivalent to those yielded by examiner testing.

In a third study, Hedl (1973) explored the effects of long-term practice with computer task procedures in the context of a computer-managed educational-psychology course. It was predicted that if students were given extensive practice on computer terminals and if this practice involved a situation of some

TABLE 9.4
Mean State-Anxiety Scores as a Function of Prior
Terminal Experience in Computer-Based Testing

Prior terminal experience	Study	Computerized Slosson Intelligence Test	
		Pretest	Posttest
None	Hedl (1973)	11.0	11.1
CAI	Hedl (1973)	8.6	9.8
Game	Hedl (1973)	10.5	11.9
CMI	O'Neil (1972)	7.0	10.0

stress similar to the intelligence-testing situation, the state-anxiety levels would be further reduced in comparison to previous studies.

Students who had completed a computer-managed instruction course (see Chapter 11) consisting of eight computer-administered tests volunteered to take the Slosson intelligence test via computer. Measures of state anxiety were obtained following each of the eight module tests as well as before and after the intelligence test.

The mean state-anxiety level for the 8 module tests was 11.9. This is a higher level of state anxiety than occurred following practice on an easy computer-assisted instructional program ($\overline{X}$ = 8.93). This elevated state anxiety may be attributed to the real evaluative stress of each module test that counted toward a course grade. Practice on the easy computer-assisted instruction program did not count toward a grade.

It was reasoned that experience during a computer-managed instruction treatment of this type constitutes more realistic practice for the evaluative stress of the intelligence test, and thus permits an adaptation to the computer testing prior to administration of the intelligence test. Evidence on this supposition can be obtained by comparing the state-anxiety data from this study with the state-anxiety data from the prior study. This comparison, as shown in Table 9.4, indicates that this supposition is wrong. Prior experience in the computer-managed instruction did not result in lower levels of state anxiety on the intelligence test.

To analyze these results further, the group with prior computer-managed-instruction testing experience was divided into two subsamples, based on data from posttest interviews: (1) those students who reported experiencing more evaluative stress during the intelligence test than during the module test; and (2) those students who reported experiencing more evaluative stress during the module tests than during the intelligence test.

The subsample who reported being more stressed during the module tests than during the intelligence test showed significantly lower state-anxiety levels during the intelligence test ($\overline{X}$ = 9.2) than those students who reported more stress during the intelligence test ($\overline{X}$ = 15.2). Apparently extended practice in computer-managed instruction-module testing did not better prepare the later group of students for computer intelligence testing; perhaps they considered these situations to be two distinct forms of evaluative stress.

Summary

In the studies reviewed in this section, state anxiety was used to evaluate a computer-based intelligence test. The performance results of these studies reported elsewhere (Hedl, 1971, 1973) indicated that the computer-administered Slosson intelligence test showed comparable test–retest reliability and validity coefficients in comparison to traditional administrations of the same test. Thus, interactive computer testing resulted in relatively equivalent psychometric data.

The major findings with respect to computer-based intelligence testing and state anxiety may be summarized as follows. High-trait-anxious students responded to the computer-testing situation in general with higher levels of state anxiety than did low-trait-anxious students. As expected, state anxiety was higher during the test than before the test. Students showed lower levels of state anxiety during a second administration of the test.

In comparison with other interactive computer activities, state-anxiety levels were higher during the computer-based intelligence test than during gamelike or relatively easy computer-assisted instructional situations.

Previous research (Spielberger *et al.,* 1970) indicates that the state-anxiety values observed within the computer test are about the same as state-anxiety scores obtained during a difficult paper-and-pencil examination. The state-anxiety levels manifested during the game and the instructional program were about the same as has been found in situations having few or no evaluative connotations. Thus, computer-administered intelligence tests resulted in levels of evaluative stress similar to those of more traditional test administrations. Similar findings were noted for the module tests.

These data suggest that the use of computers does not result in higher or lower levels of evaluative stress than normally observed during other testing procedures. From an instructional design standpoint, the uses of computers for interactive intelligence or achievement testing would better be justified along other dimensions such as immediate scoring and report generation rather than low-state-anxiety outcomes. Although the use of computers permits the presentation of test materials under carefully controlled conditions, levels of state anxiety will generally reflect conditions of evaluative stress, that is, a "test."

Computer-Managed Instruction

Hedl, O'Neil, and Richardson (1974) measured state anxiety in the formative evaluation of an undergraduate computer-managed instruction course in educational psychology. The subjects were undergraduate students enrolled in various sections of an educational-psychology teacher-preparation course. All computer-managed-instruction tests were given on a cathode-ray tube terminal of an IBM 1500 computer-assisted instructional system.

In the sequence of modules, each student studied conventional printed learning materials, guided by behavioral objectives, until completing the readings assigned for a module. The student then took a test which was keyed to the instructional objectives. Feedback at the conclusion of each testing session consisting of total score on the module and percentage score on each objective was provided. If the student failed to reach overall criterion performance of 75%, a retest at a later date was required. At the time of the retest the student was only examined over the previously failed objectives. Immediately following each test, but prior to receiving performance feedback, the student responded to a five-item state-anxiety scale administered on terminal.

During fall 1972, there were nine instructional modules. For the spring 1973 semester, the computer-managed-instruction course was revised and included a total of six instructional modules. The new criterion performance level was 80%. Although other experimental groups were included in the spring 1973 semester and are reported elsewhere, the students included in this study essentially completed the same instructional, procedural, and evaluation activities as the fall 1972 students.

The test-anxiety scale (Sarason, 1972) was administered before the CMI sequence and the five-item state-anxiety scale was administered on line before performance feedback. Performance was defined as the individual's initial score on each module test. (More detail with respect to the computer-managed-instruction course is provided in Chapter 11.)

Generalizability of anxiety findings. The purpose of this investigation was to assess the impact of the computer-managed instructional procedures on state anxiety in two different semesters. One concern was with the relationship of task difficulty to state anxiety during the computer-managed-instruction course. Based on prior research (e.g., Speilberger, O'Neil, & Hansen, 1972; Leherissey *et al.,* 1973) it was expected that state anxiety would be significantly higher during the difficult materials than easier ones. (The effects of state anxiety on performance in the computer-managed program are discussed in Chapter 11.)

A comparison of mean state-anxiety scores as a function of module content and difficulty was made. It was predicted that state-anxiety levels would increase as a function of modular difficulty. Difficulty was operationally defined as to the percentage of students who achieved criterion on their first attempt on the module tests. Although the difficulty indices ranged from 59 to 90%, the mean state-anxiety scores did not show any systematic relationship to module difficulty. For example, the mean anxiety scores for these modules were 11.06 and 11.33, respectively.

A similar descriptive comparison was made for the spring 1973 implementation of the computer-managed-instruction curriculum. The module difficulty ranged from 39 to 76%. The mean state-anxiety scores for these modules were 10.83 and 10.95 respectively. Again, at this molar level, state anxiety was not found to vary as a function of overall task difficulty.

Comparisons were then made of state-anxiety levels as a function of success or failure on module tests for both the fall 1972 and spring 1973 implementations of the computer-managed instruction curriculum. Table 9.5 presents these comparisons for fall 1972 data.

The lowest state-anxiety levels were generally observed for those students who successfully passed the module tests on their first attempt, and the highest anxiety for those students who failed the retest and had to take an oral examination by their instructor. These findings were confirmed in a series of nine one-way analyses of variance comparing the state-anxiety scores of those students who passed on their first attempt with those who passed on the second

TABLE 9.5

Means and Standard Deviations of State Anxiety Scores as a Function
of Success or Failure on a Computer-Managed Instruction Module Test in Fall 1972

Module	Passed first test	N	Failed first test	N
Computers in education	11.57	365	11.91	149
Classroom management	10.48	388	10.84	101
Cultural differences	11.00	241	12.42	148
Tests and measurements	10.76	342	12.15	134
Statistics 1	10.77	114	11.47	78
Statistics 2	10.71	125	12.00	68
Statistics 3	11.17	172	12.70	20
Statistics 4	12.11	155	12.95	37
Statistics 5	11.10	136	13.29	55

attempt and those who failed on their second attempt. It should be noted, however, that the students who failed the retests were also the highest test-anxious students in the sample.

Analysis of the spring anxiety data yielded similar findings (see Table 9.6). (Unfortunately state anxiety was not measured at the retest during this semester.) Thus, it would appear that either state-anxiety levels were dependent on the student's perception of success or failure during the testing process, or that higher levels of test anxiety led to higher levels of state anxiety during the retesting process. Although the results are confounded, the authors feel that the observed state-anxiety levels were probably a joint function of test anxiety and success–failure perception.

Use of state anxiety as a measure of value. Two broad goals were defined for the computer-managed-instruction course in educational psychology; satisfactory student performance, and moderate to low levels of state anxiety toward the instruction–evaluation system. Although the latter effect cannot be directly

TABLE 9.6

Means and Standard Deviations of State-Anxiety Scores as a Function
of Success or Failure on a Computer-Managed Instruction Module Tests in Spring 1973

Module	Passed first test	N	Failed 1st test	N
Computers in education	11.21	77	12.48	27
Classroom management	9.81	75	11.24	25
Cultural differences	9.51	35	11.67	55
Tests and measurement	10.64	72	11.27	26
Statistics 1	10.32	31	12.90	10

TABLE 9.7

Mean State-Anxiety Scale Scores as a Function of Level of Assumed Situational Stress

Experimental situation	Study	Mean state anxiety
Relaxation condition	Spielberger, Gorsuch, and Lushene (1970)	7.30 (males); 6.60 (females)
Computer game	Hedl (1973)	7.47
Easy CAI program	Hedl (1973)	8.93
Difficult CAI program	Tobias (1973c)	10.80
Fall CMI	Hedl *et al.* (1973)	11.33
Spring CMI	Hedl *et al.* (1973)	10.82
Computer-based intelligence test	Hedl (1973)	11.10
Stress film	Spielberger, Gorsuch, and Lushene (1970)	13.21 (males); 16.58 (females)

evaluated within the context of this study, since no "control" group was run, inferential evidence can be obtained by comparisons of the state-anxiety data with previous findings.

Table 9.7 presents mean state-anxiety scores from previous representative studies. These studies were chosen to exemplify the expected range of state-anxiety scores based upon assumed levels of stress inherent in the experimental situation.

The median state-anxiety mean for the nine modules of the computer-managed-instruction course during 1972 was 11.33, whereas the median state-anxiety mean for the six revised modules of the computer-managed-instruction course was 10.82. This suggests that the revision process resulted in slightly reduced state-anxiety levels within the curriculum (Hedl *et al.*, 1973).

As expected, these data suggest that relatively nonthreatening, gamelike situations result in the low state-anxiety levels, with an easy computer-assisted instructional program yielding somewhat higher levels (Hedl, 1973). As previously discussed, the difficult computer-assisted-instruction program yielded results similar to the various testing situations. High state-anxiety levels were found in a computer-based intelligence-testing situation (Hedl, 1973), as expected.

It would appear that the state-anxiety data in this study were generally consistent with other findings. These findings suggest that state anxiety is not eliminated in computer-managed-instruction testing situations.

SUMMARY AND DISCUSSION

In this chapter, the effects of several instructional variables on state anxiety were reviewed.

Behavioral objectives. The four studies reviewed concerning the presence of behavioral objectives indicated that, in general, they neither facilitated achievement nor reduced state anxiety. These results are contrary to popular belief among some modern-curriculum writers. Their importance may be more paramount in guiding the overall curriculum development and program-evaluation process.

Response modes. Another feature of modern curriculum design is the provision for active responding by the student with appropriate and immediate feedback. Eliciting frequent responses with immediate confirmation is generally viewed as a condition of optimal instructional methodology. It should be noted that McKeachie (1974) offers contrary evidence. The results of the four studies reviewed indicated that constructed responding with feedback led to higher levels of state anxiety in comparison to a reading condition within computer-assisted instruction. In fact, as may be noted in Table 9.2, the mean state-anxiety scores within the computer learning task were approximately 10. According to the state–trait-anxiety inventory norms (Spielberger *et al.,* 1970), these data match the expected level of state anxiety in a difficult examination. Apparently the requirement of active responding served as a stressor. An interesting question for future research is whether or not students can be taught to view constructed responding with feedback during the learning process in a more positive, constructive manner.

Learner control. The effects of learner control on state anxiety in both computer-assisted and computer-managed instruction were examined in a series of four studies. The results were mixed, but generally favored the use of learner control in certain situations. Given a treatment that facilitates performance and lowers state anxiety, learner control of these features cannot be expected to produce better performance or lower anxiety than continuous presence of the treatment. The only advantages of learner control in this instance would be in reduced learning time.

Two other studies (Gallagher *et al.,* 1971; Hansen, 1974) suggested that in the absence of a specific facilitating treatment, the use of learner control may enable the student to engage individual learning strategies and coping mechanisms that may serve to reduce levels of state anxiety. It would appear that learner control of instruction in the affective domain is a viable strategy since it does not result in adverse performance outcomes and does sometimes result in lower levels of state anxiety.

Computer testing. Several studies were reviewed concerning the effects of interactive computer testing in comparison to traditional testing on state anxiety. These studies indicated that interactive computer testing did not reduce state anxiety; to the contrary, in some cases it appeared to serve as a stressor. The viability of interactive computer testing may not lie in the affective domain but in those situations where on-line scoring and interpretation are advantageous.

Computer-Managed Instruction

The final section of the chapter described two studies that used state anxiety as an index of affective value in the evaluation of computer-managed instruction curriculum. The state-anxiety levels were high in the computer-managed-instruction setting, reflecting a stressful situation. All of these state anxiety measures were collected in the testing environment, however. Research needs to be done concerning the levels of state anxiety during off-line studying.

Viewed collectively, these studies suggest that state anxiety is operative and related to trait anxiety in these computer-based instructional settings. While evaluations of various computer-based instructional systems may indicate that, in general, performance levels are more than satisfactory, it would appear that a number of individuals are still stressed and therefore indicate elevated levels of state anxiety. The variables reviewed in this chapter would lead one to speculate that little progress will result if state anxiety reduction depends solely on instructional procedures.

In terms of instructional systems development, perhaps the most appropriate strategy would be to develop and refine the curricula to a point where it generally yields good performance and reasonable levels of state anxiety for most students. Then treatment programs such as the one described in the next chapter could be employed to help the high-trait-anxious individuals.

10
Development and Evaluation of an Automated Test-Anxiety-Reduction Program for a Computer-Based Learning Environment

The purpose of the research summarized in this chapter was to develop and test the effectiveness of an automated program for the reduction of test-taking anxiety in a computer-based learning environment. This program is automated in the sense that, unlike such commonly used test-anxiety treatment methods as behavior therapy (such as systematic desensitization) or study counseling, the student may complete the program independently with no contact with a counselor or therapist. Rather, the student reads a special type of manual on coping with test anxiety, observes certain videotapes, and practices anxiety-management techniques in a computer-guided practice test-taking session. The program was designed to provide, when validated, a regularly available service for high-test-anxious students in computer-based instruction.

While interested in developing a program of this specific type, the authors had a broader interest and purpose in undertaking this research. A number of prominent writers in the fields of psychotherapy and behavior modification have stressed that certain straightforward, relatively prosaic social learning processes are an overlooked but perhaps basic ingredient in most behavior-change procedures. These processes include such things as provision of new information about behavior and the environment (Lazarus, 1971; Murray & Jacobson, 1971); the direct learning of new and more effective interpersonal and self-management skills (Goldfried, 1971; Wallace, 1966); and the acquisition of general problem-solving attitudes and skills to be applied to emotional and behavioral concerns or problems in living (D'Zurilla & Goldfried, 1973; Urban & Ford, 1971).

This perspective on behavior change suggests that some of these informational and skill-learning processes could be disembedded from their traditional therapy context and made available to persons in other ways, including through such media as written information (Ellis & Harper, 1961); exposure to symbolic (filmed or videotaped) models (Bandura, 1969); and self-directed behavior-change programs applying social learning principles to behavioral concerns (Watson & Tharp, 1972). Informational- and skill-learning programs utilizing such media might effectively supplement or, in some cases, even replace traditional treatment procedures.

THE CONSTRUCT OF TEST ANXIETY

The construct of test anxiety was originated by Mandler and Sarason (1952). Sarason and Mandler held that test anxiety was a learned "drive" which results in responses which related to task completion, thereby reducing anxiety; and in responses which interfere with task completion. These latter responses include "feelings of inadequacy, helplessness, heightened somatic reaction, anticipations of punishment, or loss of status and esteem, and attempts at leaving the test situation" (Mandler & Sarason, 1952, p. 166).

However, in an article on test anxiety on the twentieth anniversary of the original study, Sarason (1972) stressed the need to direct attention to the development of therapeutic approaches to test anxiety, hopefully combining "the best features of extant behavior influence methods" (p. 399) in programs designed to alleviate it. In this review, Sarason (1972) also partially revised test anxiety theory, choosing no longer to discuss test anxiety in terms of "motivational levels and level of situationally-induced drive" (p. 387), and recast test anxiety theory in more simple and direct terms relating to attention and the uses of information or cues:

> ... what distinguishes the high test-anxious individual are (1) the manner in which he attends to the events of his environment and (2) how he interprets and utilizes the information provided by these events. These characteristics may be viewed as habits or acquired attributes whose strength is influenced by specific types of person–environment encounters. (p. 382)

THE NATURE AND TREATMENT OF TEST ANXIETY

The literature concerned with the nature and remediation of test anxiety tends to fall into two broad streams or traditions, the first dealing with test anxiety as a personality variable, the second focusing on behavior therapy treatment procedures for alleviating the problem. In very recent years, these two traditions have been drawn together and allowed to cross-fertilize one another, leading to enriched perspectives on the nature of test anxiety and improved techniques for dealing with it. This automated treatment program draws heavily on these new perspectives and techniques.

Recent research has clarified the manner in which anxious individuals approach evaluative tasks, and the nature of the interfering responses that appear to lower their performance. It appears that test-anxious persons generally are very responsive to social influences of all sorts, including modeling cues, persuasion, and conformity pressures (Sarason, Pederson, & Nyman, 1968; Wine, 1971a). Also, it has been demonstrated that high- as compared with low-test-anxious individuals have pronounced self-deprecatory, self-ruminative tendencies, that is, they engage in self-oriented thinking and describe themselves in negative terms, in evaluation situations (Sarason & Ganzer, 1962; Sarason & Koenig, 1965).

Investigation of this central feature of test anxiety has been carried on by Liebert and Morris (1967), who distinguished between "worry" (fearful, self-critical thinking) and "emotionality" (reported autonomic arousal) components of test anxiety and developed to ten-item worry–emotionality scale to measure these separate components. Several subsequent studies have indicated that "worry" shows a higher and more consistent negative correlation with task performance and performance expectancy than does "emotionality" (Doctor & Altman, 1969; Morris & Liebert, 1969, 1970; Spiegler, Morris, & Liebert, 1968).

TREATMENT OF TEST ANXIETY

Systematic Desensitization

Reviews by Chestnut (1965) and Allen (1972) present evidence that conventional group-counseling procedures or study-skills training procedures do not facilitate improved academic performance in test-anxious students. In contrast, beginning with a case-study report by Paul and Eriksen (1964) numerous studies have shown that systematic desensitization, devised and introduced by Joseph Wolpe (1958), can be effective in the treatment of test anxiety and improvement of academic performance. Paul (1969) and Allen (1972) review most of the over 20 controlled studies that have appeared since 1964 showing desensitization to be effective in reducing test anxiety (a few well-designed studies with negative results, however, should be noted; e.g., Lomont & Sherman, 1971). Many college and university counseling centers now offer student desensitization programs for test anxiety.

Research has demonstrated that systematic desensitization therapy (Wolpe, 1958, 1969) can reliably produce measurable benefits for clients with a wide range of emotional and behavioral problems in which anxiety plays a fundamental role (Paul, 1969). In desensitization therapy the client is trained in a deep-muscle-relaxation procedure (Jacobson, 1938) and then instructed to visualize, while relaxed, an ordered series of increasingly stressful scenes, called an anxiety hierarchy. Proceeding gradually through imagination up the hierarchy, the client, in the scenes, comes into progressively closer or more intense contact with the feared situation or stimulus. Following successful treatment, the client is able to approach the previously feared situation with little or no anxiety.

Wolpe (1958, 1969) and what might be called the "classical" behavior-therapy tradition view situation-specific anxiety reactions or "phobias," like test anxiety, as reflexive-conditioned emotional responses. These are usually viewed as brought on by a "traumatic" conditioning process in which a previously neutral event or stimulus (like tests) is paired with some unconditioned aversive stimulus (like punishment or humiliation) until the formerly neutral stimulus comes to elicit strong anxiety and leads to avoidance behavior. Generally, systematic desensitization has been viewed as a procedure that "counterconditions" this conditioned anxiety response.

In Wolpe's (1958) original formulation of systematic desensitization, counterconditioning effects are explained in terms of "reciprocal inhibition," that is, in terms of mutually incompatible processes occurring at the level of the autonomic nervous system. It is assumed that muscular relaxation and other responses used to counter anxiety elicit parasympathetic responsiveness which is physiologically antagonistic to and tends to inhibit the sympathetic responsiveness of anxiety. In desensitization therapy, relaxation of a response antagonistic to anxiety is made to occur in the presence of an imaginal representation of the anxiety-evoking stimuli; gradual presentation of these stimuli permits a suppression and eventual deconditioning of the anxiety response.

While continued research has established the effectiveness of desensitization as a specific, replicable treatment procedure for many anxiety problems, including test anxiety, it has not supported Wolpe's (1958) account of the mechanisms of fear reduction. Bandura (1969) and Lang (1969) summarize studies showing that anxiety cannot be identified with peripheral physiological states. It now appears doubtful that the effects of desensitization can be explained by a single principle such as counterconditioning. Expectancy of therapeutic gain and the therapist as a reinforcer of nonfear behavior may play a role in desensitization.

More recent research and theoretical speculation have focused on cognitive variables in desensitization. For example, Wilkins (1971) argues that information feedback and "instructed imagination" appear to play a central role in desensitization. He points out that desensitization subjects are given direct training in shifting their attention in a controlled manner toward and away from the threatening situation, a skill which may play a central role in coping with anxiety in real-life situations. Consistent with this, Bandura (1971) argues for a "self-arousal interpretation of conditioning" according to which fear in humans is not an automatic or reflexive emotional response to an external stimulus, but a state of emotional arousal that is cognitively self-generated by means of panicky thoughts and images by the person in the feared situation. Thus, behavior therapists are beginning to discuss anxiety and its treatment in terms that are similar to I. Sarason's (1972) attentional analysis of test anxiety. In fact, there is a close parallel between what Sarason calls "personalized, self-oriented thinking" and cognitively self-generated thoughts and images as discussed by Bandura (1971).

Many of the studies investigating the controlling variables in desensitization have shown as a by-product that the treatment procedure is a robust process not adversely affected by minor alterations in procedural details (Lang, 1969). Recently, some researchers have turned their attention directly to developing briefer, more economical forms of desensitization treatment. For example, the time required for treatment has been shortened or the ease of its administration increased through such developments as group treatment (Paul & Shannon, 1966; Suinn & Hall, 1970), the use of standardized rather than individualized hierarchies for common problems such as test and mathematics anxiety (Emery & Krumboltz, 1967; Richardson & Suinn, 1973), and accelerated treatment using only the top portion or most stressful scenes from the customary anxiety hierarchy (Richardson & Suinn, 1973; Suinn, Edie, & Spinelli, 1970). Several studies (Hall, 1970; Mann, 1972; Mann & Rosenthal, 1969; Richardson & Hall, 1974) have investigated a vicarious desensitization procedure in which clients merely observe the live or videotaped desensitization treatment of other clients, finding that this procedure may also be effective in the treatment of test anxiety.

All of these innovations create the possibility of more or less automated treatment procedures. Several studies have explored the use of audio- or video-taped recordings to conduct desensitizationlike treatments (Donner & Guerney, 1969; Suinn & Hall, 1970; Suinn & Richardson, 1971), with no apparent loss in effectiveness. A number of major university counseling centers offer students partially automated desensitization programs for test anxiety. These are usually group desensitization programs in which initial relaxation training and anxiety-hierarchy scenes are presented by audio or videotape recordings.

Cognitive Approaches

Several new approaches to the treatment of test anxiety have been developed. Wine (1971a) contends that the primary problem of the test-anxious person is the habitual withdrawal of attention from variables and activities relevant to performing on the *task* or test, and the focus of attention instead on oneself, on worried thoughts about competence, ability, or performance as compared with other students, or the consequences of doing poorly at the task. Wine stresses that this attentional view of test anxiety is concerned with how the individual uses or directs cognitive activity, divides attention between task and self, and has little concern with emotional or autonomic arousal per se.

In addition, Wine (1971a, b) has devised an "attentional training procedure that aims directly at modifying these variables." Students who receive this attentional training are given a rationale for the treatment that stresses that test-anxious individuals waste much of their time in self-evaluative worry. Then they are exposed to two brief videotapes which show two college-student models (5 minutes each) focusing their attention on themselves in an evaluative manner in a laboratory-learning and an oral-examination situation, making irrelevant comments and not paying attention to many task-relevant variables. They also view two other models (5 minutes each) who focus their attention on the task and work in a businesslike manner in similar testing situations. Finally, students are given intensive practice on a variety of testlike tasks with instructions and training to inhibit self-relevant thinking and focus attention on the task at hand. Results show that this program was highly effective in reducing self-report of anxiety and improving performance on several testlike behavioral measures.

Meichenbaum (1972) has devised a "cognitive modification" program for the reduction of test anxiety that is somewhat similar to Wine's 1971b attentional training, but undertakes to modify more systematically some of the cognitive variables thought to mediate effective test-taking behaviors. In the first phase of this cognitive modification program students undergo an "insight" therapy procedure in which they are made aware of the specific self-oriented, task-irrelevant, worried thoughts they characteristically emit in the testing situation. Then they generate alternative, incompatible "self-instructions" or "self-talk" which have the opposite effect of avoiding worry and directing attention to the task. In the second phase of treatment, students go through a brief, modified desensitization procedure in which they visualize themselves actively coping with test anxiety in a graded series of test-taking scenes. Instead of the conventional desensitization procedure of visualizing oneself perfectly calm and relaxed in the fear situation, this part of the cognitive modification treatment employs what Meichenbaum calls "coping imagery" in which the student visualizes beginning to get a little anxious but then coping successfully with anxiety by means of slow deep breaths and appropriate self-instructions and self-talk. Results showed that this cognitive modification-treatment program was significantly more successful in reducing test anxiety, as assessed by several self-report and performance measures, than a conventional systematic desensitization treatment procedure of the same length.

In Wine's (1971a, 1971b) attentional training and Meichenbaum's (1972) cognitive-modification program the two mainstreams of test-anxiety research outlined here merge, resulting in powerful new approaches for the alleviation of test anxiety. Meichenbaum (1972) explicitly adopts Sarason's (1972) and Wine's (1971a, b) interpretation of test anxiety as self-oriented thinking and inattention to the task, and argues that his cognitive modification program is simply the application of conventional behavior modification principles (modeling, reinforcement, etc.) to the phenomenon of private speech, which appears to be crucial to test anxiety. It should be noted that in spite of the comment of Wine (1971b) quoted previously, to the effect that systematic desensitization focuses on the modification of emotional rather than cognitive factors in test anxiety, current reinterpretations of desensitization within behavior-therapy circles (Bandura, 1971; Lang, 1969; Wilkins, 1971) stress the importance of cognitive variables in the desensitization process. It may be that systematic desensitization has provided clients with bits and pieces of what amounts to relaxation, attentional training, cognitive restructuring, and other effects. One task at hand for applied researchers appears to be to separate these several treatment or training processes and provide them in more concentrated and systematic doses, depending on the behavioral deficit or problem clients present.

DEVELOPMENT OF THE AUTOMATED PROGRAM

Several studies have investigated the measurement and reduction of debilitating state anxiety in a computer-assisted-instruction context (see Chapter 9). The results of these studies indicate that high anxiety often interferes with performance on tests in a computer-based learning situation, but discourage the belief that available modifications in instructional design or the manner of presentation of test material will substantially reduce test anxiety, especially in that sizeable minority of highly test-anxious individuals who appear in any student population.

In order to devise an automated test-anxiety-reduction program and literature on test anxiety and its treatment was surveyed for techniques or approaches that might be incorporated into or modified for such an automated program format. In addition, some new approaches were developed. These various techniques were then incorporated into a program, the principal components of which are described here.

Manual and Written Information

In this program each student reads and completes some written exercises in a special manual on coping with test anxiety written for the program. The entire text of this 75-page manual is available in a separate technical report (Richardson, 1973). A number of prominent writers in the fields of psychotherapy and behavior modification have stressed that the straightforward provision of new information about behavior and the environment may be an overlooked but perhaps basic ingredient in most behavior change procedures (Lazarus, 1971; Murray & Jacobson, 1971; Sarason, 1972; Urban & Ford, 1971), one that could profitably be expanded and utilized in a more systematic manner (Sarason, 1972).

Students who receive a test-anxiety treatment are usually treated in a manner based on some reasonably well-developed theory about test anxiety and its alleviation. However, they are usually not systematically provided with the full extent of available information about the behavioral and emotional dynamics of test anxiety and techniques for coping with it. Yet, in many cases, simply the provision of new and useful information about these matters and the increased awareness regarding their own functioning it triggers may enable students to modify their test-anxious behavior. Also, conveying this information in a permanent written form may be not only an economical means of communication, but an effective way of making this information available as a continuing resource to students. The manual developed for this program is an attempt to present comprehensive information about test anxiety and coping with it to anxious students in a manner most likely to assist them in implementing new behavioral strategies in the testing situation.

The manual is divided into three parts. The first part describes, in text and diagrams, the process whereby new information (such as directing attention to the task instead of to oneself during tests lowers anxiety) may lead to new coping solutions for behavioral problems, and stresses that intelligent adults are often able to utilize new, accurate information in this manner without the intervention of a professional helper. A brief section then presents some guidelines for the readers in the use of the manual. Students are encouraged to use imagination and fantasy in reading the material, to relate the material to their personal experiences, and to complete the written portions of the manual which will aid them in working the new information into their behavioral functioning. This section simply restates in nontechnical terms the rationale and expectations for the manual as a treatment device. Several sample "case histories" of test anxiety in college students are recounted, giving an idea of the range of background events and symptoms commonly found in test-anxious students. Then the reader completes a test-anxiety checklist containing a comprehensive list of symptoms of test anxiety in order to become acquainted in detail with the manner in which high anxiety manifests itself in his or her behavior and thinking on tests.

This part of the manual concludes with a relatively lengthy discussion of some different sources of test anxiety. It is claimed that high and debilitating anxiety on tests may usually be ascribed to: (1) lack of ability or preparation; (2) lack of motivation or interest; (3) a reflection of other emotional or behavioral concerns; or (4) test anxiety. Test anxiety is defined as both a kind of automatic, habitual reaction of anxiety to tests that is difficult to control, and something the individual actively does to oneself in terms of self-oriented panicky thinking and fantasizing that generates high anxiety. Detailed examples of lack of preparation, lack of motivation, and the intrusion of other concerns are given; for example, the student who is pursuing a major chosen by his or her parents is resentful, has difficulty studying, and then gets anxious on tests. The solution in this case is to become aware of one's own wishes and resolve the conflict with one's parents, not treatment for test anxiety.

The purpose of this section is to provide a self-screening procedure so that individuals for whom the program is not appropriate may deselect themselves from it. The assumption is made that in most cases students are capable of deciding for themselves whether or not the program is appropriate. They are asked to make some written notes on the extent to which these various factors play a role in their test anxiety, and to decide whether any of the factors besides test anxiety play the predominant part in their difficulties with tests. If this is the case, they are told, they may wish to consult with a faculty member or professional counselor about the matter.

The second part of the manual provides detailed information about the behavioral and emotional dynamics of test anxiety, and about a number of strategies for coping with it. First, there is a discussion of anxiety on tests that makes the point that while there is good reason to be somewhat anxious about tests, especially in this society which places a great deal of pressure on its members to compete and succeed at school and work, there is *no* good reason for the capable and prepared student to panic or "freeze up" on tests. It is asserted that the only difficulty for such students is to cope adequately with the anxiety that is ubiquitous and quite normal on tests.

Techniques for coping with test anxiety are discussed under four headings: (1) emotional state; (2) the direction of attention away from the self and to the test; (3) eliminating anxiety-arousing self-talk; and (4) the overall management of preparation, time, and pressures before and during tests. A relaxation technique of slow deep breathing and procedures for practicing it are outlined for dealing with physical tension and emotional arousal. The difference between self-oriented and task-oriented thinking on tests is discussed in detail and parallels in other behavioral spheres (such as social anxiety) are described. A number of illustrations of the process of task-oriented thinking on tests are given, such as using task-relevant fantasy and a kind of free association to assist recall, and stopping the process of reflection when a "best answer" is first determined on a multiple-choice-type test, avoiding further fruitless rumination. The manner in which self-oriented thinking usually enters the process is illustrated for the reader.

In the section on self-talk, a number of examples of panicky self-instructions and self-talk (collected for this research from students' written records of their ruminations during tests) are provided for the reader, as well as a representative list of examples of appropriate self-talk that tends to focus attention on the test rather than oneself. In the section on overall management of time and preparation several general considerations regarding behaving in a manner that fosters a sense of control over the preparation and completion of tests are discussed. It is stressed that behaving as if one felt calm and confident about tests often brings anxious feelings into line.

The third and final part of the manual contains a series of written exercises in which the student outlines behavioral strategies for coping with test anxiety. For example, the student generates a list of instances of panicky self-talk in his or her own case, and then develops a list of alternative, incompatible self-statements that might be used to counter anxiety and foster task-relevant thinking and behavior. The student is also asked to follow certain guidelines (including review of previous written material) in devising several realistic strategies for fostering a sense of control and maintaining attention to the test in his own individual case.

Symbolic Modeling

A second component of the automated program exposes students to a videotape presentation of a student modeling effective and ineffective management of anxiety on tests. The videotape presentation is composed of the following segments:

1. A therapist briefly describes (5 minutes) how panicky self-talk and inattention to the test or task interfere with smooth performance on tests for highly anxious students.

2. In order to familiarize the viewer with the exact nature of the task dealt with by the model, thereby increasing its meaning and informational value (Sarason *et al.*, 1967), the tape (5 minutes) displays instructions for operating a computer terminal and some of the intelligence test questions to be read and responded to by the model in the following segments, as they appear on the cathode-ray tube of a terminal in a computer learning situation.

3. The model (10 minutes) approaches the terminal to take a computer-based intelligence test, reads the instructions, and answers some test questions, exhibiting panicky self-talk (spoken out loud by the model), difficulty in attending to the task, worry about self and performance, and rising anxiety, eventually "freezing up" on the test.

4. The model (10 minutes) repeats the same sequence of approach—reading instructions and answering questions—but this time exhibits appropriate self-instructions and self-talk that facilitate focusing attention on the task and dealing with difficult questions; copes with anxiety and tension on 2 occasions taking several slow deep breaths, and generally proceeds in a task-oriented and business-like manner, leading to positive results and satisfaction.

Modified Desensitization Procedure

A third component of the program consists of a modified desensitization procedure along the lines of Meichenbaum's (1972) cognitive-modification treatment for test anxiety. Students are given a half-hour of deep-muscle-relaxation instructions administered by a therapist on videotape and are encouraged to practice the exercises at home. At a later date they are instructed by videotape to visualize themselves coping with mild anxiety in a graded series of test-taking scenes by slow deep breaths and the use of appropriate self-instructions to relax and pay attention to the test.

Practice Test Taking

In the fourth and final component of the program students practice responding to testlike questions at a computer terminal. Instructions presented on the cathode-ray tube remind them at the beginning of the task of the slow deep-breathing technique for combating physical tension and anxiety, and of the importance of paying attention to the test and avoiding self-oriented worry. They are encouraged to practice these anxiety management techniques while answering the questions. They are told that the questions come from a com-puterized intelligence test, but that their answers will not be scored. In a practice test-taking session, lasting about 45 minutes for most students, they are given about half of the items, ordered from easy to hard, from the computer-based Slosson intelligence test (Hedl, 1971), which has been found to elicit high levels of state anxiety in most students (Hedl, O'Neil, & Hansen, 1973).

EVALUATION OF THE AUTOMATED PROGRAM

Three studies over a period of two years were undertaken to investigate the effectiveness of the automated test-anxiety-reduction program. A preliminary study found very promising results in terms of reducing self-reported test anxiety, with some indications of improved performance on module tests for treated students. A second, larger-scale study found only very weak treatment effects for students who completed the program as compared with a control group that did not. However, it appeared that certain aspects of the procedure in this study may have led students to feel depersonalized and thus may have reduced the effectiveness of the program. Steps were taken in a third study to personalize the procedure of completing the program without altering the content of the automated program itself. The results of this study showed very substantial treatment effects, similar to the results of the first study.

Study 1

Subjects and learning materials. A preliminary study (Richardson, O'Neil, Grant, & Judd, 1973), investigating the effectiveness of the program, was undertaken during the fall semester of 1972. All students in the study were undergraduate education majors at The University of Texas at Austin taking a required introductory course in educational psychology. Part of this course consisted of five instructional modules managed by a computer and discussed in Chapter 11. All students completed the test-anxiety scale (Sarason, 1972) at the beginning of the module sequence and the subjects were selected from 200 students because their scores fell in the upper 15% of scores recorded for the normative group who had completed the module sequence a month earlier.

Twelve students from a list of high test-anxiety scale scorers were contacted by phone and asked if they would like to participate in the treatment program. Eight students (four male and four female) agreed to participate and completed the program. These students received no course credit for participation in the research but were each paid $6 for taking part in the study, which took 6–9 hours of their time during a single week. A no-contact control group was formed by selecting eight other high-test-anxiety-scale scorers who had completed the test-anxiety scale "for research purposes."

These students completed the instructional modules in the following order: (1) computers in education; (2) statistics in the classroom; (3) tests and measurement; (4) classroom management; and (5) cultural differences. A formative evaluation of this computer-managed course demonstrated that 90% of the students reached the criterion of 75% on the first modules and approximately 80% met criterion on the fifth module (Judd, O'Neil, Rogers, & Richardson, 1972).

Instruments. Two measures of general test anxiety were utilized in this study: the test-anxiety scale (Sarason, 1972) and the Suinn Test-Anxiety Behavior Scale (Suinn, 1969). The Suinn Test-Anxiety Behavior Scale (STABS) is a 50-item scale designed to identify and measure changes in test anxiety following treatment. Each item is a brief description of some event or situation relating to test taking that may evoke anxiety. Students are asked to respond to each item in terms of how much anxiety that event or situation causes them to feel, on a scale from 1 (not at all) to 5 (very much).

Both of these instruments have very adequate test–retest reliability, are supported by a variety of validity data, are positively correlated with one another, and have been used as pretest–posttest measures of test anxiety in a number of studies investigating the effectiveness of behavior therapy, chiefly systematic desensitization, for test anxiety. Information about the scales is summarized in detail in Richardson, O'Neil, Grant, and Judd (1973) and Grant (1973).

This study also utilized the short form of the state-anxiety scale of the state–trait-anxiety inventory (Spielberger, Gorsuch, & Lushene, 1970). It is designed to measure momentary feelings of anxiety or state anxiety, as opposed to trait anxiety or a general behavioral disposition to perceive a wide range of objectively nondangerous circumstances as threatening (Spielberger, 1966a). More information about these scales is given in Chapter 8.

In addition to these self-report measures, performance scores on module tests and the number of retests for students were examined for evidence of improved performance as a result of the automated program.

Testing procedure. The test-anxiety scale was completed by all students at the beginning of the module sequence, along with the rest of the 200 students enrolled in five sections of the introductory educational psychology course. At the end of four weeks of computer-managed instruction (treatment occurred during the second week of this period), following completion of the fourth module test, all students completed the test-anxiety scale for the second time.

The Suinn Test Anxiety Behavior Scale was completed by the treatment subjects only immediately before the first of three scheduled treatment sessions and immediately after the last of these sessions, at intervals varying from three to five days. The state anxiety measure was completed by students immediately after each module test and retest (before performance feedback). The items, like the module test questions, were administered by the computer and presented to students on the terminal's cathode-ray tube display.

Treatment procedure. During the first week of the computer-managed instruction period, a psychologist doctorate phoned the 12 high-test-anxiety-scoring students and invited them to participate in the test-anxiety-reduction program. He presented himself as a psychologist doing research on a test-anxiety program that was in some respects experimental, but contained a variety of procedures found effective in reducing test anxiety. Students were told that they would be interviewed by this psychologist after the treatment program was completed to glean their suggestions for its improvement. The nine students who volunteered (one of these dropped out before the treatment began) were immediately scheduled for three separate, individual treatment sessions in a sound-deadened treatment room, containing a videotape playback unit and monitor, a chaise lounge, and a computer terminal. For each student, the sessions were scheduled for the following week on separate days of that week at hours arranged, so far as possible, to the student's convenience. Finally, each student was asked to stop by the Computer-Assisted Instruction Laboratory and pick up a copy of the manual before the weekend.

The treatment procedure for each student (outlined on an explanatory sheet accompanying the manual) consisted of five parts: (1) reading the first two parts of the manual over the weekend; (2) attending the first scheduled session, consisting of watching a 1-hour videotape; the first half-hour the modeling sequence, and the second half-hour deep muscle and slow deep breathing relaxation instructions; (3) reading the third part of the manual and completing the written exercises it contained; (4) attending the second scheduled session, consisting of viewing a second 1-hour videotape presenting the modified desensitization component of the program; (5) attending the last scheduled session of the program, the practice test-taking session at the computer terminal.

A secretary on duty during that week at a desk just outside the treatment room checked students in and out, rewound the videotapes after each session using a tape, and showed students how to sign on at the terminal for the practice test-taking session. The program took about 6–9 hours of each student's time. Only 3 hours of this time, however, utilized Computer-Assisted Instruction Laboratory facility and staff time.

During the week after treatment the psychologist who initially contacted students about the program conducted a 10–20 minute interview with each student concerning the reaction to the program and suggestions for improving it. Every effort was made not to offer any advice, counseling, or further treatment of any sort during these interviews, but the effects of the treatment program may be confounded with any beneficial effects of this interview.

All treatment students completed the test-anxiety-reduction program during the second week of the computer-managed instruction period. Students completed the first module test before the treatment program (one week) began and were working on the second, statistics, module during that week. Treatment students completed the test anxiety program before taking tests on the third, fourth, and fifth modules. Therefore, the performance and state anxiety scores on the first module can be considered pretest scores, while their scores on the last three modules were examined for possible treatment effects. The data from the second module were excluded from the analyses.

Results and discussion. In general, the results showed a highly significant reduction in self-reported anxiety for the treatment as compared with the no-contact control group of highly test-anxious students. There were also some slight indications of improved performance on the modules in the treatment group.

A one-way analysis of variance performed on the pretest test-anxiety-scale scores indicated that the two groups did not differ significantly in initial level of test anxiety. A one-way analysis of variance with repeated measures was performed on the treatment group's Suinn test-anxiety behavior-scale scores obtained immediately before and after treatment. The group's mean Suinn Test-Anxiety-Behavior Scale score before treatment was 155.88 (SD = 34.61), whereas after treatment it was 126.00 (SD = 43.44). The analysis indicated a marginally significant effect ($p = .06$).

In order to investigate pretest to posttest changes on the test-anxiety scale about 2 weeks after treatment, a 2 × 2 analysis of variance with repeated measures on the last factor was performed. The first factor consisted of the presence and absence of treatment for test anxiety, and the second factor of pretest and posttest administration of the measure. The means and standard deviations of test-anxiety-scale scores before and after the first four instructional modules for the two groups are presented in Table 10.1. The scores for the no-treatment control group remained relatively constant, while the scores for the treatment group sharply decreased from pretest to posttest. The analysis of variance indicated that this treatment × trials interaction was significant.

In order to investigate the impact of the test-anxiety-reduction program on state anxiety measured immediately after each module test, a 2 × 4 analysis of variance with repeated measures on the last factor was performed on the two groups' pretest state anxiety scores (following the first module test) and posttest (following the third, fourth, and fifth module tests) state-anxiety scores. The analysis indicated a significant groups × trials interaction. Although the treat-

TABLE 10.1
Means and Standard Deviations on the Test-Anxiety Scale
for Treatment and No-Treatment Control Students

	Pretest		Posttest	
	$\overline{X}$	SD	$\overline{X}$	SD
·Treatment	27.50	3.42	16.0	6.71
Control	25.88	1.46	24.25	4.03

ment group had initially higher levels of state anxiety following treatment their state anxiety decreased relative to the no-treatment control group.

A one-way analysis of variance was performed on each module test score (mean proportion correct) for the two groups. The analysis indicated no significant differences in performance between the two groups following treatment. There were, however, some slight indications of improved performance for the treatment group—mean test scores on the two module tests immediately following the program (Modules 3 and 4) were higher for this gorup.

The results show a striking reduction in general test anxiety and state anxiety for the treatment as compared with the no-treatment control students. The pretest to posttest reduction in Suinn test-anxiety behavior-scale scores for the treatment group indicated a moderate reduction in self-reported test anxiety immediately following treatment. Two weeks after treatment, however, a greater reduction in test-anxiety-scale scores for the treatment as compared with the control group was observed. The reduction compares very favorably with the results usually found in studies investigating the effects of behavior therapy for test anxiety. Test-anxiety-scale scores for 5 of the 8 treatment students were reduced by more than 50%, making the posttest scores slightly below the mean score for 330 students used as a norm group. Also, generally speaking, the data analysis indicated a significant decrease in state-anxiety scores for the treatment group on all tests following treatment, and an apparent increase in levels of state anxiety for the control-group students over the series of tests. No clear evidence for improvement in scores on module tests for the treatment group following treatment were observed.

In the interviews following treatment the students expressed, generally, very strong positive feelings about the program. All students found the manual interesting to read and felt it communicated useful information. All students but one felt that the descriptions of text anxiety in the manual and its portrayal on the modeling videotapes were very close to their experience. Several students spontaneously related recent encounters with difficult tests other than in the computer-managed instruction program in which they were able to put to work some of the anxiety reduction techniques. Students seemed very actively involved in trying to understand and apply the information and techniques conveyed to them. Suggestions for improvement of the program centered mainly on the final, practice test-taking session. Students indicated they would have liked more information about the purpose of the session than was provided, and more structured practice of relaxation and appropriate self-talk techniques during the session.

Study 2

The encouraging results of this preliminary study stimulated another investigation (Grant, 1973) to confirm these results with a larger sample of test-anxious students and to explore the effects of the program on test anxiety and performance in a more precise manner. The students, learning materials, and testing and treatment procedures for Study 2 were very similar to those of Study 1. Only the differences between the two studies are mentioned before summarizing and discussing the results of Study 2.

Subjects. Subjects for this study were 47 test-anxious students selected in the spring of 1973 from a pool of 225 students enrolled in the same introductory educational psychology course and completing the same sequence of five instructional modules managed by a computer as in the fall semester of 1972. High-test-anxiety-scale scorers (above 66%) in this group of students were contacted by phone by an advanced graduate student and invited to participate in the test-anxiety program being offered as a service to high-test-anxious students in the course. Students were accepted until treatment and waiting-list control groups of 26 students each, equally divided between males and females, were formed. (Five students failed to complete the program, leaving a treatment group of 24 and a control group of 23 students.) Students were not paid for their participation, but were given credit for a course requirement to participate in 4 hours of research. Students were told that several measures would be used to evaluate the effectiveness of the service program as a routine matter.

Several additional measures of general and state test-anxiety were employed in this study. The measures of general or trait test anxiety included: (1) the test-anxiety scale; (2) the achievement-anxiety test (Alpert & Haber, 1960), consisting of a ten-item debilitating-anxiety scale, which measures anxiety responses that are detrimental to test performance; and the nine-item facilitating-anxiety scale, which measures anxiety responses that are beneficial to test performance; (3) the inventory of test-anxiety (Osterhouse, 1972), consisting of an eight-item trait-worry scale that measures cognitive concern over test performance, and an eight-item trait-emotionality scale, which measures autonomic reactions to the stress of the testing situation; (4) the state-anxiety scale; and (5) the worry—emotionality scale (Liebert & Morris, 1967), consisting of five items measuring worry and five items measuring emotionality in specific testing situations. (The latter scale was administered with retrospective state instructions.)

Reliability and validity information on these measures are summarized else-where (Grant, 1973). Also, performance scores on modules were examined for evidence of improved performance as a result of treatment.

Procedure. The test-anxiety scale was completed by students at the beginning of the module sequence. The achievement-anxiety test and inventory of test-anxiety were completed by treatment and control students immediately after they volunteered to participate in the study, before treatment commenced. The three state affective measures (worry—emotionality and state-anxiety scale) were completed following each module test, before receiving feedback about performance. The test-anxiety scale, inventory of test anxiety, and achievement-anxiety test were completed again at posttesting by students immediately following the final, practice test-taking component of the program, at the same time, relatively, that the Suinn Test-Anxiety Behavior Scale was completed in Study 1. Waiting-list control group students completed these instruments for the second time at about the same time the treatment group took the posttests. At that time they were scheduled for treatment during the week following completion of the fourth module test. Immediately following this treatment they completed the instruments for a third time, posttesting for this group.

The treatment procedure was nearly identical to that followed in Study 1. Treatment group students were contacted during the first week of the computer-managed module sequence and treated during the second. No posttreatment interviews were conducted with either group of students in Study 2. As in Study 1, performance, state anxiety, and state worry and emotionality scores for Module 1 were considered pretest scores, while test scores and scores on these instruments for the last three modules were examined for possible treatment effects, with state anxiety and performance data from the second module excluded from the analysis.

Results and discussion. The results of Study 2 are somewhat ambiguous, but generally indicate that the test-anxiety-reduction program was at best marginally effective in reducing self-reported test anxiety among students treated, and did not improve these students' scores on module test following treatment.

Four measures of general or trait test anxiety were used in this study to assess levels of test anxiety before and after treatment for both groups: (1) the test-anxiety scale; (2) the debilitating-anxiety scale of the achievement-anxiety test; (3) the trait-worry scale; and (4) the trait-emotionality scale. The means and standard deviations for both groups of students on these measures over the three testing sessions are reported in Table 10.2. Values are missing in Table 10.2 for Testing Session 3 for treatment students because these students were not available for follow-up posttesting.

The possibility of a significant reduction in self-reported test anxiety in the treatment as compared with the control group was investigated in a series of four 2 X 2 X 2 factorial analyses of variance. Treatment condition (treatment or

TABLE 10.2
Means and Standard Deviations for Treatment and Waiting-List Control-Group Subjects
on Four Measures of General Test Anxiety over Three Testing Sessions

		Testing session 1	Testing session 2	Testing session 3
Test-anxiety-scale	Treatment	$\overline{X}$ = 25.17	$\overline{X}$ = 22.72	–
		SD = 4.10	SD = 6.91	–
	Control	$\overline{X}$ = 24.90	$\overline{X}$ = 23.59	$\overline{X}$ = 22.57
		SD = 3.47	SD = 4.73	SD = 5.96
Debilitating-anxiety scale	Treatment	$\overline{X}$ = 35.72	$\overline{X}$ = 32.08	–
		SD = 3.76	SD = 4.06	–
	Control	$\overline{X}$ = 33.60	$\overline{X}$ = 33.18	$\overline{X}$ = 31.80
		SD = 4.77	SD = 4.84	SD = 4.74
Trait-worry scale	Treatment	$\overline{X}$ = 26.95	$\overline{X}$ = 22.54	
		SD = 6.31	SD = 7.99	
	Control	$\overline{X}$ = 25.16	$\overline{X}$ = 24.00	$\overline{X}$ = 21.35
		SD = 6.22	SD = 7.24	SD = 6.65
Trait-emotionality scale	Treatment	$\overline{X}$ = 23.52	$\overline{X}$ = 19.23	
		SD = 6.10	SD = 6.88	
	Control	$\overline{X}$ = 21.01	$\overline{X}$ = 22.04	$\overline{X}$ = 19.57
		SD = 5.93	SD = 7.58	SD = 5.81

control group), sex, and testing session (first or second) were the independent variables in each analysis; scores on the 4 instruments, the dependent variables. The treatment condition X testing session interaction was not significant in the analysis of variance performed on test-anxiety-scale scores, indicating no improvement from pre- to postperiods for the treatment as compared with the control group on this instrument. The treatment X testing session interaction in the analysis performed on debilitating-anxiety-scale scores was marginally significant (p = .09). The treatment X testing session interaction in the analysis performed on trait-worry-scale scores was statistically significant as was the interaction for the trait-emotionality-scale scores. Thus, on 3 of 4 trait-test-anxiety measures there was some evidence of improvement on the part of the treatment group students.

Analyses of variance were performed on the three state affective measures (state-anxiety scale, state-worry scale, and state-emotionality scale). No significant reduction in state anxiety due to treatment for students in the treatment as compared with the control group was found. Likewise, analyses of variance on performance test scores of both treatment and control-group students indicated no significant differences. These data provide no evidence of improved performance following administration of this treatment program.

Any encouragement that might be taken from the results showing improvement on three of four trait-test-anxiety measures for the treatment group is largley squelched by the results of additional analyses performed to detect changes, if any, in the waiting-list control group's scores from the second testing (posttesting for the treatment group) to the third testing, following the test anxiety reduction treatment for the waiting-list control group. It may be observed from Table 10.2 that the mean scores for the control group on all four measures decline following treatment. However, a series of four 2 X 2 analyses of variance, with treatment condition and testing session (second or third) as the independent variables and scores on the four measures successively as the dependent variable, found no significant changes owing to the treatment program.

Looking only at the results of Study 2 one would conclude that the test-anxiety-reduction program was, at best, marginally effective in reducing self-reported test anxiety in these students. Treatment students showed slight improvement on three of four measures of self-reported test anxiety. The mean scores of waiting-list control-group students dropped more in absolute terms from the second to the third testing session (following treatment) than they did from the first to the second testing session (following the waiting period), as may be seen from Table 10.2. But none of these changes were statistically significant. The overall picture is one of very weak treatment effects, which contrasts sharply with the results of Study 1.

It is true that students in Study 2 scored in the upper one-third of a large sample of students completing the test-anxiety scale, while Study 1 students scored in the upper 15% of a similar sample. However, a nearly identical picture of weak treatment results was obtained when pretest to posttest changes on trait-test-anxiety and state-affective-scale scores were analyzed for Study 2 subjects whost test-anxiety-scale scores fell in the upper 15% of that sample.

Of 48 students 31 returned a completed feedback form which was mailed to them after treatment. Of the 31 students 23 stated definite positive feelings about the program, four were somewhat neutral, and four expressed mainly negative feelings. Most students indicated that the manual and modeling videotape were very relevant and helpful, and many indicated that they were able to use the techniques for coping with anxiety with definite success in testing situations. The main criticisms related to the lack of fidelity of the practice test-taking session to real life (the test was not scored and no feedback about performance was given) and to the impersonality of the program, which was commented on sharply by a number of students.

The sharply contrasting results of Studies 1 and 2 may, tentatively, be attributed to both differences in the testing and treatment procedures employed. First, it should be noted that students in Study 2 were posttested immediately following treatment. Most studies of this type administer posttests several days to a few weeks after the conclusion of treatment. This delay may give students time to process and integrate the information and techniques they have acquired. It also could provide them with the opportunity to have some "success" experiences with managing anxiety more effectively in study or test situations. It is often only after such experiences that students can report that they feel or behave less anxiously on such instruments as the test-anxiety scale. Later administration of the trait-test-anxiety measures in this study might have found a greater reduction in self-reported test anxiety.

Second, a cluster of differences between the overall treatment procedures employed in the two studies may have contributed to the different results. Although they seemed relatively minor or went unnoticed at the time Study 2 was planned, it now appears that they may have been the major factor in reducing the effectiveness of the test-anxiety program in this study. In Study 1 the students were contacted by a psychologist doctorate who invited participation in a combination treatment and research project in which he was personally interested. This same psychologist was identified on the manual as its author; he introduced the modeling videotape; and he conducted the relaxation and desensitization sessions (on videotape). He personally met and briefly interviewed students after they had completed treatment. Students were aware they were part of a small group of students completing the program at that time, and that they would meet the experimenter after its conclusion.

In Study 2, the students were contacted by a graduate student who identified himself as a counseling psychology graduate student working with the Computer-Assisted Instruction Laboratory, and may have been perceived as having less status and less lofty motives for conducting the program. He never met the students in person and, of course, did not appear on any of the videotapes. Students were generally aware they were part of a larger number of students completing the program at that time, and receiving course credit for taking part in the research. No posttreatment interview, which may have personalized the program and focused the students' thinking about its benefits and uses, was conducted in Study 2.

The program appears to have been more personalized in Study 1 in a number of respects. As a result students may have developed a heightened sense of involvement in the program and greater expectations of gain from it. Most importantly, they may have put more time, effort, and thought into their participation in the various components of the program and subsequent attempts to apply it to study and test-taking situations.

If these speculations have any validity, they have implications not only for the development of a test-anxiety-reduction program of this type, but for the conduct and presentation of informational and skill-training programs in a wide variety of computer-based and other automated-learning situations, in both educational and mental-health settings. Few of these programs could be personalized in the same manner or to the same degree as was the test-anxiety program procedure in Study 1. And yet something of this nature may be required for substantial benefit to occur. In this connection it is interesting to note that a study by Morris and Suckerman (1974) found that two automated, audiotape-recorded desensitization programs, which differed only in that the therapist's voice in one condition was "warm and pleasant" and in the other was "cold and impersonal," produced quite different results. Subjects in the warm-therapist automated group improved significantly more than subjects in the cold-therapist group who did not show improvement as compared with no-treatment control group subjects.

Study 3

Study 3 was undertaken to confirm some of these speculations concerning the reasons for the divergent results of Study 1 and Study 2, and to investigate some feasible procedures for ensuring that participants in a program of this type do not feel depersonalized, but participate fully in the program, and achieve a higher level of benefit from treatment.

The students, learning materials, testing, and treatment procedures for this study were similar to those of Studies 1 and 2. Subjects for this study were 19 test-anxious students selected from a pool of 167 students enrolled in the fall of 1973 in the same introductory educational psychology course and completing a sequence of six instructional modules (the same five as previous with one added) managed by a computer.

Procedure.   Certain specific steps were taken to: (1) personalize the program and ensure full participation on the part of students taking it; and (2) utilize procedures to do this that were economical of professional time and could easily be carried out by paraprofessional-level personnel. A graduate student in educational psychology was assigned the task of contacting possible program participants and monitoring their progress through the program. Contact and activities with students fell into three categories: (1) making very brief face-to-face personal contact with each student before and after the program; (2) stressing the need to complete all parts of the program in the initial personal contact and informally contracting for full participation in return for the service program; and (3) being available to students during certain office hours during the course of the program for consultation about any problems that might arise.

The testing and treatment procedures for Study 3 are outlined in Figure 10.1 The test-anxiety scale was completed by 167 students before the beginning of the module sequence. Those whose scores fell above 82% for this group were contacted by phone by the graduate-student program monitor and invited to participate in what was billed as a regularly offered service program for high-test-anxious students in the computer-managed instruction course. Of 25 students contacted, 21 (4 males and 17 females) volunteered to participate. Students were randomly assigned, before being called, to either a treatment of a waiting-

	Week 1	Week 2	Week 3	Weeks 4–7	Week 8
Treatment Group	Phone contact. Initial interview with monitor. STABS 1 (pretest), Module test 1, SAS 1. Module Test 3,	Three treatment sessions. Module Test 2, SAS 2.	Check-out session with monitor, TAS and STABS 2 (immediate post-test). Module Test 3, SAS3.	Module Tests and SAS 4 and 5.	Module Test 6, SAS 6, TAS and STABS 3 (delayed posttest).
Waiting-List Control Group	Initial interview with monitor. STABS 1 (pretest), Module Test 1, SAS 1.	Module Test 2, SAS 2.	Module Test 3, SAS 3.	Module Tests, and SAS 4 and 5.	Module Test 6, SAS 6, TAS, and STABS 3 (posttest).

TAS 1 (pretest)

Three Treatment sessions.

FIG. 10.1 Testing and treatment procedures for Study 3.

TAS – test-anxiety scale
STABS – Suinn test-anxiety behavior scale
SAS – five-item state-anxiety scale

list control group. Students were told that their participation in the program did satisfy the course's 4-hour research requirement because of certain information they would be asked to provide about the program's usefulness to them, but the service nature of the program was emphasized and all students expressed sharp concern over test anxiety. At this time the program monitor made an appointment to meet briefly (for up to 15 minutes) with each volunteer during the next few days.

The monitor met with each student during the first three days of the first week of the 8-week module sequence. (Modules were completed at the rate of approximately one module per week, but during two weeks students were involved in other course activities.) Each student in the treatment group was greeted warmly and given a 1-page handout describing the program and a copy of the manual on coping with test anxiety. Any questions were answered following reading the handout, and each subject was signed up for three individual treatment sessions on separate days during the following week, the second week of the 6-week module sequence. The student was asked to read that night the first part of the manual, which contained information about different sources of anxiety on tests and some guidelines and procedures for self-screening with regard to the appropriateness of the program, and check back the next day if there were any questions. Students were told that most persons who wanted the program were appropriate for it, but that they should consider this issue carefully. The student was then informed that the monitor would keep regular office hours during the program and was encouraged to consult with the monitor if any problems or questions arose. It was mentioned that at the last treatment session students would be signing up for a final brief check-out session with the monitor and that they would be asked to bring their manuals to that session with completed checklists, exercises, and so on for anonymous perusal by the staff in order to consider possible ways of improving the manual, in return for which they would receive the 4-hours of research credit. Finally, it was stressed that in order to get the full benefit of the program it was usually necessary to complete carefully all parts of it and that signing up for the program meant agreeing to so complete it if at all possible. Each student then completed the Suinn Test Anxiety Behavior Scale.

Each waiting-list control-group student was given a copy of the handout describing the program, and any questions were answered. Then they were signed up for three individual sessions during the first week after the module sequence was completed, or in six weeks. They were told that they would be called a week before the program began for them and reminded about the sessions, and that at that time they would be asked to pick up a copy of the manual and begin the program. They also completed a copy of the Suinn Test Anxiety Behavior Scale before leaving.

The treatment procedure was nearly the same as that followed in Studies 1 and 2. The third, practice test-taking, treatment session was modified so that students were informed that they would be given feedback after the practice test concerning the number of questions they answered correctly, and actually were given this feedback, in order, hopefully, to make the practice test somewhat more realistic.

Before leaving the third and final session students signed up for a brief check-out interview with the monitor during the first few days of the following week. At this interview the monitor chatted briefly with the subjects about their experience with the program, answered any questions, collected the manuals (to be returned to students in a week), and asked students to fill out the test-anxiety scale and the Suinn Test-Anxiety Behavior Scale for a second time. Six weeks later, immediately following their last module test, all students were requested to complete the test-anxiety scale and the Suinn Test-Anxiety Behavior Scale again, the treatment group for the third time, the control group for the second time. The waiting-list control group then received treatment during the next week and at a check-out interview with the monitor during the week after that, following treatment, completed the test-anxiety scale and the Suinn test-anxiety behavior scale for the third time. As in the previous studies all students completed the five-item state-anxiety scale immediately following module tests, before receiving feedback about their performance on the test.

Results. The results of Study 3 indicate that the test-anxiety-reduction program was highly successful in reducing self-reported test anxiety in treatment as compared with control students. There were, also, some indications of improved performance on module tests for treatment-group students, although these results did not reach statistical significance.

The scores of one student in each group could not be utilized because of computer misrecordings of their responses during the first administration of the test-anxiety scale. Comparisons of the mean pretest test-anxiety scale and Suinn test-anxiety behavior scale scores for the two groups indicated no significant differences between the mean scores of the nine treatment and ten control students on these instruments before treatment.

Two 2 X 2 analyses of variance with repeated measures on the last factor were performed on the groups' test-anxiety scale and Suinn test-anxiety behavior-scale scores. Levels of the first factor were the presence and absence of treatment for test anxiety while levels of the second factor were pretest and posttest administration of the measures. Pretest measures were the initial test-anxiety scale and the Suinn Test Anxiety Behavior Scale completed at the first interview with the monitor. Posttest measures were the test-anxiety scale and Suinn Test Anxiety Behavior Scale completed six weeks after the treatment group received treatment. This constituted a second pretesting for the control group and a delayed or follow-up posttesting for the treatment group (which had also been posttested immediately after treatment). The means and standard deviations of these scores before and after treatment for the two groups are presented in Table 10.3. Values are missing for control students at the time of immediate posttesting of treatment students because the design excluded an

TABLE 10.3
Pretest, Immediate Posttest, and Follow-Up Means and Standard Deviations on the
Test-Anxiety Scale and Suinn Test-Anxiety Behavior Scale
for Treatment and Control Students

	Pretest		Immediate posttest		Follow-up	
	TAS[a]	STABS[b]	TAS	STABS	TAS	STABS
Treatment	$\bar{X}$ = 28.56	$\bar{X}$ = 150.22	$\bar{X}$ = 23.78	$\bar{X}$ = 123.78	$\bar{X}$ = 20.78	$\bar{X}$ = 116.00
	SD = 2.92	SD = 41.8	SD = 6.04	SD = 51.2	SD = 6.86	SD = 42.42
Control	$\bar{X}$ = 27.60	$\bar{X}$ = 177.70	–	–	$\bar{X}$ = 29.70	$\bar{X}$ = 182.70
	SD = 1.89	SD = 31.9	–	–	SD = 5.65	SD = 34.60

[a]Test-anxiety score.
[b]Suinn Test Anxiety Behavior Scale.

administration of the scales at this time to control students. As may be observed in Table 10.3, the mean test-anxiety scale and the Suinn Test Anxiety Behavior-Scale scores for the control group rise slightly, while the mean scores for the treatment group drop sharply from pretest to immediate posttest, and drop a small amount more from posttest to follow-up. The analysis indicated that these interactions were significant for the test-anxiety scale and for the Suinn Test-Anxiety Behavior Scale.

A *t* test for independent samples indicated no significant difference between the state-anxiety-scale mean scores for the two groups at the time of the first module test. Some subjects had completed parts of the test-anxiety program when they responded to the state-anxiety scale after the second module test, and these scores were not considered in the analysis. In order to determine the effects of the program on state anxiety measured immediately after the module tests, a 2 X 4 analysis of variance with repeated measures on the last factor was performed on the two groups' state-anxiety scores following the third, fourth, fifth, and sixth module tests, all obtained after the treatment group had completed the program. The means and standard deviations of the two groups' scores on this measure following the first and the third through sixth module tests are contained in Table 10.4. The analysis indicated a significant groups effect. The mean of the four posttreatment state-anxiety means for the treatment group was 12.06, for the control group 16.39. Thus, the treatment group state anxiety mean was lowered to a point just above the mean for all students completing the scale.

Performance scores (mean number of questions correct) for the two groups over the six modules were analyzed by means of separate one-way analyses of variance for each module. While none of the differences between groups on any module test was statistically significant, a trend was indicated. On the first

TABLE 10.4

State-Anxiety Means and Standard Deviations on Module Tests before
and after Treatment for Treatment and Control Students

	Pretreatment: Module test	Posttreatment: Module tests			
	1	3	4	5	6
Treatment	$\bar{X}$ = 14.89	$\bar{X}$ = 10.78	$\bar{X}$ = 11.22	$\bar{X}$ = 13.11	$\bar{X}$ = 13.11
	SD = 3.69	SD = 1.82	SD = 2.98	SD = 3.85	SD = 4.05
Control	$\bar{X}$ = 15.44	$\bar{X}$ = 15.22	$\bar{X}$ = 15.89	$\bar{X}$ = 18.22	$\bar{X}$ = 16.22
	SD = 3.02	SD = 3.10	SD = 2.79	SD = 2.28	SD = 3.59

module test, prior to treatment, the treatment group scored slightly lower than the control group. On the last four modules, however, following treatment, the treatment group scored higher on each test than did the waiting list control group.

DISCUSSION

The partially automated test-anxiety-reduction program proved highly successful in reducing self-reported test anxiety when steps were taken to ensure that clients did not feel depersonalized and when care was taken to obtain their active and full participation in the program. The program format utilized in Study 3 seemed feasible and economical, and one that could easily be used in other learning centers. Only a few hours of the paraprofessional program monitor's time was involved in meeting briefly with students before and after the program. A few students sought the monitor for consultation during the program but mostly for answers to questions about appointment times or procedures.

The results of Studies 1 and 3 compare favorably with the outcomes of behavior-therapy treatment programs for test anxiety reported in the literature. It is our opinion that Study 3 was successful because of the steps taken to personalize the program. However, the results of the three studies do not demonstrate conclusively that this is so. The procedure in Study 3 differs from that in Study 2 in two confounded respects. Study 3 both a more personalized program format and a delayed posttest administration of the general or trait test anxiety measures were employed, raising the possibility that a different testing procedure rather than the personalized format may have accounted for the more favorable results obtained in Study 3.

Study 3 subjects were first posttested several days after treatment, and posttested again after six weeks. As may be seen in Table 10.3, most of the drop in test-anxiety-scale and Suinn Test Anxiety Behavior Scale scores for these subjects occurred from pretest to the first posttest, with only a slight further decline from the first to the second posttest. However, in Study 2 subjects were posttested immediately after completing the final, practice test-taking component of the program and a second posttest was not given. In support of the notion that personalization of the program led to its success in Study 3, it should be noted that in Study 2 no reduction in state anxiety, measured immediately after the three module tests following treatment, was found for the treatment as compared with control subjects.

The results of Studies 1 and 3 provide no clear evidence for improvement in scores on module tests for the treatment groups. A number of factors need to be considered in interpreting these results and in planning for future research.

It appears that improvement in academic performance is much more likely to occur if behavior-therapy programs are accompanied by instruction in study-counseling techniques (Allen, 1972). High-test-anxious individuals typically engage in some of the same ineffective approaches to studying and preparing for tests as they do for taking tests. For example, they delay any systematic preparation for tests until the last moment and then anxiously cram (Wittmaier, 1972). Improvement in academic performance may not occur until study behavior as well as test-taking behavior is altered, or they may alter only slowly and gradually unless specifically addressed in the treatment program. The students in these studies received only a small amount of study counseling in the form of suggestions and illustrations in the manual on coping with test anxiety. In fact, a number of subjects commented that they found these suggestions helpful and wished there had been more of them.

Third, a common clinical observation by behavior therapists is that some students requesting treatment for test anxiety indicate that high anxiety seriously interferes with their performance on tests. However, other high test-anxious students report only slight interference with their performance on tests. A reduction of test anxiety in individuals of this sort is certainly a worthwhile outcome, and the results of the studies reviewed here indicated that this occurred for many participants.

IMPLICATIONS FOR FURTHER RESEARCH

It is recommended that further development of the test-anxiety-reduction program and research with it involve four major modifications in the program. First, a section should be added to the manual that will provide students with information and some planning and training exercises on improving their general study and specific test-taking skills. The study and test-taking information should focus on the type of learning materials and test utilized in the computer-managed instructional sequence.

Second, changes are recommended in the relaxation training and desensitization component of the program. Conventional relaxation training might appropriately be replaced by training, via written instructions and reading, in the use of relaxation and "positive self-talk" as active, anxiety-countering responses in actual study and test-taking situations (Goldfried, 1973).

Third, the practice test-taking component of the program, which now uses items from a general intelligence test, might better utilize multiple-choice items similar to the module tests used in the course. It is felt that such a test would make for a more realistic and effective practice session and better facilitate transfer to actual course exams.

Finally, the computerized test-taking procedure might be modified so that new learning about coping with test anxiety will more effectively transfer to the actual test-taking situation. Sarason (1972) has suggested that engineering certain aspects of the learning and test-taking situation to reduce debilitating anxiety may represent an alternative or perhaps a useful addition to treatment for test anxiety that takes place away from these situations.

Developing some of Sarason's suggestions concerning the use of programed experiences during actual performance in an evaluative situation, a revised program might include the presentation of pertinent instruction concerning relaxing and directing one's attention and thinking in a functional manner. Reminders about basic "test-wise" approaches to taking objective tests immediately before (and perhaps during) the presentation of test questions to the student at the computer terminal might also be utilized. The computer-based learning situation offers some unique opportunities for structuring learning and test-taking experiences in a manner designed to minimize the interference of anxiety.

Some other directions are suggested by the apparent success of this program. The program might, for example, be modified to apply broadly to most types of academic testing situations. The program in inexpensive and could be used to impart valuable knowledge and coping skills to an almost unlimited number of interested persons in the university population. Such a program might usefully be offered to incoming first-year university students. A preventative mental health effort of this type might be able to reach more individuals earlier than would be possible through existing campus counseling or student service programs. It is also possible that similar semiautomated program formats could be developed to increase students' coping skills and personal competence in a number of different areas of academic and social functioning.

11

State Anxiety and Performance in Computer-Based Learning Environments

The focus in this chapter is on the effects of state anxiety on the learning process in the context of computer-based learning environments. In this chapter, state anxiety is employed as an independent variable and its effects on performance are examined. The question asked here is: How does state anxiety affect the learning process? In contrast, in Chapter 9 state anxiety was employed as a dependent variable. The question asked in Chapter 9 was: Do instructional strategies affect state anxiety? Thus, in this chapter, we are not concerned with the variables which influenced the level of state anxiety in the situation; rather, we are concerned that, given that state anxiety is present, what are its effects on performance? Further, the studies reviewed in this chapter are, in most cases, originally designed to investigate the impact of various instructional treatments on state anxiety. The relationship of state anxiety to performance was of secondary interest. For this chapter, of course, these relationships are of primary interest.

Hypotheses about the effects of anxiety on learning were derived from drive theory. Spielberger's trait–state-anxiety theory provided a further specification of the construct of anxiety and a tool with which to measure this construct. These theories provided the conceptual framework within which the research to be reported was conceived.

DRIVE THEORY

Drive theory, as formulated by Spence and Spence (1966), attempts to integrate both associative and motivational variables that are operative in the learning process. The theory makes three major assumptions concerning the learning process:

1. Both correct and erroneous response tendencies are voked by a learning

task and that the latter continue to be elicited even as the correct response is being learned.

2. Drive theory posits that the strength of both the correct response and competing error tendencies are multiplied by drive.

3. Performance is jointly determined by level of drive and the relative strengths of correct and competing response tendencies.

Anxiety is equated with Hull's (1943) concept of drive and level of drive is usually inferred from scores on the Taylor manifest-anxiety scale. That is, it is assumed that individual differences in the Taylor manifest-anxiety-scale scores reflect differences in drive. (See Chapter 2 for further details on the relationship between drive theory and the measurement of anxiety.)

Drive theory predicts that the performance of high-anxious students will be inferior to that of low-anxious students on complex or difficult learning tasks in which competing error tendencies may be as strong as correct responses. In contrast, on simple learning tasks, in which correct responses are dominant relative to incorrect response tendencies, it would be expected that the performance of high-anxious students would be superior to that of low-anxious students. Following Spence (1958), we assume that the level of difficulty of a task is assumed to be a positive function of the number and strength of competing erroneous response tendencies elicited by the task.

Although many studies utilizing the Taylor manifest-anxiety scale as a measure of drive have provided support for drive theory (e.g., Lucas, 1952; Montague, 1953; Raymond, 1953; Spence, 1964; Spence & Spence, 1966; Taylor & Chapman, 1955), other investigators have reported results inconsistent with the theory (e.g., Hughes, Sprague, & Bendig, 1954; Kamin & Fedorchak, 1957).

TRAIT–STATE-ANXIETY THEORY

Research on anxiety in general, and on anxiety and learning in particular, has suffered from the ambiguity of anxiety as a theoretical construct. Spielberger (1966a) has emphasized the necessity of distinguishing between anxiety as a transitory state and as a relatively stable personality trait. According to Spielberger (1966a):

> Anxiety states (A-states) are characterized by subjective, consciously perceived feelings of apprehension and tension, accompanied by or associated with activation or arousal of the autonomic nervous system. Anxiety as a personality trait (A-trait) would seem to imply a motive or acquired behavioral disposition that predisposes an individual to perceive a wide range of objectively nondangerous circumstances as threatening, and to respond to these with A-state reactions disproportionate in intensity to the magnitude of the objective danger. (pp. 16–17)

Most previous work on anxiety and learning used measures of anxiety such as the Taylor manifest-anxiety scale to select students on the assumption that high scorers were higher in drive than low scorers. Since the Taylor manifest-anxiety scale appears to be a measure of trait anxiety (Spielberger, 1966a), this procedure is questionable in that the concept of drive is logically more closely associated with state anxiety than with trait anxiety.

Spielberger, O'Neil, and Hansen (1972) suggested that the results of research on anxiety and learning are consistent with the hypothesis that high-trait anxious students respond with higher levels of state anxiety than do low trait anxious students in situations that are made stressful by failure or by ego-involving instructions. It follows from drive theory that the high drive associated with high levels of state anxiety should facilitate performance on simple tasks in which correct responses are dominant and lead to performance decrements on difficult tasks. In accord with this reasoning, measures of state anxiety have been employed as predictor variables in all of the research discussed in this chapter. (The data pertaining to the validity and reliability of the measure employed are discussed in some detail in Chapter 8.)

EFFECTS OF STATE ANXIETY ON PERFORMANCE

The effects of anxiety on computer-assisted learning were investigated in a series of studies in which the short form of the state-anxiety scale was employed. All of the research involved computer-based learning situations, either computer-assisted or computer-managed; and, with one exception, use of the IBM 1500 computer-assisted instruction system. (A more extended discussion of computer-assisted and managed instruction, in general, and of the IBM 1500 instructional system in particular, can be found in Chapter 8.)

Computer-based learning tasks provide a means of carefully controlling the presentation of learning materials, and the conditions and materials more closely resemble school learning environments than do traditional laboratory learning tasks. An additional advantage of using computer-based instruction is that it is possible to measure anxiety and student performance during actual learning tasks.

EFFECTS OF STATE ANXIETY ON PERFORMANCE
IN COMPUTER-ASSISTED INSTRUCTION

Both mathematical and verbal–graphical computer-assisted learning tasks were investigated. The two kinds of learning tasks provide somewhat different ways of operationalizing the task difficulty variable that is crucial to testing drive-theory predictions. The research that employed the mathematical learning tasks is reported first, followed by those employing the verbal–graphical material.

Computer-Assisted Instruction Mathematical Tasks

In each of 5 studies reviewed, the instruction consisted of a brief (1–2 hour) computer-assisted instruction tutorial lesson on the field properties of complex numbers. With the exception of the initial study, all were conducted on the IBM 1500 system. The terminals for this system consisted of a cathode-ray tube for the presentation of materials and a typewriter keyboard for entering student responses. All of the studies were conducted at Florida State University.

To test the drive-theory hypothesis that the performance of high-anxious students will be inferior to that of low-anxious students on complex or difficult learning tasks in which competing error tendencies may be as strong or stronger as correct responses, but that the reverse is true on simple tasks where the dominant response is strongest, it was necessary to specify the difficulty level of the learning tasks.

For the difficult materials, the student was presented with a series of definitions and examples concerning the field properties of complex numbers (like substitution of terms, commutivity with respect to addition, associativity with respect to addition, and so on). This was followed by a series of three sets of five problems each. Each problem was presented in the format indicated below:

Step 1: We will show, for all pairs of elements in C, that their sum is also an element of C. To do this, we will select two arbitrary elements $Z1 = (a, b)$ and $Z2 = (c, d)$ and show that $Z1 + Z2$ is an element of C.

Step 2: $Z1 + Z2 = (a, b) + (c, d)$ (type the abbreviation to justify this step).

Step 3: The subject types C to indicate that he thinks the answer is COMMUTIVITY.

Step 4: Make sure that you are using the correct abbreviation. If $R = 8$ and $S = 7$, then $8 + 7$ may be written in place of $R + S$. Try again.

The problem itself was presented in Step 1, followed by a proof statement (Step 2), as in the proof of a geometric theorem. The student then selected a validating property from a sheet listing the field properties of complex numbers and types his answer (Step 3). If the student responded incorrectly, another example of the correct validating property would be given (Step 4), and the student would be told "wrong, try again." The student was required to respond to each item correctly before being allowed to attempt the next one. In this case, "S," (substitution), the computer would respond "correct" and the next problem would be presented.

On an intuitive basis and subsequent post hoc analysis of error rates, this task was divided into two problem sets: a more difficult set (Problems 1–5) for which the error rate was relatively high; and a less difficult set (Problems 6–15) for which the error rate was relatively low. The less difficult set was further subdivided in subsequent research to yield a least difficult subset consisting of Problems 11–15. In Studies 1 and 2 a second set of easier problems on compound fractions was used.

Study 1.   O'Neil, Spielberger, and Hansen (1969) investigated the relationship between state anxiety and performance for male and female college students learning both difficult and easy mathematics concepts. The materials were presented on an IBM 1440 computer-assisted instructional system. It was hypothesized that students who were high in state anxiety would make more errors than would low-state-anxious students on the difficult materials and that this relationship would be reversed on the easy materials.

High-state-anxious students, defined by a median split, made significantly more errors than did low-anxious students on the more difficult problems (Problems 1–5), whereas this relationship was reversed on the less difficult problems (Problems 6–15). However, the latter difference was not statistically significant. These data support the prediction from drive theory that the effects of anxiety on learning depend upon the relative strengths of correct responses and competing error tendencies. State anxiety appeared to influence performance by activating error tendencies on the initial, more difficult, section of the task.

Study 2. A second study (O'Neil, Hansen, & Spielberger, 1969), employing male students only, selected from a population of 1100 on the basis of extreme scores (upper and lower 20%) on the trait-anxiety scale of the state–trait-anxiety inventory. The learning materials used in the prior study were presented on an IBM 1500 instructional system.

The number of student errors on the easy materials (compound fractions) was so slight as to rule out any possible differences due to state-anxiety level. Consequently, the analyses discussed will be limited to only the difficult materials. For purposes of analysis, the difficult materials were divided into three subtasks of decreasing difficulty: Problems 1–5, 6–10, and 11–15. High- and low-state-anxious students were defined on the basis of a median split of state anxiety measured after Problems 1–5. High-state-anxious students made significantly more errors than did low-anxious students on the more difficult sections of the task (Problems 1–5) while they performed as well as the low-state-anxious students on the less difficult sections (Problems 6–10, 11–15). There was only a minimal change in error rate for low-state-anxious students as they progressed from one level of task difficulty to another. In addition, there was no effect of trait anxiety on performance. These results replicated those of the first study and were consistent with predictions from drive theory.

Study 3. O'Neil (1972) investigated the relationship of state anxiety and performance in a computer-assisted instruction task in which students were given either neutral or negative feedback (stress) regarding their performance. The computer-assisted instruction task was the same as Study 2 except that the compound fraction materials were dropped. Female students were selected from a population of 583 on the basis of extreme scores (upper and lower 20%) on the trait-anxiety scale of the state–trait-anxiety inventory.

Performance was evaluated as a function of state anxiety measured after each problem set. High-state-anxious students made more errors than the low-state-anxious students on all three sections of the learning task. Surprisingly, the differences between these groups were statistically significant for Problems 6–10 and 11–15, but not for the more difficult Problems 1–5. These results differed from the results of Studies 1 and 2, in which high-state-anxious students made significantly more errors than low-state-anxious students on Problems 1–5 but not on the less difficult Problems 6–10 and 11–15. Consistent with Study 2, there was no effect of trait anxiety on performance. In addition, there was no effect of stress on performance.

The findings of the Studies 1 and 2 were consistent with drive-theory predictions of interference on difficult tasks. However, the results of Study 3 were consistent with neither the previous research nor predictions from drive theory. Perhaps these differences could be attributed to the use of female subjects in Study 3, while male subjects were used in Study 2.

Study 4. James and O'Neil (1971) attempted to replicate and extend the previous research by using the same task conditions and procedures as in the prior study but employing both male and female students. The subjects were selected on the basis of extreme scores (upper and lower quartiles of normative group) of the trait anxiety scale.

For both sexes, the observed mean number of errors per problem was greater for the high-state-anxiety group than for the low-state-anxiety group on all 3 tasks. The results indicated that for females only the difference on Problems 11–15 was significant ($p < .10$). For males, there were significant main effects of state anxiety on Problems 1–5 and 11–15, but not for Problems 6–10.

The results for females were consistent with Study 3 in that there was no difference between high- and low-state-anxious students on the most difficult Problems 1–5, whereas high-anxious female students performed significantly worse on the less difficult Problems 11–15. With respect to males, the results were similar to Study 2 in that high-state-anxious students made significantly more errors than did low-state-anxious students on Problems 1–5. The finding that high-state-anxious males made significantly more errors than did low-state-anxious males on the median difficulty Problems 11–15 was inconsistent with the prior research with males. These findings, which replicated in general those of Studies 2 and 3, were clearly not in accord with the predictions from drive theory.

Study 5. Leherissey, O'Neil, and Hansen (1971) attempted to improve the performance of high-state-anxious male students by providing memory support. They used the same difficult mathematics materials used in Studies 1–4 but also supplied students in the experimental group with a list of their previous errors as a memory support. Memory support was not provided to the control group. Students were rank ordered and then divided into high-, medium-, and low-state-anxiety groups on the basis of their mean state-anxiety scores averaged across Problems 1–5, 6–10, and 11–15. Memory support and no memory support group students were then separated yielding unequal but proportional Ns for each 6 groups. The criterion variable was mean number of errors answered across all 15 problems.

A significant state anxiety by memory-support treatment interaction was found. Consistent with predictions, high-state-anxious students given memory support made fewer errors than did the high-anxious students without memory support, whereas there was little difference for low- and medium-state-anxious students. In general, high-state-anxious students made significantly more errors ($\bar{X}$ = 5.04) than did either medium- ($\bar{X}$ = 2.54) or low-state-anxious students ($\bar{X}$ = 2.27).

For this chapter the data were reanalyzed for the no-memory-support condition, which was exactly the same as the nonstress conditions of Studies 3 and 4, so as to investigate relationship of state anxiety to performance on each of the three sections. Male high-state-anxious students made significantly more errors than did low-state-anxious students on Problems 1–5 and 11–15 but did not differ significantly from low-anxious students on Problems 6–10. These results for male students replicated Study 4.

Summary. Five studies of the relationship between state anxiety and performance have been reported. Studies 2–5 divided the difficult materials into three sections and were all run on the IBM 1500 system, and thus are directly comparable. One clear finding emerging from these studies is that high levels of state anxiety are indeed debilitating. The details of the interactive effect of state anxiety, task difficulty, and sex on performance remains unclear, however.

The findings of the four studies are summarized in Table 11.1 with a note as to the statistical significance of the differences between performance of high- versus

TABLE 11.1
The Statistical Significance of the Differences bewteen Performances
of High- versus Low-State-Anxious Students

Sex	Study	Problems 1–5 (Difficult)	Problems 6–10	Problems 11–15 (Least Difficult)
Male students				
O'Neil, Hansen, and				
Spielberger 1969	2	Significant	Nonsignificant	Nonsignificant
James and O'Neil				
1971	4	Significant	Nonsignificant	Significant
Leherissey *et al.*				
1971	5	Significant	Nonsignificant	Significant
Female students				
O'Neil 1972	3	Nonsignificant	Significant	Significant
James and O'Neil				
1971	4	Nonsignificant	Nonsignificant	Significant

low-state-anxious students. High states of anxiety consistently interfered with the performance of male students on Problems 1–5, the most difficult part of the program. In contrast, there were no statistically significant differences between the performance of high- and low-anxious female students on this subtask. It should be noted that throughout the task in all studies, females made fewer errors than did males. With only one exception, high anxious students made significantly more errors than did low anxious students on the least difficult section (Problems 11–15), regardless of sex. In only one case was there a significant difference between the performance of high- and low-anxious students on the intermediate difficulty Problems 6–10.

These findings were inconsistent with drive theory predictions, that for difficult tasks, (Problems 1–5), high state anxiety should be debilitating for both male and female students. This expectation was confirmed only for males. Further, drive theory leads to the expectation that on easy tasks, high state anxiety should facilitate performance or at least not interfere with it. Clearly, the data in Table 11.1 for Problems 11–15 indicate that this prediction was *not* confirmed. Thus, for meaningful computer-assisted instruction tasks of varying levels of difficulty, drive theory seems to have limited utility in predicting the relationships between state anxiety and performance.

This state of affairs, in retrospect, could have been predicted based on Spence's (1958) remark:

> In order to derive implications concerning the effects of drive variable in any type of complex task, it is necessary to have, in addition to the drive theory, a further theoretical network concerning the variables and their interacting that are involved in the particular learning activity. (p. 137)

We have been unable to generate such a network in the context of meaningful tutorial computer-assisted instruction contexts and thus drive theory is not further discussed in this chapter.

Review of Findings with Verbal–Graphical Computer-Assisted Instruction Materials

The prior studies suggest that, in general, high levels of state anxiety interfered with performance. Conclusions from these computer-assisted-learning studies were based on the use of a single set of mathematics-learning materials using acquisition data (errors). To test the generality of these findings across content, a second series of computer-assisted-instruction experiments was conducted using the set of verbal–graphical problem-solving materials documented by Tobias in Chapter 6. In addition to acquisition data, retention data (a posttest) were also available. As was previously noted, no theoretical network concerning drive theory was derived for these studies.

These materials dealt with two types of content: (1) familiar materials concerning the incidence and risk of contracting heart disease; and (2) technical materials concerning the diagnosis of myocardial infarction (heart attack). The materials were revised, with minimal adaptations, for computer presentation on the IBM 1500 system.

Four response-mode versions of the basic instructional program were prepared, each containing exactly the same subject matter and frame structure. Tobias' (1969) two response modes, reading and constructed response, were retained, and two additional modes were added: a covert-response version, requesting students to "think" answers to questions, but requiring no overt response; and a modified multiple-choice version, which required students to answer multiple-choice questions. As in the Tobias study, the reading version did not require students to make overt responses but merely to read each successive frame. The constructed-response version was identical to the modified multiple-choice on the verbal frames but on the frames requiring EKG drawings students had to construct EKG tracings before receiving the correct answer. The program was preceded and followed by paper-and-pencil pre- and posttests requiring constructed responses. Two state-anxiety studies using these materials were reported by Leherissey, O'Neil, Heinrich, and Hansen (1973).

Study 6. The first of these studies sought to investigate the effects of both trait anxiety and response mode on state anxiety and performance. On the basis of prior research with the complex numbers program, it was anticipated that high-state-anxious students would make fewer correct responses on the achievement measures than would low-state-anxious students. On the basis of Tobias' (1969) findings, the constructed-response group was expected to make more correct responses on the technical portion of the posttest than would the reading group, with the performance of students assigned to the other response modes falling between the performance levels of these two groups. To ensure a distribution of anxiety levels in each experimental treatment, female students were randomly assigned to one of the four response mode conditions on the basis of their level of trait anxiety: high, medium, or low (upper and lower quartiles of norms).

For purposes of data analysis, students were divided into high-, medium-, and low-state-anxiety groups by ranking the total distribution of scores on the appropriate state-anxiety scale and dividing the resulting distribution into thirds. This procedure was followed in all three studies reported here.

The initial analyses examined the effects of response mode and level of state anxiety, as measured following the posttest, on posttest performance. On the familiar material, there was a significant main effect for response mode, but neither the effect of state anxiety nor its interaction with response mode was significant. Results for the technical portion revealed that the main effect of state anxiety did approach significance ($p < .10$), with low-state-anxious students making more correct responses ($\bar{X} = 59.35$) than medium- ($\bar{X} = 54.39$) or high-state-anxious students ($\bar{X} = 51.71$). These findings were consistent with the results of prior research in that anxiety detrimentally affected performance on more difficult, technical content.

The other factor of interest in this study was the effect of response mode and state anxiety measured during the learning program on within-program performance of those students who responded overtly during acquisition, that is, the modified multiple-choice and constructed-response groups. There were no significant main effects of anxiety or interactions on the familiar materials. On the technical materials, a significant main effect was found for response mode but not for anxiety. Thus, level of state anxiety was not related to performance during acquisition for either group. The finding that in-task performance was not related to level of state anxiety on the more difficult portions of the program was inconsistent with the results of the previous studies with mathematical materials. This inconsistency may be due to the fact that, unlike the previous studies, students were not required to give the correct response before progressing to the next problem. This nonforced mastery procedure could have reduced the debilitating effects of state anxiety on performance during acquisition, while the expected relationship between state anxiety and performance on difficult materials was observed in the more stressful posttest situation.

Study 7. The second of the two studies reported by Leherissey, O'Neil, Heinrich, and Hansen (1973) sought to determine if the effects of state anxiety of female students would be reduced and if their performance would be improved if the amount of time students were required to spend on the task was shortened. Time was reduced in the experimental groups by reducing the amount of technical material to be learned. A secondary objective was to replicate the findings of the prior study using only the reading and constructed-response modes of the program. Only those findings concerned with treatments identical to those of Study 6 will be discussed.

The posttest was divided into "familiar," "initial-technical," and "remaining-technical" sections since the technical materials of the previous study had been subdivided into two sections (initial versus remaining) in order to reduce time spent on the task. Analyses of the familiar portions of the posttest revealed a significant state anxiety by response-mode interaction. For the reading group, performance was relatively consistent for all levels of state anxiety, whereas increasing levels of state anxiety was debilitating for the constructed-response group. No significant main effect for anxiety nor any other significant interactions were found. Performance on the initial and remaining-technical portions of the posttest revealed no significant main effects or interactions for state anxiety or response mode.

In summary, analyses of familiar posttest performance indicated that in both studies, students in the reading groups performed better than students in the constructed-response groups and that, in general, state anxiety was unrelated to performance on the familiar posttest. On the technical posttest, there was no main effect for state anxiety on performance in Study 7 as there had been in Study 6.

Study 8. Leherissey (1971) sought to investigate the hypothesis that stimulating state epistemic curiosity within a computer-assisted-instruction task would reduce state anxiety and improve performance. Further, this study was designed to explicate the inconsistencies between Studies 6 and 7. The familiar materials were dropped; otherwise, the content of the instructional program consisted of the same materials as were employed in the prior two studies. The posttest, however, was revised to more validly sample the behavior taught in the program; that is, rather than being required to draw the EKG tracings, students were instructed simply to write the numbers corresponding to the EKG components as they did in the instructional sequence. As in the Tobias (1969) study, therefore, the learning program and posttest required the same behaviors. State anxiety was assessed periodically. Female undergraduates were selected on the basis of extreme scores on the trait-anxiety scale of the state-trait-anxiety inventory. They were then assigned to either a curiosity-stimulating instruction or no-instruction condition within a reading or constructed-response version of the program.

Analysis of the initial-technical posttest data indicated that students in the constructed-response groups made significantly more correct responses than did students in the reading group. In addition, there was a significant interaction between curiosity instruction conditions and state-anxiety levels. Whereas there was relatively little difference in the performance of students in the curiosity-stimulating-instruction groups as a function of state anxiety, in the no-instruction group, high-state-anxious students performed more poorly than did medium- or low-anxious students. No other main effects or interactions were significant. The remaining-technical posttest data revealed that students in the constructed-response groups again performed significantly better than students in the reading groups. No other main effects or interactions were significant. These findings indicated that the changes made in the technical posttest improved the constructed-response group's performance, thus replicating the earlier programmed instruction research reported by Tobias (1969).

In addition to these posttest results, the effect of anxiety on within-program performance was analyzed as in Study 6. Only the data of the constructed-response group were used as they were the only group to respond overtly during the program. Results of the analysis on the initial-technical portion of the program revealed no significant main effects. Results on the remaining-technical portion of the program indicated that, as predicted, low-state-anxious students made significantly more correct responses ($\bar{X}$ = 94.90) than did medium ($\bar{X}$ = 89.56) or high-state-anxious students ($\bar{X}$ = 78.65). No other main effects or interactions were found to be significant.

Summary. The findings of these studies were consistent in revealing little relationship between state anxiety and familiar posttest performance. These findings were also consistent with prior research using easy compound fractions materials. On the technical materials, there were some inconsistencies. It was expected that the high-state-anxious students would perform more poorly on this difficult posttest than would less anxious students. In Study 6 these expectations were confirmed, with high-state-anxious students performing most poorly ($p < .10$); however, in Study 7, there was no effect of state anxiety on performance. Finally, in Study 8, high-state-anxious students performed more poorly than did low-anxious students on the initial but not on the remaining-technical portion of the posttest.

Since there was no posttest for the complex-numbers materials, comparisons cannot be drawn between these findings and the heart-disease program. It is consistent with expectation, however, that high states of anxiety were debilitating to performance on the technical portions of the posttest.

The data were also somewhat inconsistent with respect to in-task performance on the technical materials. There was no significant effect of state anxiety on performance in Study 7. Unfortunately, within-program performance data were unavailable for Study 7. In Study 8, the technical materials were divided into two parts for purposes of analysis. No relationship was found between state anxiety and performance on the relatively less difficult initial-technical materials. The expected relationship was found on the more difficult remaining-technical materials with high-state-anxious students having fewer correct answers than low-state-anxious students. Thus, the effect of state anxiety on performance was only evident during the most difficult portions of the learning program.

Some interesting observations concerning explicitness of feedback and the contingencies following errors emerge when the three studies presented here are compared with the complex-mathematics materials. Within the learning programs themselves, both the extent to which explicit feedback was provided and the action taken following an error differed from one set of studies to the other. In the verbal/graphical materials (Studies 6–8), it was left to the student to compare responses to the correct answers and judge correctness. Irrespective of whether the answer was correct, the program proceeded to the next instructional frame. In contrast, the mathematics program (Studies 1–5) either confirmed the student's response or replied "wrong, try again." The student was not allowed to proceed to the next instructional item until the current item had been answered correctly.

In view of the fact that, in general, stronger relationships were found between state anxiety and performance in the context of the mathematical materials than in the verbal/graphical materials, it is suggested that either explicitness of feedback, or the action that follows an incorrect response (for example, forced mastery), or a combination of both factors may be paramount in determining the relationship between anxiety and performance. On difficult materials with high error rates, the presence of explicit failure feedback and the requirement that the student remain in the failure situation until a correct response was made could well have affected the student's cognitive appraisal of the situation. In line with the suggestion made by Spielberger (1966a), students would be expected to respond to this stressful situation with high levels of state anxiety. If state anxiety does indeed interfere with the learning process, it is to be expected that the error–feedback–anxiety cycle would be cumulative, resulting in both higher error rates and higher levels of state anxiety. On the other hand, other students would tend not to view the explicit feedback as threatening and would have lower levels of state anxiety. Without the interfering effect of anxiety, these students would be more able to use the explicit feedback constructively and would, as a result, demonstrate lower error rates.

When, as in the verbal–graphical materials, and in all forms of linear programmed instruction, explicit error feedback is not provided and the student is allowed to immediately escape the specific failure situation, one would not expect as strong an effect of the vicious error–anxiety–error cycle. Similarly, the absence of explicit feedback would deprive low-state-anxious students of the opportunity to use this feedback constructively. The net result would be a less marked difference between the performance of high and low-state-anxious students.

EFFECTS OF STATE ANXIETY ON PERFORMANCE IN COMPUTER-MANAGED INSTRUCTION

The previous research was conducted under relatively well-controlled, time-limited conditions using carefully developed experimental learning materials. With both the mathematical material and verbal/graphical materials, a number of studies found that high levels of state anxiety were associated with poor performance. Although the learning materials used were probably more meaningful to students than is typically the case in traditional laboratory experiments, the research was limited to observations of performance in a single experimental session. For the purpose of generalizing beyond the laboratory, the relationships on retention measures were investigated in an instructional context over the period of a semester.

In this section we focus on the relationship of state anxiety to performance on two computer-managed-instruction systems, one at Florida State University and the other at The University of Texas at Austin. In computer-managed instruction (CMI), the instruction is not presented by the computer. Rather, the instruction is presented via a conventional, less expensive form of media. The student determines the rate of study, while the computer is used to monitor and direct progress through the curriculum. Monitoring occurs by frequent resting to diagnose the student's strengths and weaknesses, providing learning prescriptions, and scheduling student use of available resources. (A more extended discussion of computer-managed instruction is found in Chapter 8.)

Study 9. Gallagher, O'Neil, and Dick (1971) investigated the effects of state anxiety on performance in a course on "techniques of programed Instruction." State anxiety was measured before and after each of 13 module tests. (This CMI course is described in Chapter 9.)

Little evidence of any systematic relationship between pretest state anxiety and test grades was found. Only 2 of 13 correlations were statistically significant (−.30 and −.32, respectively). In contrast, 9 of the 13 correlations between test grades and the state-anxiety measures administered after the tests were statistically significant (ranging from −.30 to −.53). All correlations were negative. Thus, while there was little relationship between test grades and state anxiety prior to the test (anticipation), students who reported higher levels of state anxiety during the test did less well than those who reported lower state anxiety. There are at least two possible interpretations of these findings. The poorer performance of the high-state-anxious students could be attributed to their higher levels of state anxiety. An equally plausible alternative is that higher levels of state anxiety resulted from students' reactions to their poor performance.

Study 10. The computer-managed instructional sequence developed at The University of Texas comprised a portion of an introductory educational-psychology course. (This CMI system is also described in Chapter 9.)

The relationship of performance on the initial posttest to state anxiety measured immediately following the test was investigated for each module. Higher states of anxiety were consistently associated with poorer performance. For six of the nine modules these findings were statistically significant. However, even when significant, the absolute magnitude of these negative correlations was small. The observed range for all modules was from −.06 to −.21, whereas Gallagher, O'Neil, and Dick (1971) reported correlations ranging from −.30 to −.53.

The two computer-managed instruction studies differed on a number of dimensions. Gallagher, O'Neil, and Dick (1971) used graduate students as opposed to the undergraduates of this study; feedback was given concerning the correctness of each test item by Gallagher and co-workers, whereas no feedback was given concerning adequacy of performance in this study until after state anxiety has been measured. In addition, content varied dramatically between the two studies.

Study 11. During the semester that Study 10 was conducted, pilot data were also collected for validation of the automated test-anxiety-reduction program described in Chapter 10. These data suggested an explanation for the conflicting CMI findings. One aspect of this pilot data was focused on the relationship of "worry" and "emotionality" to performance. The subjects of the pilot study were students in the introductory educational-psychology course who volunteered to fill out a number of affective measures and to be interviewed by an experimenter concerning their test anxiety following two of the five statistical modules.

As will be recalled from Chapter 9, Sarason's (1972) test-anxiety scale was administered to all students before they took any of the nine computer-managed instruction tests and state anxiety was measured by the five-item state-anxiety scale following each of the nine tests. In addition, immediately before and after the third and fourth statistics-unit tests, the students in the pilot study filled out a paper-and-pencil form of the worry–emotionality-scale (Liebert & Morris, 1967).

Wine (1971b) suggested that a cognitive factor is the principle component accounting for the inverse relationship between task performance and test anxiety. Liebert and Morris (1967) reviewed Sassenrath's (1964) factor-analytic study and named his cognitive factors "worry"; autonomic arousal factors were called "emotionality." Worry was defined as cognitive concern over performance; emotionality signified reported autonomic arousal due to the stress of an immediate testing situation. On this basis, a scale composed of five "worry" and five "emotionality" items drawn from the text-anxiety questionnaire was constructed. Items were modified so that the responses reflected the subject's immediate feelings relative to a specific testing situation.

In general, these studies indicate that the "worry" component of test anxiety correlated significantly with performance on subscales of a timed IQ test, and examination grades, while the "emotionality" component did not correlate with these variables. Based on these findings, Morris and Liebert (1970) concluded that worry accounted for more of the debilitating effects of test anxiety on performance than did emotionality. The relationships of each of these measures to performance were investigated in this pilot study. The data in Table 11.2 clearly indicate that both worry and emotionality were more highly correlated with performance than either test or state anxiety. Worry about performance correlated the highest with performance.

In addition to being different constructs, however, the worry and state-anxiety scales also differed on other dimensions in this computer-managed-instruction study, that is, the state-anxiety scale was administered online, whereas worry and emotionality were given offline. The pertinent consequence of this procedural difference was that state anxiety was assessed before performance feedback, that is, before students were informed explicitly whether they had passed

TABLE 11.2
Correlation of Performance with Various Affective Measures

	N	Statistics-unit Test 3 performance	Statistics-unit Test 4 performance
Worry	64	−.60*	−.45*
Emotionality	64	−.43**	−.30**
State anxiety	182	−.18	−.18
Test-anxiety scale	182	−.18	−.19

*p < .05
**p < .01

or failed, whereas worry was assessed following performance feedback. Thus, differences in constructs were confounded with procedural differences. The next study was explicitly designed to investigate the relationship between state anxiety, worry, emotionality, and performance both before and after performance feedback.

Study 12. The computer-managed-instruction system was undergoing revisions and summative evaluation and the results of these activities are reported elsewhere (Dixon & Judd, 1974; Judd, O'Neil, Rogers, & Richardson, 1973).

For exploratory purposes, 5 additional items from the long form of the state-anxiety scale were selected for administration with the short five-item form. As was done during the preceding semester, the modified, ten-item state-anxiety scale and the worry—emotionality scales were administered online with retrospective instructions following each module test. Only data pertaining to the original five-item state-anxiety scale are discussed. To investigate the effect of performance feedback on students' reported anxiety levels, students were randomly assigned to one of two groups, the first of which was always administered the scales immediately following the test and prior to performance feedback. For the second group, scales were administered following performance feedback.

Collapsing across the points at which the scales were administered, correlations were computed for each of the 5 module tests between worry, emotionality, and state anxiety. As may be seen in Table 11.3, the various measures of anxiety were all highly intercorrelated. For example, on the computers-in-education module, state anxiety correlated .66 with worry, and .80 with emotionality. This pattern of state anxiety being more highly correlated with emotionality than with worry was true for all five tests and statistical tests of the difference between correlation coefficients (Guilford & Fruchter, 1973) indicated that these differences were all significant.

In order to investigate the effect of availability of performance feedback (present versus absent) on the relationships between the various affective measures and performance, separate correlation coefficients were computed for the 2 groups of students to whom the scales were administered prior to or following feedback. These data, which are presented in Table 11.4, suggest that performance feedback was a salient variable. After performance feedback, 10 of the 15 negative-correlation coefficients were significant, whereas before performance feedback, only 5 of the 15 were statistically significant. These findings are congruent with the differences noted bewteen the results of Study 9, in which explicit feedback was provided following each task item, and Study 10, in which state anxiety was measured prior to the provision of feedback.

Following performance feedback, worry was more highly correlated with performance than was state anxiety on all five module tests. These differences were significant only on the first three modules. Thus, following performance

TABLE 11.3
Intercorrelations of Various Anxiety Measures

Module	N	Emotionality	State Anxiety[a]
Computers in education	215		
worry	–	.72	.66
emotionality	–	–	.80
Classroom management	207		
worry	–	.81	.72
emotionality	–	–	.86
Statistics unit 1	86		
worry	–	.67	.63
emotionality	–	–	.78
Tests and measurement	203		
worry	–	.80	.66
emotionality	–	–	.76
Cultural Differences	186		
worry	–	.74	.61
emotionality	–	–	.78

All correlation coefficients in this table are significantly greater than zero ($p < .01$).

feedback, worry appears to be a better predictor of performance in the computer-managed-instruction testing environment than does state anxiety.

It must be concluded that, in general, the five-item state-anxiety scale has not proven to be as useful a predictor of performance in computer-based-learning situations as is worry. It is hypothesized that the limited relationship found between state anxiety and performance is due, at least in part, to the procedures used to establish the scale's validity. It will be recalled from Chapter 8 that in discussing the validity of a state anxiety measure, Spielberger (1972c) emphasized the scale's ability to reflect stress. As was discussed in the description of the scale's validation procedures in Chapter 8, the five-item state-anxiety scale has been shown to provide a valid and reliable measure of the responsiveness of individuals to stress situations. No aspect of these validation procedures, however, concerned the relationship of individuals' responses to the scale to their performance on a learning task.

One research strategy that emerged from this conclusion is to develop a new scale by selecting items from the 20-item state-anxiety scale on the joint requirement of their ability to predict performance as well as to reflect stress. Items from the worry and emotionality scales would also be included. Such a strategy was implemented within the context of the CMI system at the Texas

TABLE 11.4
Correlational Relationship of Affective Measures and Performance

Module	Before performance feedback	N	After performance feedback	N
Computers in education		104		111
worry–performance	−.25*		−.43**	
emotionality–performance	−.14		−.21*	
state anxiety–performance	−.14		−.10	
Classroom management		100		107
worry–performance	−.20		−.54**	
emotionality–performance	−.20		−.42**	
state anxiety–performance	−.17		−.40**	
Statistics Unit 1		41		45
worry–performance	−.60**		−.25	
emotionality–performance	−.39*		−.08	
state anxiety–performance	−.24		−.03	
Tests and measurement		98		105
worry–performance	−.19		−.33**	
emotionality–performance	−.15		−.15	
state anxiety–performance	−.09		−.26*	
Cultural differences		90		96
worry–performance	−.19		−.33**	
emotionality–performance	−.21*		−.25**	
state anxiety–performance	−.26*		−.24*	

$*p < .05.$ $**p < .01.$

campus. It seems upon reflection, however, to be more reasonable, given the plethora of anxiety scales, that a new scale not be developed. The necessary reliability and validity studies needed would be costly both in terms of time and money. Since the five-item state anxiety scale is a good index of stress and the five-item worry scale is a good predictor of performance on retention tests, our future research will use both scales.

SUMMARY AND DISCUSSION

What is the relationship between state anxiety and performance in a computer-based-learning environment? On the mathematical computer-assisted-instruction material, high states of anxiety were, in general, found to interfere with performance. The data reported with respect to verbal/graphical computer-assisted-instruction materials provides some replication for the findings of the mathematical materials but in the main, more questions are raised than are answered. For example, on the mathematics material, the data pertaining to errors committed during the task were relatively clear, that is, high states of anxiety were debilitating. In contrast, for the heart-disease technical material, high states of anxiety were debilitating on only the most difficult parts of the task.

A suggestion regarding the importance of the explicitness feedback emerges from these two sets of studies. Although both tasks had difficult components, resulting in high in-task error rates, the mathematical materials provided explicit feedback in a forced-mastery setting, whereas the verbal–graphical materials provided only implicit feedback and had no forced-mastery requirement.

It is suggested that both explicit feedback and forced mastery could effect students' cognitive appraisal of a difficult instructional task with high error rates. For some students, like high-trait-anxious students, the implication of failure from feedback and/or the requirement of a correct response before proceeding would lead to a perception of threat and higher levels of state-anxiety leading, in turn, to poorer performance. Other students—those less prone to perceive the situation as threatening, like low-trait-anxious students—would be less likely to increase their levels of state anxiety. It would be expected that these students could use the explicit error feedback constructively, resulting in improved performance. Thus, marked differences in performance between high- and low-state-anxious students would not be expected to occur in situations in which the feedback was less explicit or mastery was not required, or the learning situation was less difficult and hence less stressful.

A weak generalization from the posttest data for the verbal/graphical materials would be that high states of anxiety were debilitating, but this was true only for relatively less difficult initial technical materials. Unexpectedly, there was no differential effect of state anxiety on performance for the posttest over the most difficult materials.

The above generalizations were based on research in the context of computer-assisted instruction paradigms, using materials of a 1–2 hour duration. For purposes of replication and increased generalizability, a computer-managed curriculum was developed, implemented, and evaluated. The data for the first computer-managed instruction study at the Texas campus (Study 10) indicated that the relationship between state anxiety and performance was weaker than in prior studies. For example, over the series of nine module tests, the correlations ranged from −.06 to −.21.

These low correlations between state anxiety and performance were in striking contrast to the correlations found between worry and performance for two of the nine modules (−.45 and −.60). These data were confounded with procedural differences—affective states measured before or after performance feedback. Thus, another study was designed for the computer-managed-instruction setting. The resulting data supported both the power of the worry construct, that is, worry was more highly correlated with performance than was state anxiety, and the relevance of performance feedback, that is, after performance feedback, relationships were more consistent than before performance feedback.

While the state-anxiety scale has provided a reliable and valid measure of the responsiveness of individuals to stress situations (see Chapters 8, 9, and 10), no aspect of these validation procedures concerned the relationship of individuals' item responses to their performance on a learning task. Thus, there is a need to use a measure which is more responsive to those affective factors which influence performance (worry).

The evidence reported in this chapter indicates that drive theory as a framework to relate anxiety and performance was inadequate in meaningful situations. A different framework has been suggested by Wine (1971b) and Sarason (1972). Wine suggests that performance differences between high- and low-test-anxious students may largely be accounted for by the fact that the low-test-anxious student is attentive to task-relevant variables, while the high-test-anxious student focuses on internal, self-evaluative, self-deprecatory thinking and perception of his autonomic responses. Since difficult tasks, in general, require full attention, the highly test-anxious student cannot perform as well on these as can the low-test-anxious student owing to a division of attention between internal cues and task cues. It should be noted, however, that such a theory does not explain the replicated sex effects found with the mathematical computer-assisted instruction materials.

The evidence for these cognitive/attentional conclusions was derived from the use of the test-anxiety scale as a measure of specific trait anxiety. Spielberger (1972c) indicates that test anxiety measures more accurately predict performance decrements in test-like situations than do trait anxiety measures. He also cites evidence that indicates that situation-specific trait measures in the areas of speech anxiety and fear of shock predicted better than general trait measures. If situation-specific trait-anxiety measures are better predictors than are general trait measures, it would be expected that situation-specific state measures would be better predictors than would general state measures. Thus, if one were to conceptualize worry as a situation-specific state measure, then the data reported in the computer-managed instructional section provides empirical support for this position.

Finally, it is striking that despite careful design of the computer-managed instructional materials, a substantial number of students did report high levels of state anxiety (see Chapter 9). Further, the data reviewed in this chapter suggest that state anxiety and/or worry are debilitating to performance, particularly for those types of individualized instruction contexts which provide explicit feedback and employ a forced-mastery approach. Thus, it must be concluded that anxiety is as much a concern in an individualized-instruction context as it is with traditional educational methodology.

Part IV

A MODEL FOR EXAMINING INTERACTION EFFECTS OF ANXIETY AND INSTRUCTIONAL PROCEDURES ON PERFORMANCE

Seven years have transpired since the research program described here was initiated. In the course of that time, our ideas have developed and changed considerably. It is now clear that there are better ways of achieving the aims we have been pursuing.

In Chapter 12, a model is presented that improves on the research designs that have been employed up to now, and recommendations are made for future research.

12
A Model for Research on the Effect of Anxiety on Instruction

In the review of research on the interaction between anxiety and different instructional treatments (see Chapter 6) few consistent interactions were reported. Similarly, many inconsistent findings have been reported in other chapters of this book dealing with the relationship between anxiety and instruction. My purpose in this chapter is to elaborate a tentative model for heuristic purposes which attempts to bring order out of some of the discrepant research findings, and hopefully serve as a guideline for research strategy on the effects of anxiety on instruction.

AN INFORMATION-PROCESSING MODEL
OF ATTRIBUTE–TREATMENT INTERACTIONS

An adaptation of an information-processing model developed previously (Tobias, 1976) may clarify the process by which anxiety can affect learning from different instructional methods. The implications of this model for attribute–treatment interactions in general are discussed first, followed by the implications of the model for research on the effect of anxiety on instruction.

The model displayed in Figure 12.1 is divided into three major components: input, processing, and output. The input section of the model connotes different instructional methods, such as, for examples, lectures, workbooks, programed or computer-assisted instruction. *Input* refers to the way the instructional content has been organized by the instructional designer or teacher. In other words, input refers to the organization of stimuli prior to the student's response to them.

The *processing* section of the model refers to any operations the student performs on the input, such as registering, storing, or transforming it so as to produce a solution as output. This section of the model includes such processes

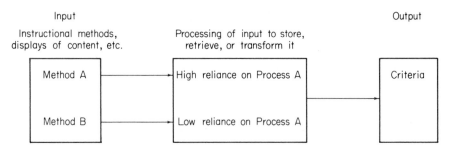

FIG. 12.1   Model of cognitive attributes in interaction with instructional methods

as attention, coding, deduction and induction, retrieval from memory, and any organization performed on the input in order to store it and render it more accessible for retrieval.

The *output* part of the model denotes all of the behaviors students perform allowing an external observer to determine whether instructional objectives have been attained. This section is identical to the dependent or criterion variable in most research on the outcome of instructional methods.

An example may clarify the implications of the model. Let us suppose that the objective of a task was for students to solve a set of mathematical problems somewhat similar to those used by Leherissey, O'Neill, and Hansen (1971). In order to solve these problems students need both relevant prior mathematical skills, and access to a set of rules. Method *A* might require students to memorize the relevant rules, and then start off on the problem. Method *B,* on the other hand, might display the rules in advance, but, in addition, enables the student to refer to them at will. Clearly Method *A* is presumed to rely heavily on processes involved in the student's effectively memorizing, storing, and retrieving rules from memory; these processes are symbolized by *A* in the model. Method *B* places little emphasis on memory and retrieval.

In order to conduct an attribute treatment interaction study using Methods *A* and *B,* a measure of memory abilities would be required. Then, subjects who score low on memory abilities would be expected to do well with Method B and poorly with method A, which relies heavily on memory, whereas students high on memory ability would be expected to perform equally well with either Method *A* or *B.*

It has been pointed out elsewhere (Berliner & Cahen, 1973; Cronbach & Snow, 1969; Tobias, 1976) that treatments in attribute-treatment studies have often been defined somewhat carelessly. That is, instructional methods, the inputs in the model, may have differed from one another in only minor details. Sometimes instructional methods appeared to differ sharply from one another in the way the materials were arranged, yet relied on essentially similar internal psychological processes. Such superficial, or phenotypic differences which fail to rely on different types of psychological processing of the input stream are unlikely to yield interactions, or even overall achievement differences.

IMPLICATIONS OF THE MODEL
FOR RESEARCH ON ANXIETY–TREATMENT INTERACTIONS

In the example of attribute–treatment interactions presented in the previous section, the interaction between the instructional method and memory ability were symbolized by the model presented in Firure 12.1. In order for anxiety to affect instructional outcomes, an additional step is required. Anxiety does *not* generally affect instructional outcomes directly. Instead, anxiety affects the cognitive processes required by the instructional methods, and these, in turn, affect outcome.

In terms of the example discussed in the previous section, anxiety may interfere with the student's ability to utilize memory processes effectively, as indicated in the research of Sieber, Kameya, and Paulson (1970), and by Leherissey *et al.* (1971). Students high in anxiety are less able to utilize memory processes, and hence would learn more from Method B, which does not require memorization. In contrast to attribute–treatment interaction studies in general, in which the attribute involved is presumed to affect instructional outcomes directly, anxiety affects outcome indirectly.

The possible effects of anxiety on instructional outcomes are displayed in Figure 12.2. Logically, it seems clear that anxiety may affect output in three ways, as indicated by the broken lines and barriers in Figure 12.2: prior to processing, during processing, and after processing has been completed. The first two sources of interference may be conceptualized as occurring during acquisition, and the third after acquisition and just prior to posttest.

Preprocessing

The first possible effect of anxiety on instruction is prior to processing. Anxiety may, in some manner, reduce or restrict the effectiveness of input. This may occur when the anxious student's ability to attend to the material presented is reduced and nominal stimuli fail to become effective since the student is less able to represent input internally. Such a hypothetical deficit can be remediated in one of two ways:

1. The student will have to have the input presented again in order to attend to a greater portion of it.

2. The student will have to infer the characteristics of the input unsuccessfully attended to previously from that proportion of input which did register effectively.

Interference During Processing

The second route by which anxiety can affect instructional outcome is by working on the processes transforming the input information and generating a solution to the problem. The previous example of anxiety interfering with

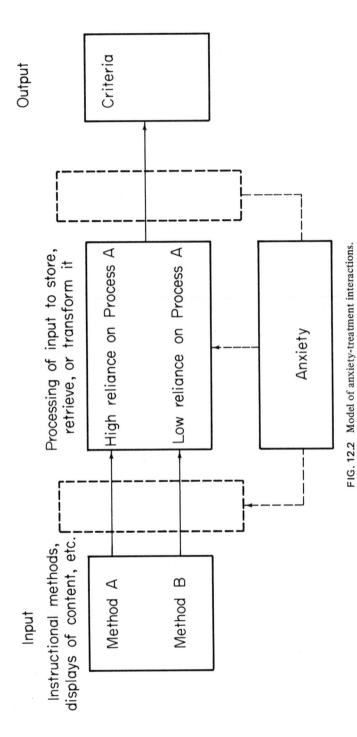

FIG. 12.2 Model of anxiety-treatment interactions.

students' ability to retrieve the rules for solving mathematical problems is an instance of interference during processing. At this point, input has effectively registered, and the student's task is to bring memory and problem-solving techniques to bear in order to make an answer. As indicated, anxiety may interfere in the efficiency with which memory processes are brought to bear for the solution of the task.

Interference by anxiety at the processing stage can be differentiated—at least conceptually—from interference prior to processing. Preprocessing interference should make it harder for the student to identify which of several alternatives are presented during input right after these are displayed. Interference during processing, on the other hand, should enable the student, prior to the presentation of succeeding problems, to select among several choices shown at input with greater accuracy.

Output Interference

The third possible effect of anxiety would occur after processing and before output. When anxiety affects learning prior to and during processing, such effects may be conceptualized as occurring during the acquisition stage of learning. This effect of anxiety may be conceptualized as occurring after acquisition, and just prior to posttest. To continue with the example described, at this stage the student has solved the arithmetic problem and is ready to make an answer. It seems possible that anxiety may interfere with the accurate rendering of that response in output. Phenomenologically we are all familiar with occasions in which the solution of a problem has been grasped and then lost. For example, one may hit upon an intuitive answer to an arithmetic problem, or the sudden identification of a melody, quotation or poem, which is then inexplicably "forgotten" before one is able to verbalize or record it. Such interference would appear to have occurred after processing has been completed, but before it has been reproduced effectively as output.

It should be possible to differentiate between interference just prior to output and processing interference in the following manner: if students have made an answer or solved a problem during acquisition which they are incapable of during posttest, postprocessing interference may be inferred. Furthermore, for interference at the conclusion of processing students would be able, on immediate recall, to produce a greater number of steps in the process of reaching a solution than they would if interference had occurred during processing.

Typically, the various sources of interference by anxiety are probably not independent. It is quite possible that very anxious individuals are subject to interference at all three stages and, furthermore, that such interference may be cumulative. That is, interference which restricts the proportion of effective input places a greater burden on processing to figure out that proportion of input which has not been successfully registered previously. If processing itself is also subject to interference, the deficit attributable to restricted input is magnified by the reduced efficiency of the ongoing processing. In turn, interference in producing the results as output increases this deficit even further.

The advantages of such a model would appear to be that it permits specification of the type of effects one might expect, and thus focus as the attention of researchers on the useful kinds of behavioral measures, as well as on promising independent variables. Furthermore, if verified by research, the model can suggest appropriate remedial procedures to instructional designers to compensate for the effects of anxiety.

AROUSAL AND MAINTENANCE OF ANXIETY
IN INSTRUCTIONAL RESEARCH SITUATIONS

Irrespective of the particular model regarding the effects of anxiety on instruction, one underlying assumption is vital for all such research: that anxiety is actually operative within the research situation. Researchers generally assume that the student's trait anxiety will affect the instructional manipulations much the way they affect the student's functioning in day-to-day life, especially within scholastic situations. It has been pointed out elsewhere (Tobias, 1969; Tobias & Williamson, 1968) that there are ample reasons for questioning the accuracy of this assumption.

Precisely the same question has been addressed in the test anxiety literature. Wine (1971b) and Sarason (1972) have indicated that test-anxiety effects are observed primarily in those situations where ego-involving instructions are used. Such instructions typically indicate that the experimental task is one which has been highly related to overall success in school. Reviews of this test-anxiety research, such as those by Wine (1971b) and Sarason (1972), have generally indicated that under ego-involving conditions, teamed with difficult material, test anxious students tend to perform more poorly than individuals who are low on test anxiety.

A review of anxiety–treatment-interaction research suggests that ego-involving instructions appear to have less influence on anxiety effects in that area than in the typical contexts in which test-anxiety research is done. Several of the experiments reviewed in Chapter 6 provided some empirical data regarding the degree to which anxiety was actually aroused in the research situation. In Hall's (1970) study, half of the sample was subjected to ego-involving instructions. It was assumed that these students, by virtue of the instructions, should have higher state anxiety than the nonstress group. This assumption was not verified by the results; not only did stress fail to increase A-state scores significantly, but the results actually indicated an effect approaching significance ($p < .10$) that nonstress students actually had higher anxiety scores than those under the stress condition. Tobias and Abramson (1971) also manipulated egoinvolvement by instructions. In that investigation, state-anxiety indices were not available; however, there was no main effect attributable to stress instructions either on posttest performance for the familiar program, the posttest for the technical program, or the number of errors committed on either the familiar or the technical program.

These two anxiety treatment interaction studies manipulating stress in instructional contexts are revealing because they indicate that even in conditions in which experimenters have attempted to induce anxiety, the evidence suggested that such procedures were unsuccessful. These data raise serious questions regarding the degree to which one can assume that, in general, anxiety is aroused and/or maintained within instructional contexts. Until there is greater reassurance that anxiety is, in fact, operative while the student works on the task, all other discussion regarding the effects of anxiety become mere speculation.

For anxiety to be induced in the research task, the student must view the research as an evaluative situation of equal importance to evaluations in classroom lectures, homework assignments, course examinations, and so on. Building the instructional task into an ongoing course would appear, on the face of it, to be the best way of arousing student motivation similar to that existing in school. For college students, especially, it seems specious to assume that any task labeled as research for which the student is frequently forced to "volunteer" actually engages the same intensity of anxiety and stress as a classroom procedure. This may well be less true of elementary-school students who are not as "testwise" as college students. It should be noted, however, that few anxiety–treatment-interaction studies have been conducted with other than college students.

Since anxiety–treatment-interaction studies attempt to generalize to the instructional task, it should prove possible to build various instructional manipulations directly into college courses. Such procedures would circumvent the problem of students viewing the activity as "meaningless" participation in an experiment rather than as an important performance that will be evaluated. The use of brief state-anxiety or worry indices as a check that anxiety is differentially engaged within the research task is especially valuable. The state-anxiety scale, in such situations, provides definitive evidence that the researcher's perception of the relative degree of stress actually coincides with that of most students.

APPLICATIONS OF THE MODEL
IN ANXIETY–TREATMENT-INTERACTION RESEARCH

My purpose in this section is to analyze the reviews of anxiety–treatment-interaction-research in the previous chapters in terms of the model elaborated above. It is hoped that such an analysis will bring some order to these discrepant research findings, as well as suggest more practical leads for future research on the interaction between anxiety and instructional treatments.

It will be recalled that anxiety interaction studies utilizing instructional programs, whether programed or computer based, had few significant interactions which were consistently replicated. It is, of course, possible to ascribe these inconsistencies to procedures, subjects, or, in the case of the heart-disease program, to modifications in the program format. On the other hand, the model suggests that there may have been some other reasons for these inconsistencies.

Studies using instructional programs typically compare the effect of presenting a program in the manner for which it was designed, and then prepare an altered version for comparison. The alteration may involve changing the mode of responding, the organization of the program, or some other characteristic. But, do such alterations change the degree to which the instructional method is affected by anxiety? This question is reviewed below in terms of the types of experimental manipulations which are most likely to yield ultimate achievement differences between students high and low in anxiety.

In anxiety–treatment-interaction research instructional methods or materials are adapted so that students differing in anxiety may profit optimally from the instructional method designed for them. Another approach would be to design the materials in such a way that the student's anxiety is altered so that ultimately the need for alternate tracks would be reduced. Such a possibility would be an enormously exciting outcome of instruction. A number of approaches towards the reduction of test anxiety by essentially instructional means are discussed in Chapter 9. Altering anxiety levels has not been studied from an anxiety–treatment-interaction point of view since it is generally believed that altering the attributes is a much more difficult chore than adapting the instructional methods to the attributes. The optimistic results reported in the test-anxiety-reduction chapter suggest that reducing anxiety as opposed to modifying the instructional treatment, may well merit more serious consideration. Whether changes in cognitive and motivational attributes other than anxiety can be affected as readily as test anxiety remains to be seen. Since this problem was discussed extensively in Chapter 10, it is not pursued here.

To return to the problem of altering the instructional strategy to adapt to individual differences in anxiety, an example may clarify this discussion. Suppose that an instructional program is altered from constructed responding to reading the program cast in the form of completed sentences. How has this alteration affected the psychological processes required by the task, or the point at which anxiety interferes? If anxiety enters at a preprocessing stage, the student is able to compensate for such interference by rereading the instructional materials. Thus, if a student's attention is diverted from the task by anxiety, a rereading of the materials is possible, whether the student is constructing responses or merely reading from the program.

If interference by anxiety occurs during processing, students can remediate this situation since constructed responding and other response modes do not limit the amount of time the student can spend on the problem, nor do they substantially alter the difficulty of the problem.

The same considerations suggest that interference which occurs at the end of processing can be remediated similarly. It appears, then, that these two response modes are not differentially affected by anxiety.

What are the types of instructional manipulations, then, from which it might be possible to expect differences attributable to anxiety? There are various stages of the model at which anxiety effects are expected. These are now reviewed, and the type of experimental manipulations that may make a difference at each stage are discussed. Finally, the results of the literature reviewed here are reinterpreted in terms of that discussion.

Preprocessing Effects

One way of analyzing how anxiety affects the instructional sequence at this stage is to determine what a hypothetical student could do whose performance is affected. If the input stream has in some way been interfered with by anxiety (such as by reducing attentiveness), the student could attempt to reinstitute it by rereading a text, rewinding an audio- or videotape, or restarting a calculation. Interference at the preprocessing stage, then, can be reduced by any procedures that permit reinspection of the input materials or checking the input against a standard. One would expect, therefore, that instructional methods which are affected by anxiety at this stage are ones that prevent the student from reinspecting input materials, or that make it more difficult to reinspect or check.

A prediction from the model would be that any instructional method that prevents the student from such checking would be differentially sensitive to being affected by anxiety. Specifically, achievement of high-anxiety students should be negatively affected when they are unable to reinspect input, whereas such an opportunity should be unimportant to low-anxiety students. For example, a comparison between a live lecture in which the instructor does not pause for questions, and an audio- or videotape of the same lecture which the student is free to rewind as needed ought to be differentially affected by anxiety. Support for such anxiety effects comes from the study by Oosthoek and Ackers (1972). It will be recalled that these investigators found that for students above the mean on debilitating anxiety, achievement from a taped lecture was higher than from a conventional lecture. Furthermore, a correlation was found between the number of times students rewound the tape to reinstitute input and debilitating anxiety. While these effects appeared small, further research would be required to manipulate these variables more rigorously and to check on the size of this effect.

The generally pessimistic findings regarding anxiety interactions when different formats of programed or computer-based instructional materials were compared can be easily understood from this formulation. Neither programed nor computer-based instruction vary with respect to the student's ability to reinstitute parts of the input. In programed instruction students are generally free to go back and reread any part of the instructional material desired, irrespective of the format or organization of the materials. Interactions with anxiety at the preprocessing stage would, therefore, not be expected. In computer-based instructional environments, on the other hand, irrespective of the particular condition, students are generally unable to go back and reinspect any part of the content. Again, then, interactions with anxiety would not be expected since none of the instructional methods permit reinstituting of the input stream.

Another variable related to the opportunity to reinspect part of instructional input, but not identical to it, is control of the pace of instruction. Anxious students who have difficulty focusing attention on task relevant concerns (Sarason, 1972; Wine, 1971b) should have greater difficulty under group-paced compared to self-paced instruction. When students have no control over instructional pace it appears likely that more anxious students are more likely to miss part of the instructional input since anxiety diverts their attention. Hence, they would have greater difficulty processing the material. It is important that the instructional rate in such pacing experiments be such that frequent repetitions of instructional content are not built into the instructional sequence.

Comparisons between conventional classroom instruction, which tends to be teacher paced, and some individualized procedures, which generally are student paced, are not as revealing about the issue of reinspecting content as one would at first expect. Teachers typically repeat content and give different examples that review the content selectively so that even though the instructional input is not under student control, there is a fair amount of repetition to it. Ripple *et al.* (1969) reported that in their comparison of instruction by teachers in classrooms and by programed instruction, the teacher groups typically took *longer* on the instructional content than the average class working under self-paced programed instruction. Clearly, in this example at least, the repetition of input would not have been much of a problem in the classroom conditions. Furthermore, teachers can be stopped and asked questions if part of the input has been missed, thus restoring the missing input element.

It seems clear that the potential effect of anxiety at the preprocessing stage is best manipulated by strictly controlled instructional sequences in which repeating the input, or manipulating the pace of instruction are the specific independent variables in the research. In such experiments, students in the appropriate groups should be encouraged to repeat selected parts of the input as they need to, and such repetition should be made convenient.

The convenience factor is of some importance, especially in programed and computer-based instructional situations. Skimming an instructional program tends to be something of a chore since the sequence of ideas is tightly controlled by the program, making it difficult for the student to find exactly the part of the content to be checked. In computer-based instructional environments these difficulties are enlarged since the student does not have all of the instructional material in view. In order to implement such a condition, programmers would have to make it convenient for students to transfer to previous frames, perhaps by numbering them consecutively so that students could easily go back to any one, or several previous frames.

Finally, to minimize the effect of anxiety at the preprocessing stage, and all other points, it is vital that students' anxiety be actively engaged during the instruction. The instruction has to matter enough so that students will be concerned about those aspects that they might have missed, and motivated enough to reinspect the input. Without effective involvement of the student and consequent engagement of anxiety, none of the procedures outlined would matter.

In summary, the effects of anxiety at the preprocessing stage can most effectively be studied by comparing conditions in which the students' ability to reinspect instructional input is varied. This can be done either by directly implementing an instructional condition in which students can go back to selected parts of input, or cannot do so; or by manipulating a student-paced versus group-paced condition. In the latter event, it is important that the group pacing does not include extensive repetition which would be synonymous with allowing students to reinspect selected parts of the input. Problems in implementing such a condition in programed and computer-based instructional systems were identified, and finally, the importance of insuring that anxiety is effectively aroused and maintained was reemphasized.

The Effect of Anxiety during Processing

Conceptually, at this stage, the student processes the instructional material by encoding it; storing in either short- or long-term memory; bringing problem solving, or organizational processes to bear on the task; or by invoking retrieval processes that relate this problem to previously stored content or skills. It is quite probable that this list of cognitive processes includes many which are differentially sensitive to the effects of anxiety. Unfortunately, little is known regarding the types of cognitive processes required by different curricular areas, or by different instructional methods within the same curricular area. Specification of the types of processes that are involved in a specific content area, or by an instructional method is thus premature. It may be possible, however, to specify some task parameters which are clearly involved during the processing stage of acquisition, which are differentially susceptible to the effects of anxiety, irrespective of the cognitive process involved.

In order for anxiety to have significant consequences at the processing stage the anxiety state must affect the cognitive processes transforming the input rather than the input materials themselves. Such an effect would have to be differential, that is, high anxiety should affect the cognitive processes in a different way than does low anxiety. The previous research suggests that a differential effect is most likely to be mediated by manipulating the following task parameters: (1) difficulty of content; (2) organization of the task; and (3) the degree to which the task relies on memory processes.

Difficulty

One of the most frequently replicated findings in research relating anxiety to learning is that anxiety interferes with learning only on relatively difficult subject matter. As indicated elsewhere in this book (see Chapter 3), drive theory predicts a facilitating effect of anxiety on learning for relatively easy subject matter, and an interfering or debilitating effect on more difficult content. The state-anxiety research reported in Chapter 9 has also indicated that, as one might expect, state anxiety appears closely related to subject matter difficulty: it is relatively low when subject matter is easy, and increases as subject matter becomes more difficult. Similarly, research on test anxiety (Wine, 1971b; Sarason, 1972) shows that the debilitating effects of test anxiety are most likely to be seen in situations in which both difficult material and ego-arousing conditions are utilized.

An important and unanswered question is precisely what level of difficulty is necessary for anxiety to exert its debilitating effect. In experiments relating anxiety to learning, researchers typically report the number of errors students committed on the easy and difficult material. Frequently, then, a test of the difference in the numbers of errors is reported justifying the description of one task as easy, and the other as difficult. What is not reported, however, is the *percentage of errors* committed. This percentage may be computed by dividing the erroneous responses by the total number of possible responses, or by the total number of correct responses. In some experimental situations, such as concept-formation tasks in which subjects have to keep generating hypotheses until the task is solved, the total number of responses may well be infinite, and hence percentage of erroneous responses cannot be obtained. In free-recall experiments students may respond with words not a part of the learning materials in the first place, the number of errors of this type is also unknown, since students can "recall" many responses they were never asked to learn initially. In this instance, however, a report of what proportion of the responses made by the student were incorrect would be useful. Report of such data may prove enlightening regarding when anxiety effects can be expected in instructional situations.

The inconsistent findings, and generally pessimistic state of affairs regarding anxiety treatment interactions in studies using programed or computer-based instruction can be understood when the relative ease of these materials is considered. There are two factors contributing to making such materials easy: (1) low error rates; and (2) opportunity for self-correction.

Low error rates. The heart-disease instructional program, for example, has error rates around 3% for the familiar, and about 20% for the technical part of the program. Differences between these error rates (Tobias, 1968) were highly significant, but how difficult is a task in which persons pass approximately 80% of the material? From the point of view of norm-referenced evaluation, an item which is passed by 80% of the population would be considered relatively easy, as would tests with mean scores of 80%. For instructional programs employed in anxiety–treatment-interaction studies, error-rate data in terms of proportion of errors are not reported. It is safe to assume, however, that generally these error rates are comparable to those obtained for the heart-disease instructional program, since a widely held conviction among instructional developers is that effective instructional materials should have relatively low error rates. One study in an instructional context in which relatively large anxiety effects were observed (O'Neil *et al.,* 1969a) indicated an interaction between task difficulty and state anxiety. Some difficult materials were used which consisted of mathematical problems and proofs, and had approximate error rates of 73% and 60% for two different sections. These materials were difficult by any standard. Error rates for the easy material used in that investigation were virtually 0%. The question then arises, how difficult, in terms of proportion of errors, should material be to induce high anxiety, and in order for anxiety to have a differential effect?

Surprisingly enough there are no answers to this question. Despite the voluminous research on anxiety in experimental and clinical contexts, few benchmarks for specific difficulty levels can be offered beyond the vague generalization that anxiety is likely to impair performance on difficult content, and facilitate, or have no effect, on easy subject matter. This is certainly an area deserving intensive further investigation so as to establish some benchmark regarding the precentage of errors that may be considered indication of "easy" and "difficult" material. Until such results become available, significant progress in anxiety–treatment-interaction research is unlikely since a "difficult" task in one study may be quite different from a "difficult" task in another study. Further research in both experimental and instructional contexts is urgently needed to clarify this question.

Opportunity for correction.   Another factor contributing to the relative simplicity of programed or computer-based self-instructional materials deals with the opportunity for correction. In experimental tasks and in lectures and textbooks, an error is quite likely to have cumulative effects, since the opportunities for self-correction tend to be limited. With self-instructional materials, on the other hand, self-corrective features are built into these materials. In those conditions in which feedback regarding the accuracy of responses is provided, correction occurs by virtue of the learner getting the right answer. When instructional programs are altered by removing feedback or by converting them into a reading mode, correction still occurs due to the frame-by-frame structure of most programs in which prior material is implicitly rehearsed before new material is introduced. These considerations are discussed further in the next section on organization of the task. Here, it is sufficient to suggest that the opportunities for correction of misconceptions in most self-instructional tasks limits the debilitating effects of anxiety by reducing the probability of the cumulative effect of error.

The preceding discussion suggests an explanation for Hall's (1970) surprising findings. It will be recalled that Hall used an easy (error rate = .25, .22) and difficult (error rate = .55, .57) task. The error rate should certainly have been high enough to induce interfering anxiety effects (although it should be re-emphasized that evidence for this assumption is lacking), yet there was no evidence of difficulty level by anxiety interaction in this study. It seems likely that this program had enough opportunities for correction built in to reduce the debilitating effect of anxiety.

In summary, then, it has been suggested that one of the variables mediating the effects of anxiety on instruction at the processing stage is the difficulty of the instructional content. A widely reported finding that anxiety interferes with learning of relatively difficult material cannot easily be applied to instructional contexts since difficulty levels are undefined. Finally, it is suggested that in most self-instructional contexts, either programed or computer based, materials are generally too easy to induce interference by anxiety, since they have self-corrective features built into the materials, and low error rates.

Organization of the Task

The research suggests that the degree to which a task is well organized is another variable mediating the effect of anxiety during the processing stage. Recall that replicated anxiety–treatment-interaction findings were reported in classroom-based studies. Dowaliby and Schumer (1973) and Domino (1974) both found that anxious students achieved more from a teacher-organized lecture, than from a student-centered recitation-discussion section. Similarly, the finding of Grimes and Allinsmith (1961), that high-anxious students learned more from a well-structured phonics method than from a more casually organized whole-word method, also supports this formulation. In these studies, the more organized presentation led to superior achievement for the high-anxiety students compared to the less organized presentation.

Self-instructional materials (programed or computer-based) tend to be better organized than lectures or textbooks. Even when the program is altered to a reading format or any other of the response modes, the tight organization of the program still persists and interactions with anxiety would, therefore, be minimized. The organization of programs is destroyed, of course, by randomizing the frame sequence, yet such studies have also failed to yield interactions with anxiety. As has been suggested in Chapter 6, in such studies students are most likely to ascribe their difficulties to the grossly distorted sequence, rather than to their own perceived inadequacy. Consequently, interactions with anxiety cannot be expected.

It has been suggested previously that at the preprocessing stage, the effects of anxiety are mediated by the students' ability to review, or reinspect input. At that point, lectures were considered more prone to be affected by anxiety because it was difficult to review input material under such conditions. But it is also suggested that lectures are superior to student-centered discussions, at least, in terms of organization of subject matter. These expectations are not directly paradoxical. When material is equally well organized, opportunities for reinspecting the content are likely to determine differentially which method is superior for high-anxious students. On the other hand, when both instructional methods have opportunities for reviewing selected parts of the content, the organization of the material is likely to be decisive with respect to which method is most advantageous for anxious students.

The term "well organized" is, of course, extremely vague, and subject to some misinterpretation. One possible way out of such ambiguity is to suggest that for intellectual skills, well-organized materials are those following the hierarchical formulation advocated by Gagné (1968). When intellectual skills cannot be rigorously differentiated from verbal information, or facts, an organizational scheme such as that advocated by Ausubel (1968) would be one definition of a well-organized sequence. While the work of these writers provide criteria by which the organization of content can be judged, it is well known (Bunderson, 1973) that developing a hierarchy is not as reliable as one might wish. When different individuals are asked to develop a hierarchy of the same subject matter, they invariably tend to develop different ones. For our purposes it is assumed that while there may be a good deal of individual difference with respect to which of a number of hierarchies is optimal, there is likely to be substantial reliability regarding whether a particular set of material is well organized or poorly organized. This area, and many others in the field of instructional research remains to be clarified by future investigation.

Memory Support

The third variable mediating anxiety effects at the processing stage appears to be the degree to which the student has to to rely on memory without referring to external prompts while processing an instructional task. As has been discussed elsewhere in this book (Chapter 4), the achievement of anxious students in situations in which they ordinarily would have to rely on their own memory is facilitated by being given external aids reducing the degree to which they have to rely on their own memory for task solution. Typically, there are no differences for low-anxiety students between conditions in which memory supports are and are not provided. This is a condition which has not been widely manipulated in anxiety—treatment-interaction experimentation, though the evidence indicates that this might be a fruitful variable for systematic manipulation in instructional research.

To some degree, providing memory support is similar to being able to review the input. Conceptually, reviewing input refers to a situation in which instructional material has not registered for processing. Providing memory support, on the other hand, refers to a situation in which the elements of a problem have been processed, however, the student has to resort to previously processed rules, explanations, or aids which at the moment are not accessible. In other words, varying memory support is presumed to represent a condition of reliance on retrieval from long-term memory. Rewinding input, on the other hand, is supposed to represent a condition in which material has not been subjected to processing or storage into short- or long-term memory. The two processes can be operationally differentiated. In reinspecting input the student is unable to reproduce some of the material from the input stream. In varying memory support, however, the student was at some time able to reproduce the desired information; may be able to do so when asked for the information specifically; but is unable to retrieve the information at a time when it is needed for the solution of problems on which the student is working.

Summary

It has been suggested that effects of anxiety at the processing stage are mediated by the difficulty of the content, the tightness of organization of material, and the degree to which it relies on memory-retrieval processes. Material which is "difficult" and not "well organized"—two terms requiring better definition from future research—and requires retrieval of previously mastered material for problem solution would be especially subject to interference for students high in anxiety. Conversely, content which is easy, well organized, and does not require extensive retrieval would be especially advantageous to students high in anxiety. Low-anxiety students, on the other hand, may well function equally effectively under both situations. It is recognized that if material were simultaneously difficult, disorganized, and provided no external memory support, no student would do well. Future research will have to vary these conditions selectively in order to ascertain their parameters.

Postprocessing Effects

As indicated above, in this model of the effects of anxiety on instruction, postprocessing effects by anxiety occur when students have solved the problem, understood the message in text or lecture, and in some inexplicable way become unable to do so when required on posttest. Some examples of this effect are: being unable to retrieve a melody, fact, or equation even though one is quite sure one "knows" it. When applied to instruction this effect is similar to the memory-support condition in the processing stage. In other words, previously stored material cannot be effectively retrieved when it is required for task solution on criterion tests.

Conceptually, interference by anxiety at the postprocessing stage is different from that at processing. In the former, students have solved the problem at some point, but are unable to reproduce the solution at posttest. During processing, problem solution has not occurred and the interference consists of an inability to recall the previously stored concepts, facts, or rules that are required to generate the answer.

There appear to be no anxiety–treatment-interaction studies manipulating this variable. It would seem possible to implement such an investigation by comparing posttest performance of students who have gone though a similar instructional sequence. During instruction, students would be permitted to take notes or to make some record of the instructional content and their work on those materials. When required to report for posttest, some students would be given access to this information while others would be prevented from looking at them. It would be predicted from the present model that having notes available would be especially advantageous to high-anxiety students as they are more prone to interference from anxiety at this stage than would be low-anxiety students.

SUMMARY

The research model presented in this chapter has conceptualized the instructional process into input, processing, and output sections. It has been suggested that anxiety can affect the instructional process at a number of points, and that these have not always been systematically and rigorously manipulated in research studying the interaction between anxiety and instruction, as well as in the effects of anxiety in general.

Preprocessing interference is presumed to occur when the input of the instructional material has in some way been restricted. It is suggested that such restriction of input is more likely to occur for high-anxiety students than for their low-anxiety counterparts. Interference at this stage can be studied most effectively by manipulating the opportunity students have to review the input, or check it in general. In instructional contexts, opportunity for review has rarely been made a variable in research designs. Typically students in any condition could either review at will, or were prevented from doing so by the conditions or equipment utilized in the experiments.

Processing interference is presumed to occur when the input has registered and cognitive processes are brought to bear in order to master and solve the task. While it is premature to speculate on the specific cognitive processes that different curricular areas, or instructional methods utilize, it is argued that systematic variation of the following task parameters should yield significant anxiety effects:

1. *Difficulty of the content:* Research has generally demonstrated that students low in anxiety do better on difficult content than high-anxious individuals. The implications of these findings for instruction are obscure, since the absolute levels of difficulty required to invoke and maintain anxiety have not been specified. Further research in this area is urgently needed.

2. *Organization of the task:* Research has indicated that differences between high- and low-anxious students are most likely to occur on instructional material which is loosely organized. The tighter the organization, the less likely are anxiety effects to be found.

3. *The degree to which the task calls for memory:* Tasks with minimal reliance on memory tend to be less impaired than those requiring memory for task solution.

Interference after processing is presumed to occur between the time content or skills have been acquired from instruction, and the student is required to demonstrate these on posttest. Such interference occurs when students solve problems during the instructional sequence that they are unable to during posttest. This source of interference has been little studied in the effects of anxiety on instruction.

References

Allen, G. J. Effectiveness of study counseling and desensitization in alleviating test anxiety in college students. *Journal of Abnormal Psychology*, 1971, *77*, 282–289.

Allen, G. J. The behavioral treatment of test anxiety. *Behavior Therapy*, 1972, *3*, 253–262.

Allen, G. J. Private communication, September, 1972.

Alpert, R., & Haber, R. M. Anxiety in academic achievement situations. *Journal of Abnormal and Social Psychology*, 1960, *61*, 207–215.

American Psychological Association, Ad hoc Committee on Ethical Standards in Psychological Research. *Ethical principles in the conduct of research with human participants.* Washington, D.C.: APA, 1973.

Anderson, R. C. Educational psychology. *Annual Review of Psychology*, 1967, *18*, 103–164.

Anderson, R. C., Kulhavy, R. W., & André, T. Feedback procedures in programmed instruction. *Journal of Educational Psychology*, 1970, *62*, 148–156.

Atkinson, J. W. *An introduction to motivation.* Princeton, N.J.: Van Nostrand-Reinhold, 1964.

Atkinson, R. C. Teaching children to read using a computer. *American Psychologist*, 1974, *29*, 169–178.

Atkinson, R. C., & Wilson, H. A. (Ed.). *Computer-assisted instruction: A book of readings.* New York: Academic Press, 1969.

Ausubel, D. P. *Educational psychology: A cognitive view.* New York: Holt, Rinehart, & Winston, 1968.

Baker, F. B. Computer-based instructional management systems: A first look. *Review of Educational Research*, 1972, *41*, 51–70.

Bandura, A. *Principles of behavior modification.* New York: Holt, Rinehard, & Winston, 1969.

Bandura, A. *Social Learning Theory.* Morristown, N. J.: General Learning Press, 1971.

Barnes, I. D. The effect of learner controlled computer assisted instruction on performance in multiplication skills. Unpublished doctoral dissertation, University of Southern California, 1970.

Bechtoldt, H. P. Response defined anxiety and MMPI variables. *Iowa Academy of Science*, 1953, *60*, 495–499.

Bellewicz, W. The efficiency of matched samples: An empirical investigation. *Biometrics*, 1965, *11* 623–644.

241

Berliner, D. C., & Cahen, L. S. Trait-treatment interactions and learning. In F. N. Kerlinger (Ed.), *Review Of Research In Education. 1,* Itasca, Ill.: Peacock, 1973.

Bloom, B. S., *Taxonomy of educational objectives. Handbook I: Cognitive domain.* New York: McKay, 1956.

Bloxom, B. Relationship of test anxiety and need for achievement to academic achievement. *American Psychologist,* 1964, *19,* 708.

Bowers, K. S. Situationism in psychology: An analysis and a critique. *Psychological Review,* 1973, *80,* 307–335.

Bracht, G. H. Experimental factors related to aptitude-treatment interactions. *Review of Educational Research.* 1970, *40,* 627–645.

Briggs, L. J., Campeau, P. L., Gagne, R. M. & May, M. A. *Instructional media: A Procedure for the design of multi-media instruction, a critical review of research, and suggestions for future research.* Pittsburgh, Pa.: American Institutes for Research, 1966.

Bunderson, C. V. Team production to learner-controlled courseware: A progress report (Technical Report No. 1, Institute for Computer Uses in Education). Provo, Utah: Brigham Young University Press, 1973.

Cameron, N. *The psychology of behavior disorders: A bio-social interpretation.* Boston: Houghton Mifflin, 1947.

Campeau, P. L. Test anxiety and feedback in programmed instruction. *Journal of Educational Psychology,* 1968, *59,* 159–163.

Carrier, N. A., & Jewell, D. O. Efficiency in measuring the effect of anxiety upon academic performance. *Journal of Education and Psychology,* 1966, *57,* 23–26.

Castaneda, A., Palermo, D., & McCandless, B. Complex learning and performance as a function of anxiety in children and task difficulty. *Child Development,* 1956, *27,* 327–332.

Chestnut, W. J. The effects of structured and unstructured group counseling on male college students' underachievement. *Journal of Consulting Psychology,* 1965, *12,* 388–394.

Cohen, I. S. Programmed learning and the Socratic Dialogue. *American Psychologist,* 1963, *17,* 772–775.

Cohen, J. Multiple regression as a general data analytic system. *Psychological Bulletin,* 1968, *70,* 426–443.

Collier, R., Poynor, L., O'Neil, H. F., Jr., & Judd, W. A. Effects of learner control on performance and state anxiety in a computerized learning task. Paper presented at the annual meeting of the American Educational Research Association, New Orleans, February 1973.

Cronbach, L. J. The two disciplines of scientific psychology. *American Psychologist,* 1957, *12,* 671–684.

Cronbach, L. J. How can instruction be adapted to individual differences? In R. M. Gagne (Ed.), *Learning and individual differences.* Columbus, Ohio: Merrill, 1967.

Cronbach, L. J., & Furby, L. How we should measure "change"—or should we? *Psychological Bulletin,* 1970, *74,* 68–80.

Cronbach, L. J., & Snow, R. E. Individual differences and learning ability as a function of instructional variables (Final Report, United States Office of Education, Contract No. OEC 4-6-061269-1217, School of Education, Stanford University). Palo Alto, Cal.: 1969.

Cronbach, L. J., & Snow, R. E. *Aptitudes and instructional methods.* New York: Irvington, 1977.

Darwin, C. R. *The expression of the emotions in man and animals.* London: Murray, 1872.

Datta, L. E. On the unidimensionality of the Alpert–Haber achievement anxiety test. *Psychological Reports,* 1967, *20,* 606.

De Boer, J. J., & Dallmann, M. *The teaching of reading.* New York: Holt, Rinehart, & Winston, 1970.

Delbecq, A. L., & VandeVen, A. H. A group process model for problem identification and program planning. *Journal of Applied Behavioral Science,* 1971, *7,* 466–492.

Dick, W., & Gallagher, P. Systems concepts and computer-managed instruction: An implementation and validation study. *Educational Technology,* 1972, *12,* 33–39.

Dixon, P. N., & Judd, W. A. Summative evaluation of a CMI system in educational psychology. Paper presented at Chicago, April 1974.

Doctor, R. M., & Altman, F. Worry and emotionality as components of test anxiety: Replication and further data. *Psychological Reports,* 1969, *24,* 563–568.

Domino, G. Aptitude by treatment interaction effects in college instruction. Paper presented at a meeting of the American Psychological Association, New Orleans, September 1974.

Donner, L., & Guerney, B., Jr. Automated group desensitization for test anxiety. *Behavior Research and Therapy,* 1969, *7,* 1–14.

Dowaliby, F. J., & Schumer H. Teacher-centered versus student-centered mode of college classroom instructions related to manifest anxiety. *Journal of Educational Psychology,* 1973, *64,* 125–132.

Duchastel, P. C., & Merrill, P. F. The effects of behavioral objectives on learning: A review of empirical studies. *Review of Educational Research,* 1973, *43,* 53–69.

D'Zurilla, T. J., & Goldfried, M. R. Problem solving and behavior modification. In C. M. Franks & G. T. Wilson (Eds.), *Annual review of behavior therapy and practice.* New York: Brunner/Mazel, 1973.

Easterbrook, J. A. The effect of emotion on cue utilization and the organization of behavior. *Psychological Review,* 1959, *66,* 183–201.

Ellis, A., & Harper, R. A. *A guide to rational living.* North Hollywood, Calif.: Wilshire, 1961.

Elwood, D. L. Automation of psychological testing, *American Psychologist,* 1969, *24,* 287–289.

Elwood, D. L. Automated versus face-to-face intelligence testing: Comparison of test–retest reliabilities. *International Journal of Man–Machine Studies,* 1972, *4,* 363–369. (a)

Elwood, D. L. Reliability of automated intelligence testing using a three-month test–retest interval. *International Review of Applied Psychology,* 1973, *22,* 157–163.

Emery, J. R., & Krumboltz, J. D. Standard versus individualized hierarchies in desensitization to reduce test anxiety. *Journal Counseling Psychology,* 1967, *14,* 204–209.

Endler, N., & Hunt, J. McV. Sources of behavioral variance as measured by the S–R inventory of anxiousness. *Psychological Bulletin,* 1966, *65,* 366–346.

Erikson, E. H. *Childhood and society.* New York: Norton, 1950.

Ericksen, S. E. Symposium: The bridge between the learning research laboratory and the classroom. Introduction to the symposium. *Educational Psychologist,* 1973, *10,* 105–106.

Evans, W. M. & Miller, J. R. Differential effects on response bias of computer vs. conventional administration of a social science questionnaire: An exploratory methodological experiment. Behavioral Science, 1969, 14, 216–227.

Flynn, J. T., & Morgan, J. H. A methodological study of the effectiveness of programmed instruction through analysis of learner characteristics. *Proceedings of the Annual Convention of the American Psychological Association,* 1966, *1,* 259–260. (Summary)

Freud, S. [*The problem of anxiety.*] New York: Psychoanalytic Quarterly Press & Norton, 1936.

Gagne, R. M. (Ed.) *Learning and individual differences.* Columbus, Ohio: Merrill, 1967.

Gagne, R. M. Learning hierarchies. *Educational Psychology,* 1968, *6,* 1–9.

Gagne, R. M. *Conditions of learning* (2nd ed.). New York: Holt, Rinehart, & Winston, 1970.

Gagne, R. M., & Briggs, L. J. *Principles of instructional design.* New York: Holt, Rinehart, & Winston, 1974.

Gallagher, P., O'Neil, H. F., Jr., & Dick, W. Effects of trait and state anxiety in a computer-managed instruction course. Paper presented at a meeting of the American Educational Research Association, New York, February, 1971.

Gantt, W. H. The origin and development of nervous disturbances experimentally produced. *American Journal of Psychiatry*, 1942, *98*, 475–481.

Glaser, R. Psychology and instructional technology. In R. Glaser (Ed.), *Training research and education*. Pittsburgh: University of Pittsburgh Press, 1962.

Glaser, R. Some implications of previous work on learning and individualized differences. In R. M. Gagne (Ed.), *Learning and individual differences*. Columbus, Ohio: Merrill, 1967.

Glaser, R. Individuals and learning: The new aptitudes. *Educational Research*, 1972, *1*, 5–12.

Glaser, R. Educational psychology and education. *American Psychologist*, 1973, *28*, 557–566.

Goldberg, L. R. Student personality characteristics and optimal college learning conditions: An extensive search for trait-by-treatment interactions. *Instructional Science*, 1972, *1*, 153–210.

Goldfried, M. R. Systematic desensitization as training in self-control. *Journal of Consulting and Clinical Psychology*, 1971, *37*, 228–235.

Goldfried, M. R. Reduction of generalized anxiety through a variant of systematic desentization. In M. R. Goldfried & M. Merbaum (Eds.), *Behavior change through self control*. New York: Holt, Rinehart, & Winston, 1973.

Gonzalez, H. A comparison of three methods in the treatment of test anxiety. Unpublished master's thesis, University of South Florida, 1976.

Goulet, L. R. Anxiety (drive) and verbal learning: Implications for research and some methodological considerations. *Psychological Bulletin*, 1968, *69*, 235–247.

Grant, R. D., Jr. Validation of an automated test anxiety reduction program. Unpublished doctoral dissertation, The University of Texas at Austin, 1973.

Grimes, J. W., & Allinsmith, A. W. Compulsivity, anxiety, and school achievement. *Merrill-Palmer Quarterly*, 1961, *7*, 247–271.

Grossnickle, F. E., Brueckner, L. J., & Reckzeh, J. *Discovering meanings in elementary school mathematics*. New York: Holt, Rinehart, & Winston, 1968.

Guilford, J. P., & Fruchter, B. *Fundamental statistics in psychology and education* (5th ed.). New York: McGraw-Hill, 1973.

Hall, B. W. Anxiety, stress, task difficulty and achievement via programmed instruction. Paper presented at a meeting of the American Educational Research Association, Minneapolis, March, 1970.

Hall, R. A. Desensitization of test anxiety. Unpublished doctoral dissertation, Colorado State University, 1970.

Hansen, J. B. Effects of feedback, learner control, and cognitive abilities on state anxiety and performance in a computer-assisted instruction task. *Journal of Educational Psychology*, 1974, *66*, 247–254.

Hedl, J. J., Jr. An evaluation of a computer-based intelligence test (Tech. Report No. 21). Tallahassee Fla.: Florida State University, 1971.

Hedl, J. J., Jr. State anxiety considerations within computer-based testing environments. Paper presented at a meeting of the American Psychological Society, Montreal, Canada, August 1973.

Hedl, J. J., Jr., O'Neil, H. F., Jr., & Hansen, D. N. Affective reactions toward computer-based intelligence testing. *Journal of Consulting and Clinical Psychology*, 1973, *40*, 217–22.

Hedl, J. J., Jr., O'Neil, H. F., Jr., & Richardson, F. C. Affective considerations in computer-managed instruction. Paper presented at a meeting of the American Educational Research Association, Chicago, April, 1974.

Heidegger, M. [*Existence and being.*] Chicago: Regnerg, 1949.

Hill, K. T., & Sarason, S. B. A further longitudinal study of the relation of test anxiety and defensiveness to test and school performance over the elementary school years. *Child Development Monographs*, 1966, *31*, 1–76.

Hodges, W. F. The effects of success, threat of shock and failure on anxiety. *Dissertation Abstracts*, 1968, *28*(10-B), 4296. Order No. 68-5388.

Holland, J. G. A quantitative measure for programmed instruction. *American Educational Research Journal*, 1967, *4*, 87–101.

Holtzman, W. H. (Ed.). *Computer-assisted instruction, testing, and guidance*. New York: Harper & Row, 1970.

Hops, H. & Cobb, J. Initial investigations into academic skill training, direct instruction and first grade achievement. *Journal of Educational Psychology*, 1974, *66*, 548–559.

Horowitz, F., & Armentrout, J. Discrimination learning, manifest anxiety and effects of reinforcement. *Child Development*, 1965, *36*, 731–748.

Hughes, J. B., II, Sprague, J. L., & Bendig, A. W. Anxiety level, response alteration, and performance in serial learning. *Journal of Psychology*, 1954, *38*, 421–426.

Hull, C. L. *Principles of behavior*. New York: Appleton. 1943.

Hunt, D. E. Person-environment interaction: A challenge found wanting before it was tried. *Review of Educational Research*, 1975, *45*, 209–230.

Jacobson, E. *Progressive relaxation*. Chicago: University of Chicago Press, 1938.

James, T. G., & O'Neil, H. F., Jr. Effects of sex and stress on state anxiety and performance in computer-assisted learning. Paper presented at a meeting of the American Educational Research Association, New York, February, 1971.

Johnson, D. F., & Mihal, W. C. Performance of blacks and whites in computerized versus manual testing environments. *American Psychologist*, 1973, *28*, 694–699.

Johnson, P. O., & Neyman, J. Tests of certain linear hypotheses and their applications to some educational problems. *Statistical Research Memoirs*, 1935, *1*, 57–93.

Jones, H. E. The study of patterns of emotional expression. In M. L. Reymert (Ed.), *Feelings and emotions*. New York: McGraw-Hill, 1950. Pp. 161–168.

Joy, V. L. Repression-sensitization and interpersonal behavior. Paper presented at a meeting of the American Psychological Association, Philadelphia, August, 1963.

Judd, W. A. Learner controlled computer-assisted instruction. Paper presented at the International School of Computer in Education, Pugnochiuso, Italy, July 1972.

Judd, W. A., Daubek, K. & O'Neil, H. F., Jr. Individual differences in learner controlled computer-assisted instruction. Paper presented at the annual convention of the American Educational Research Association, Washington, D.C., March 1975.

Judd, W. A., O'Neil, H. F., Jr., Rogers, D. D., & Richardson, F. C. Development and formative evaluation of a five module computer-managed instructional system for educational psychology. (Tech. Report No. 19) Austin: Computer-Assisted Instruction Laboratory, The University of Texas at Austin, 1973.

Judd, W. A., O'Neil, H. F., Jr., & Spelt, P. F. Individual differences and learner control I: Program development and investigation of control over mnemonics in computer-assisted instruction. (Interim Report, U.S. Air Force, Human Resources Laboratory, Contract AFHRL-TR-74-3.) Austin: Computer-Assisted Instruction Laboratory, The University of Texas at Austin, July 1974. (a)

Kamin, L. J., & Fedorchak, O. The Taylor scale, hunger and verbal learning. *Canadian Journal of Psychology*, 1957, *2*, 212–218.

Kelly, F. J., Beggs, D. L., McNeil, K. A., Eichelbeigel, T., & Lyon, J. *Research design in the behavioral sciences: Multiple Regression approach*. Carbondale, Ill.: Southern Illinois University Press, 1971.

Kerlinger, F. N. (Ed.). *Review of Research in Education*. Itasca, Ill.: Peacock, 1973.

Kerlinger, F. N. & Carroll, J. B. (Ed.). *Review of Research in Education*. Itasca, Ill.: Peacock, 1974.

Kerlinger, F. N., & Pedhazur, E. *Multiple regression in behavioral research.* New York: Holt, Rinehart, & Winston, 1973.

Kierkegaard, S. [*The concept of dread.*] (W. Lowrie, trans). Princeton, N. J.: Princeton University Press, 1944. (Originally published, 1844).

Kight, H. R., & Sassenrath, J. M. Relation of achievement motivation and test anxiety to performance in programmed instruction. *Journal of Educational Psychology,* 1966, *57,* 14–17.

Klein, S. P., Frederiksen, N., & Evans, F. R. Anxiety and learning to formulate hypotheses. *Journal of Educational Psychology,* 1969, *60,* 465–475.

Krathwohl, D. R., Bloom, B. S., & Masia, B. B. *Taxonomy of Educational Objectives: Handbook II: Affective Domain.* New York: McKay, 1964.

Lache, S. I. Auto-instructional response mode and anxiety as factors in the retention of simple verbal materials. Paper presented at a meeting of the American Educational Research Association, New York, New York. February, 1967.

Lacey, J. I. Psychophysiological approaches to the evaluation of psychotherapeutic process and outcome. In E. A. Rubinstein and M. B. Parloff (Eds.), *Research in Psychotherapy.* Washington, D. C.: Amer. Psychol. Ass., 1959. Pp. 160–208.

Land, K. C. Principles of path analysis. In E. F. Borgatta (Ed.), *Sociological Methodology.* San Francisco: Jossey-Bass, 1969.

Lang, P. J. The mechanics of desensitization and the laboratory study of human fear. In C. Franks (Ed.), *Behavior therapy: Appraisal and status.* New York: McGraw-Hill, 1969.

Lanzetta, J. T. Information acquisition in decision making. In O. J. Harvey (Ed.), *Motivation and social interaction.* New York: Ronald Press, 1963. Pp. 239–265.

Lazarus, A. A. *Behavior therapy and beyond.* New York: McGraw-Hill, 1971.

Lazarus, R. S., & Opton, E. M., Jr. The study of psychological stress. In C. D. Spielberger (Ed.), *Anxiety and behavior.* New York: Academic Press, 1966.

Leherissey, B. L. The effect of stimulating state epistemic curiosity on state anxiety and performance in a complex computer-assisted learning task. Unpublished doctoral dissertation, Florida State University, 1971.

Leherissey, B. L., O'Neil, H. F., Jr., & Hansen, D. N. Effects of memory support upon anxiety and performance in computer-assisted learning. *Journal of Educational Psychology,* 1971, *62,* 413–420.

Leherissey, B. L., O'Neil, H. F. Jr., Heinrich, D. & Hansen, D. N. Effect of anxiety, response mode and subject matter familiarity in computer-assisted learning. *Journal of Educational Psychology,* 1973, *64,* 310–324.

Lekarczyk, D. T., & Hill, K. T. Self-esteem, test anxiety, stress and verbal learning. *Developmental Psychology,* 1969, *1,* 147–154.

Levien, R. E. *The emerging technology: Instructional uses of the computer in higher education.* New York: McGraw-Hill, 1972.

Levinson, D. J., Darrow, C. M., Klein, E. B., Levinson, M. H., & McKee, B. The psychosocial development of men in early adulthood and the midlife transition. In D. F. Ricks, A. Thomas, & M. Roff (Eds.), *Life History Research in Psychopathology (Vol. 3).* Minneapolis: University of Minnesota Press, 1974.

Lewin, K. *Field theory in social science.* New York: Harper, 1951.

Liebert, R. M., & Morris, L. W. Cognitive and emotional components of test anxiety: A distinction and some initial data. *Psychological Reports,* 1967, *20,* 975–978.

Lomont, J. F., & Sherman, L. J. Group systematic desentization and group insight therapies for test anxiety. *Behavior Therapy,* 1971, *2,* 511–518.

Lorr, M., McNair, D. M., Michaux, W. W., & Raskin, A. Frequency of treatment and change in psychotherapy. *Journal of Abnormal and Social Psychology,* 1962, *64,* 281–292.

Lucas, J. D. The interactive effects of anxiety, failure, and intra-serial duplication. *American Journal of Psychology,* 1952, *65,* 59–66.

Lushene, R. L., O'Neil, H. F., Jr., & Dunn, T. G. Equivalent validity of a completely computerized MMPI. *Journal of Personality Assessment*, 1974, *38*, 353–361.

Lykken, D. T. A study of anxiety in the sociopathic personality. *Journal of Abnormal and Social Psychology*, 1957, *55*, 6–10.

Mager, R. F. On the sequencing of instructional content. *Psychological Reports*, 1961, *9*, 405–413.

Mager, R. F., & McCann, J. *Learner-controlled instruction.* Palo Alto, Calif.: Varian, 1962.

Maier, N. R. F. *Problem-solving, discussions and conferences: Leadership methods and skills.* New York: McGraw-Hill, 1963.

Mandler, G., & Sarason, S. B. A study of anxiety and learning. *Journal of Abnormal and Social Psychology*, 1952, *47*, 166–173.

Mandler, G., & Watson, D. L. Anxiety and the interruption of behavior. In C. D. Spielberger (Ed.), *Anxiety and behavior.* New York: Academic Press, 1966.

Mann, J. Vicarious desensitization of test anxiety through observation of videotaped treatment. *Journal of Counseling Psychology*, 1972, *19*, 1–7.

Mann, J., & Rosenthal, T. L. Vicarious and direct counterconditioning of test anxiety through individual and group desensitization. *Behaviour Research and Therapy*, 1969, *7*, 359–367.

Marantz, J., & Dowaliby, F. J. Aptitude X treatment interactions with movie and lecture instruction. Paper presented at the Northeastern Research Association annual convention, Ellenville, New York, November 1973.

Maslow, A. H. *Motivation and personality.* New York: Harper, 1954.

Masserman, J. H. *Behavior and neurosis.* Chicago: University of Chicago Press, 1943.

Matarazzo, R. G., Matarazzo, J. D., & Saslow, G. The relationship between medical and psychiatric symptoms. *Journal of Abnormal and Social Psychology*, 1961, *62*, 55–61.

McCombs, B. L., Eschenbrenner, A. J., Jr., & O'Neil, H. F., Jr. An adaptive model for utilizing learn characteristics in computer-based instructional systems. *Educational Technology*, 1973, *13*, 47–51.

McKeachie, W. J., Pollie, D. & Speisman, J. Relieving anxiety in classroom examinations. *Journal of Abnormal and Social Psychology*, 1955, *50*, 93–98.

McKeachie, W. J. Students, groups and teaching methods. *American Psychologist*, 1958, *13*, 580–584.

McKeachie, W. J. Interaction of achievement cues and facilitating anxiety in the achievement of women. *Journal of applied Psychology*, 1969, *53*, 147–148.

McKeachie, W. J. Instructional psychology. *In Annual Review of Psychology.* Palo Alto, Cal.: Annual Reviews, 1974.

McManus, M. Group desensitization of test anxiety. *Behavior, Research and Therapy*, 1971, *9*, 51–56.

McMurchie, T. D., Krueger, S. E., and Lippert, H. T. A Programming Language. Systems Memo #8. Florida State University, Computer Assisted Instruction Center, Tallahassee, Florida, 1970.

Meeker, M. N. *The structure of intellect: Its interpretation and uses.* Columbus, Ohio: Merrill, 1969.

Meichenbaum, D. Cognitive modification of test anxious college students. *Journal of Consulting and Clinical Psychology*, 1972, *39*, 370–380.

Meichenbaum, D. Clinical implications of modifying what clients say to themselves. Unpublished manuscript, University of Waterloo, (Waterloo, Ontario) 1974.

Merrill, P. F., Steven, M. H., Kalish, S. J. & Towle, N. J. The interactive effects of the availability of objectives and/or rules on computer-based learning: A replication (Technical Memo No. 59). Computer-Assisted Instruction Center, Florida State University, 1972.

Merrill, P. F., & Towle, N. J. Interaction of abilities and anxiety with availability of objectives and/or test items on computer-band task performance (Technical Memo No. 61). Computer-Assisted Instruction Center. Florida State University, 1972.

Milgram, S. *Obedience.* New York: New York University Film Library, 1965.

Mitchell, K. R., & Ng, K. T. Effects of group counseling and behavior therapy on the academic achievement of test anxious students. *Journal of Counseling Psychology,* 1972, *19,* 491–497.

Montague, E. K. The role of anxiety in serial rote learning. *Journal of Experimental Psychology,* 1953, *45,* 91–96.

Morris, L. W. & Liebert, R. M. Effects of anxiety on timed and untimed intelligence tests. *Journal of Consulting and Clinical Psychology,* 1969, *33,* 240–244.

Morris, L. W. & Liebert, R. M. Relationship of cognitive and emotional components of test anxiety to psychological arousal and academic performance. *Journal of Consulting and Clinical Psychology,* 1970, *35,* 332–337.

Morris, R. T., & Suckerman, K. R. Therapist warmth as a factor in automated systematic desensitization. *Journal of Counseling and Consulting Psychology,* 1974, *42,* 244–250.

Morris, V. A., Blank, S., McKie, D., & Rankin, F. C. Motivation, step size and selected learner variables in relation to performance with programmed instruction. *Programmed Learning and Educational Technology,* 1970, *7,* 257–267.

Mowrer, O. H. The basis of psychopathology: Malconditioning or misbehavior? In C. D. Spielberger (Ed.), *Anxiety and behavior.* N. Y.: Academic Press, 1966. Pp. 143–156.

Murray, E. J., & Jacobson, L. I. The nature of learning in traditional and behavioural psychotherapy. In A. Bergin & S. Garfield (Eds.), *Handbook of psychotherapy and behavior change.* New York: Wiley, 1971.

Newell, A., Shaw, J. C., and Simon, H. A. Elements of a theory of human problem solving. *Psychological Review,* 1958, *65,* 151–166.

O'Neil, H. F., Jr. Anxiety reduction and computer-assisted learning. Paper presented at a meeting of the American Psychological Association, as part of a symposium entitled Anxiety in Educationally Relevant Situations, Honolulu, September 1972.

O'Neil, H. F., Jr., Hansen, D. N., & Spielberger, C. D. Errors and latency of response in computer-assisted learning as a function of anxiety and task difficulty. Paper presented at a meeting of the American Educational Research Association, Los Angeles, February 1969.

O'Neil, H. F., Jr., Spielberger, C. D., & Hansen, D. N. The effects of state anxiety and task difficulty on computer-assisted learning. *Journal of Educational Psychology,* 1969, *60,* 343–350.

O'Reilly, R. P., & Ripple, R. E. The contribution of anxiety, creativity and intelligence to achievement with programed instruction. Paper presented at a meeting of the American Educational Research Association, New York, February, 1967.

Oosthoek, H. & Ackers, G. The evaluation of an audio-taped course (II). *British Journal of Educational Technology,* 1973, *4,* 55–73.

Osterhouse, R. A. Private communication, 1972.

Paul, G. L. *Insight and desensitization in psychotherapy.* Palo Alto, Calif.: Stanford University Press, 1966.

Paul, G. L. Outcome of systematic desensitization II: Controlled investigations of individual treatment, technique variations, and current status. In C. Franks (Ed.), *Behavior therapy: Appraisal and status.* New York: McGraw-Hill, 1969.

Paul, G. L. & Eriksen, C. W. Effects of test anxiety on "real-life" examinations. *Journal of Personality* 1964, *32,* 480–494.

Paul, G. L., & Shannon, D. T. Treatment of anxiety through systematic desensitization in therapy groups. *Journal of Abnormal Psychology,* 1966, *71,* 124–135.

Phillips, B. N., Martin, R. P., & Meyers, J. Interventions in relation to anxiety in school. In

C. D. Spielberger (Ed.), *Anxiety: Current Trends in Theory and Research.* (Vol. 2). New York: Academic Press, 1972. Pp. 408–464.

Raymond, C. K. Anxiety and task as determiners of verbal performance. *Journal of Experimental Psychology,* 1953, *46,* 120–124.

Raynor, J. O. Relationships between achievement-related motives, future orientation and academic performance. In J. W. Atkinson & J. O. Raynor (Eds.), *Motivation and achievement.* Washington: Halstead, 1974.

Review of Educational Research, Cumulative Index, 1973, *43,* 488–492.

Richardson, F. C. A self-study manual on coping with test anxiety (Tech. Report No. 25). Austin, Tex.: Computer-Assisted Instruction Laboratory, The University of Texas at Austin, 1973.

Richardson, F. C., & Hall, R. A. Vicarious desensitization of test anxiety. Unpublished manuscript, The University of Texas at Austin, 1974.

Richardson, F. C., O'Neil, H. F., Jr., Grant, R. D., Jr., & Judd, W. A. Development and preliminary evaluation of an automated test anxiety reduction program for a computer-based learning situation. (Tech. Report No. 20) Austin: Computer-Assisted Instruction Laboratory, The University of Texas at Austin, April, 1973.

Richardson, F. C., & Suinn, R. M. A comparison of traditional systematic desensitization, accelerated massed desensitization, and anxiety management training in the treatment of mathematics anxiety. *Behavior Therapy,* 1973, *4,* 212–218.

Ripple, R. E., Millman, J., & Glock, M. D. Learner characteristeristics and instructional mode: A search for disordinal interactions. *Journal of Educational Psychology,* 1969, *69,* 113–120.

Roback, H. B. Human figure drawings: their utility in the clinical psychologists armamentarium for personality assessment. *Psychological Bulletin,* 1968, *70,* 1–19.

Rosenthal, R. *Experimenter effects in behavioral research.* New York: Appleton-Century-Crofts, 1966.

Ruebush, B. K. Interfering and facilitating effects of test anxiety. *Journal of Abnormal and Social Psychology,* 1960, *60,* 205–212.

Sarason, I. G. Effects of verbal learning, reassurance, and meaningfulness of material. *Journal of Experimental Psychology,* 1958, *56,* 472–477. (a)

Sarason, I. G. Empirical findings and theoretical problems in the use of anxiety scales. *Psychological Bulletin,* 1960, *57,* 403–415.

Sarason, I. G. Characteristics of three measures of anxiety. *Journal of Clinical Psychology,* 1961, *17,* 196–197.

Sarason, I. G. Experimental approaches to test anxiety: Attention and the uses of information. In C. D. Spielberger (Ed.), *Anxiety: Current trends in theory and research* (Vol. 2). New York: Academic Press, 1972. Pp. 381–403.

Sarason, I. G., & Glanzer, V. J. Anxiety, reinforcement and experimental instructions in a free verbalization situation. *Journal of Abnormal and Social Psychology,* 1962, *65,* 300–307.

Sarason, I. G., & Glanzer, V. J. Effects of test anxiety and reinforcement history on verbal behavior. *Journal of Abnormal and Social Psychology,* 1963, *67,* 87091.

Sarason, I. G., & Harmatz, M. G. Test anxiety and experimental conditions. *Journal of Personality and Social Psychology,* 1965, *1,* 499–505.

Sarason, I. G., & Koenig, K. P. The relationship of test anxiety of self and parents. *Journal of Personality and Social Psychology,* 1965, *2,* 617–621.

Sarason, I. G., Pederson, A. M., & Nyman, B. Test anxiety and the observation of models. *Journal of Personality,* 1968, *36,* 493–511.

Sarason, S. B. The measurement of anxiety in children. In C. D. Speilberger (Ed.), *Anxiety and behavior.* New York: Academic Press, 1966. Pp. 63–79.

Sarason, S. B., Davidson, K. S., Lighthall, F. F., Waite, R. R., & Ruebush, B. K. *Anxiety in elementary school children.* New York: Wiley, 1960.

Sarason, S. B., Hill, K. T., & Zimbardo, P. G. A longitudinal study of the relation of test anxiety to performance on intelligence and achievement tests. Monographs of the Society for Research in Child Development, 1964, *29,* (2, Serial No. 7).

Sarason, S. B., Mandler, G., & Craighill, P. G. The effect of differential instructions on anxiety and learning. *Journal of Abnormal and Social Psychology,* 1952, *47,* 561–565.

Sartre, J. P. [Freedom.] In Cormier, R., Chinn, E., & Lineback, R. H. (Eds.) *Encounter: An introduction to philosophy.* Glenview, Ill.: Scott, Foresman, 1970. Pp. 369–381.

Sartre, J. P. [*Being and nothingness.*] New York: Philosophical Library, 1956.

Sassenrath, J. M. A factor-analysis of rating scale items on the Test Anxiety Questionnaire. *Journal of Consulting Psychology,* 1964, *28,* 371–377.

Schachter, S. The interaction of cognitive and psysiological determinants of emotional state. In C. D. Spielberger (Ed.), *Anxiety and Behavior.* New York: Academic Press, 1966.

Schachter, S. *Emotion, obesity, and crime.* New York: Academic Press, 1971.

Schilpp, P. A. *Philosophy of Karl Jaspers,* New York: Tudor, 1957.

Schmuck, R., & Van Egmond, E. Sex differences in the relationship of interpersonal perceptions to academic performance. *Psychology in the schools,* 1965, *2,* 32–40.

Schultz, C. B., & Dangel, T. R. The effects of recitation on the retention of two personality types. *American Educational Research Journal,* 1972, *9,* 421–430.

Shrable, K., & Sassenrath, J. M. Effects of achievement motivation and test anxiety on performance in programmed instruction. *American Educational Research Journal,* 1970, *7,* 209–220.

Shuford, E. H. Personal communication, November 1972.

Shuford, E. H., Albert, A., & Massengill, H. E. Admissible probability measurement procedures. *Psychometrika,* 1966, *31,* 125–145.

Sieber, J. E. A paradigm for experimental modification of the effects of test anxiety on cognitive processes. *American Educational Research Journal,* 1969, *6,* 46–61.

Sieber, J. E. The effects of anxiety on ability to generate warranted subjective uncertainty. *Journal of Personality and Social Psychology,* 1974, *30,* 688–695.

Sieber, J. E., Clark, R. E., Smith, H. H., & Depue, N. S. The effects of learning to generate warranted uncertainty on children's knowledge and use of drugs. Palo Alto, Cal.: Stanford Center for Research and Development in Teaching, 1976.

Sieber, J. E., & Crockenberg, S. B. The teacher and the anxious child. *Today's Education,* 1970, *59,* 76–77.

Sieber, J. E., Kameya, L. I., & Paulson, F. L. Effects of memory support on the problem solving abilities of test-anxious children. *Journal of Educational Psychology,* 1970, *61,* 159–168.

Silverman, R. E., & Blitz, B. Learning and two kinds of anxiety. *Journal of Abnormal and Social Psychology,* 1956, *52,* 301–303.

Slosson, R. L. *The Slosson Intelligence Test for Children and Adults.* East Aurora: Slosson Education Publication, 1973.

Smith, R. E., Ascough, J. C., Ettinger, R. F., & Nelson, D. A. Humor, anxiety, and task performance. *Journal of Personality and Social Psychology,* 1971, *19,* 243–246.

Smith, W. F., & Rockett, F. C. Test performance as a function of anxiety, instructor and instructions. *Journal of Educational Research,* 1958, *52,* 138–141.

Spence, K. W. A theory of emotionally based drive (D) and its relation to performance in simple learning situations. *American Psychologist,* 1958, *13,* 131–141.

Spence, K. W. Anxiety (drive) level and performance in eyelid conditioning. *Psychological Bulletin,* 1964. *61.* 129–139.

Spence, J. T., & Spence, K. W. The motivational components of manifest anxiety: Drive and drive stimuli. In C. D. Spielberger (Ed.), *Anxiety and behavior.* New York: Academic Press, 1966.

Spiegler, M. D., Morris, L. W., & Liebert, R. M. Cognitive and emotional components of test anxiety: Temporal factors. *Psychological Reports,* 1968, *22,* 446–451.

Spielberger, C. D. Theory and research on anxiety. In C. D. (Ed.), *Anxiety and behavior.* New York: Academic Press, 1966. (a)

Spielberger, C. D. The effects of anxiety on complex learning and academic achievement. In C. D. Spielberger (Ed.), *Anxiety and behavior.* New York: Academic Press, 1966. (b)

Spielberger, C. D. Trait-state anxiety and motor behavior. *Journal of Motor Behavior,* 1971, *3,* 265–279. (a)

Spielberger, C. D. *Current topics in clinical and community psychology* (Vol. 3). New York: Academic Press, 1971. (b)

Spielberger, C. D. *Anxiety: Current trends in theory and research* (Vol. 1). New York: Academic Press, 1972. (a)

Spielberger, C. D. (Ed.). *Anxiety: Current trends in theory and research* (Vol. 2). New York: Academic Press, 1972. (b)

Spielberger, C. D. Anxiety as an emotional state. In C. D. Spielberger (Ed.), *Anxiety: Current trends in theory and research.* (Vol. 1). New York: Academic Press, 1972. Pp. 23–49. (c)

Spielberger, C. D. Anxiety: State-trait process. In C. D. Spielberger & I. G. Sarason (Eds.), *Stress and anxiety* (Vol. 1). Washington, D. C.: Hemisphere, 1975.

Spielberger, C. D., Anton, W. D., & Bedell, J. The nature and treatment of test anxiety. In M. Zuckerman & C. D. Spielberger (Eds.) *Emotions and anxiety: New concepts, methods, and applications.* New York: Lawrence Erlbaum Associates, 1976.

Spielberger, C. D., Gorsuch, R. L., & Lushene, R. E. *Manual for the state-trait anxiety inventory.* Palo Alto, Cal.: Consulting Psychologists Press, 1970.

Spielberger, C. D., O'Neil, H. F., Jr., & Hansen, D. N. Anxiety drive theory and computer-assisted learning. In B. A. Maher (Ed.) *Progress in experimental personality research.* New York: Academic Press, 1972.

Spielberger, C. D., & Smith, L. H. Anxiety (drive), stress and serial-position effects in serial-verbal learning. *Journal of Experimental Psychology,* 1966, *72,* 589–595.

Stennett, K. G. The relationships of performance level to level of arousal. *Journal of Educational Psychology,* 1957, *54,* 54–61.

Stevenson, H., & Odom, R. The relation of anxiety to children's performance on learning and problem-solving tasks. *Child Development,* 1965, *36,* 1003–1012.

Straughan, J. H., and Dufort, W. H. Task difficulty, relaxation, and anxiety level during verbal learning and recall, *Journal of Abnormal Psychology,* 1969, Vol. *74,* 621–624.

Suinn, R. M. The STABS, a measure of test anxiety for behavior therapy: Normative data. *Behaviour Research and Therapy.* 1969, *7,* 97–98.

Suinn, R. M., Edie, C., & Spinelli, P. Accelerated massed desensitization: Innovation in short term treatment. *Behavior Therapy,* 1970, *1,* 303–311.

Suinn, R. M., & Hall, R. A. Marathon desensitization groups. *Behaviour Research and Therapy,* 1970, *8,* 97–98.

Suinn, R. M., & Richardson, F. C. Anxiety management training: A non-specific behavior therapy program for anxiety control. *Behavior Therapy,* 1971, *2,* 498–510.

Taylor, J. A. A personality scale of manifest anxiety. *Journal of Abnormal and Social Psychology,* 1953, *48,* 285–290.

Taylor, J. A. Drive theory and manifest anxiety. *Psychological Bulletin,* 1956, *53,* 303–320.

Taylor, J. A., & Chapman, J. P. Anxiety and the learning of paired-associates. *American Journal of Psychology,* 1955, *68,* 671.

Tennyson, R. D. & Boutwell, R. C. Pretask versus within-task anxiety measures in predicting performance on a concept acquisition task. *Journal of Educational Psychology,* 1973, *65,* 88–92.

Terman, L. M. & Merrill, M. A. *Measuring intelligence.* Boston: Houghton Mifflin, 1937.

Thomas, D. B. Two applications of simulation in the educational environment (Technical Memo No. 31). Computer-Assisted Instruction Center, Florida State University, 1971.

Tobias, S. Effect of verbal reinforcement and response changes in a non-reinforced situation. Paper presented at a meeting of the American Psychological Association, Chicago, September 1960.

Tobias, S. *The effect of creativity, response mode, and subject matter familiarity on achievement of programmed instruction.* New York: MSS Educational Publ., 1968.

Tobias, S. Effect of creativity, response mode, and subject matter familiarity on achievement from programmed instruction. *Journal of Educational Psychology,* 1969, *60,* 453–460.

Tobias, S. A history of an individualized instructional program of varying familiarity to college students (Technical Memo No. 43). Tallahassee, Fla.: Computer-Assisted Instruction State University, 1972.

Tobias, S. Review of the response mode issues. *Review of Educational Research,* 1973, *43,* 193–204. (a)

Tobias, S. Sequence, familiarity, and attribute-treatment interactions in programmed instruction. *Journal of Educational Psychology,* 1973, *64,* 133–141. (b)

Tobias, S. Distraction, response mode, anxiety, and achievement in computer-assisted instruction. *Journal of Educational Psychology,* 1973, 65, 233–237. (c)

Tobias, S. Achievement treatment interactions. *Review of Educational Research,* 1976, *46,* 61–74.

Tobias, S., & Abramson, T. The relationship of anxiety, response mode, and content difficulty to achievement in programmed instruction. *Journal of Educational Psychology,* 1971, *62,* 357–364.

Tobias, S. & Duchastel, P. C. Behavioral objectives, sequence, and anxiety in CAI. *Instructional Science,* 1974, *3,* 231–242.

Tobias, S., & Williamson, J. *Anxiety and response mode to programmed instruction.* Paper presented at AERA, Chicago, February 1968.

Tomkins, S. S. *Affect, imagery, consciousness.* Vol. I: *The positive affects.* New York: Springer Publ., 1962.

Tomkins, S. S. *Affect, imagery, consciousness.* Vol. II: *The negative affects.* New York: Springer Publ., 1963.

Travers, R. M. W. (Ed.). *Second handbook of research on teaching.* Chicago: Rand McNally, 1973.

Traweek, M. T. The relationship between certain personality variables and achievement through programmed instruction. *California Journal of Educational Research,* 1964, *15,* 215–220.

Urban, H. B., & Ford, D. H. Some historical and conceptual perspectives on psychotherapy and behavior change. In A. Bergin & S. Garfield (Eds.), *Handbook of psychotherapy and behavior change.* New York: Wiley, 1971.

Waite, R. R. *Test performance as a function of anxiety and type of task.* Unpublished doctoral dissertation, Yale University, 1959.

Wallach, M. A., & Kogan, N. *Modes of thinking in young children.* New York: Holt, Rinehart, & Winston, 1965.

Wallace, J. An abilities conception of personality: Some implications for personality measurement. *American Psychologist,* 1966, *21,* 132–138.

Watson, D., & Tharp, R. *Self-directed behavior: Self-modification for personal adjustment.* Belmont, Calif.: Brooks-Cole, 1972.

Webb, E. J., Campbell, D. T., Schwartz, R. D., & Sechrest, L. *Unobtrusive Measures: Nonreactive Research in the Social Sciences.* Chicago: Rand McNally, 1971.

Wilkins, W. Desensitization: Social and cognitive factors underlying the effectiveness of Wolpe's procedure. *Psychological Bulletin,* 1971, *76,* 311–317.

Wine, J. An attentional approach to the treatment of test anxiety (Counseling Services Report). Waterloo, Ontario: University of Waterloo, February 1971. (a)

Wine, J. Test anxiety and direction of attention. *Psychological Bulletin,* 1971, *76,* 92–104. (b)

Wine, J. Cognitive-attentional approaches to test anxiety modification. Paper presented at a meeting of The American Psychological Association, Honolulu, September, 1972.

Wine, J. Cognitive-attentional approaches to test anxiety modification. Paper presented as part of a symposium entitled "Anxiety and Instruction" at a meeting of The American Psychological Association, Montreal, August 1973.

Wittmaier, B. C. Test anxiety and study habits. *Journal of Educational Research,* 1972, *65,* 352–354.

Wolf, M., Risley, T., Johnston, M., Harris, F., & Allen E. Application of operant conditioning procedures to the behavior problems of an autsitic child: A follow-up and extension. *Behavior Research and Therapy,* 1967, *5,* 103–111.

Wolpe, J. The conditioning and deconditioning of neurotic anxiety. In C. D. Spielberger (Ed.), *Anxiety and behavior.* New York: Academic Press, 1966.

Wolpe, J. *The practice of behavior therapy.* London: Pergamon Press, 1969.

Wolpe, J. *Psychotherapy by reciprocal inhibition.* Stanford, Calif.: Stanford University Press, 1958.

Wonderlic, E. F. *Personnel test manual* (Rev. and enl. ed.). Northfield, Ill.: Author, 1961.

Author Index

Subject Index

UNIVERSITY LEXINGTON